PRESENTED TO

....

BY

....

DATE

....

365

FOR MEN

GLENN HASCALL

365 ENCOURAGING PRAYERS FOR MEN

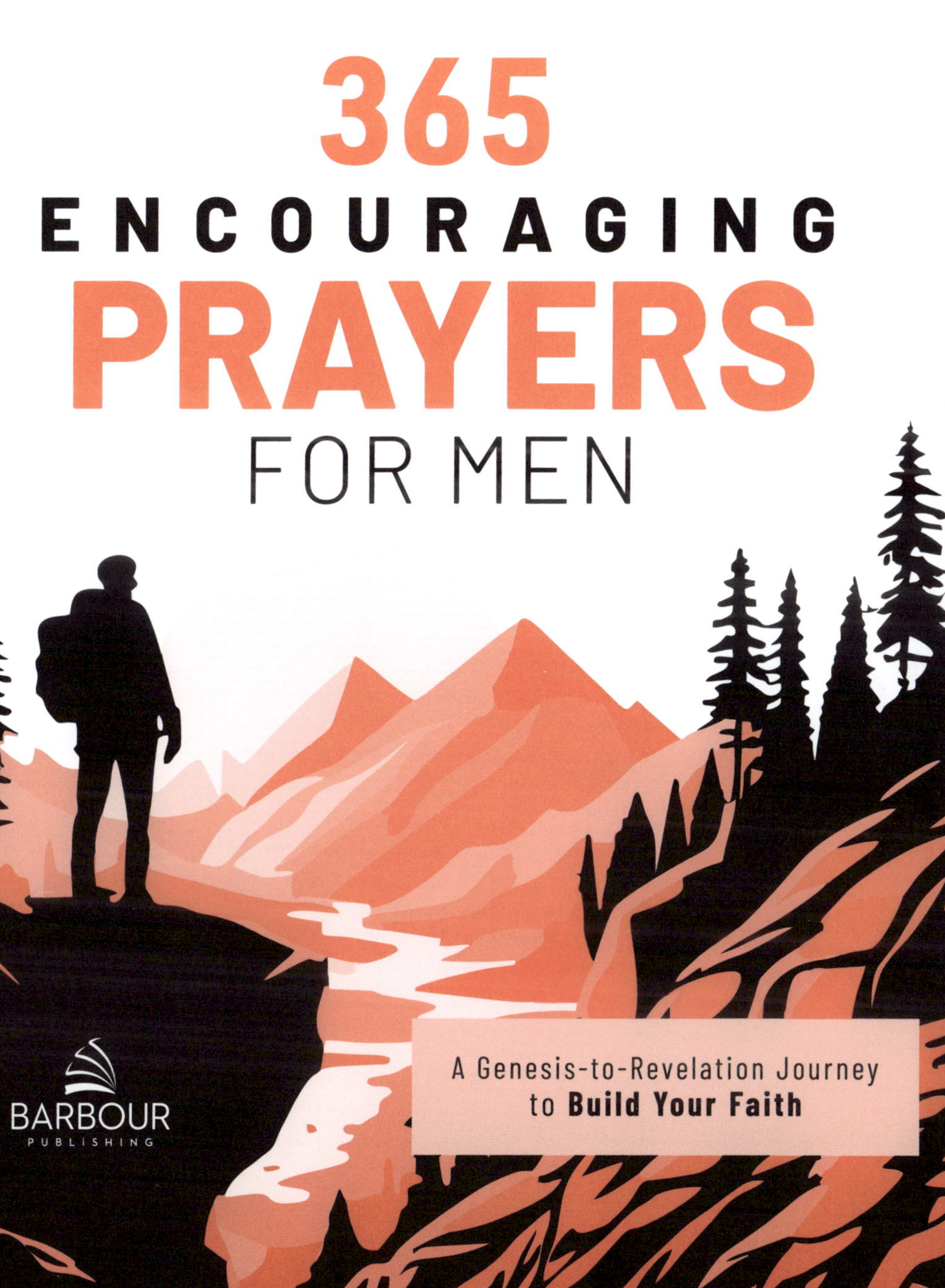

A Genesis-to-Revelation Journey to **Build Your Faith**

BARBOUR PUBLISHING

ISBN 979-8-89151-195-8

Published by Barbour Publishing, Inc., 1810 Barbour Drive, Uhrichsville, Ohio 44683, www.barbourbooks.com

Our mission is to inspire the world with the life-changing message of the Bible.

Printed in China.

WELCOME TO
365 ENCOURAGING PRAYERS FOR MEN

The struggles you experience aren't unknown to God or uncommon to man. Read through each page of this book and confront the struggle and joy found in living life while experiencing God's love.

Witness the unheeded warnings and lawlessness that resulted in a story of correction and redemption. And know that in so many bad circumstances God steps in and moves in ways no one could have predicted. This book is a year-long chronicle of man's misdirection and God's restoration.

In that year, you'll meet many well-known men as well as less-familiar ones. Each has a connection to prayer. You will see positive examples and some demonstrations of what to avoid. Perhaps you'll find this book relatable because you'll encounter so many reasons for prayer. The common thread of struggle also illustrates humanity's desperate need for prayer.

Come just as you are and understand that those biblical figures who needed to pray needed God. They needed to recognize His goodness and that they couldn't do life without Him. These are the same things every generation from the beginning of time has needed to learn.

Allow God to help you make meaningful connections discovered in the stories and experiences of those who've been where you are and chose rescue over what we might call "the great walkaway."

DAY 1
GENESIS 1–3

Prayer Scripture

When the woman saw that the tree was good for food, and that it was pleasant to the eyes, and a tree to be desired to make one wise, she took some of its fruit and ate, and gave also to her husband with her, and he ate. And the eyes of them both were opened, and they knew that they were naked.
Genesis 3:6–7

Prayer Thought for the Day

Before the Bible ever mentions prayer, it shows the trouble caused by *not* praying. Adam and Eve should certainly have talked with God before touching that forbidden fruit. As Jesus would teach, "Watch and pray, that you do not enter into temptation. The spirit indeed is willing, but the flesh is weak" (Matthew 26:41).

Prayer Starter

Lord God, I don't want a lack of prayer to bring me the trouble it brought to Adam and Eve, and I know You don't want that either! Please give me a hunger to talk with You about everything. Give me a thirst to pray without ceasing. Protect me from temptation and guide me into Your wise ways, because I know You're the perfect Creator, sustainer, and Redeemer. Today, Lord, right now, here are the things that concern me most. . .

DAY 2
GENESIS 4:1–7:9

Prayer Scripture

And in process of time it came to pass that Cain brought from the fruit of the ground an offering to the Lord. And Abel also brought from the firstlings of his flock and from the fat from them. And the Lord had respect for Abel and for his offering, but for Cain and for his offering, He did not have respect. And Cain was very angry, and his countenance fell.

Genesis 4:3–5

Prayer Thought for the Day

An offering was a solemn event that signified the close connection between God and His people. It recognized God's authority and was an outward sign of a willingness to obey. Cain and Abel were the sons of Adam and Eve. They were both preparing for this time set aside to present an offering to God. Abel followed the rules, and Cain created his own playbook. This decision was disrespectful and the opposite of obedience. This infraction did not go unnoticed by God. It led to anger within Cain, which eventually resulted in the murder of his brother. Sin that's not turned away from results in more sin.

Prayer Starter

Father, when I pray to You, I'm acknowledging Your presence, power, and perfection. I don't want to assume I know what You want without reading Your instructions. Help me to use this time to turn from everything that keeps me at a distance from You. Some of those things include. . .

DAY 3
GENESIS 7:10–10:32

Prayer Scripture

The LORD said. . . "I will not again curse the ground anymore for man's sake, for the imagination of man's heart is evil from his youth. Neither will I again strike any more everything living, as I have done. While the earth remains, seedtime and harvest, and cold and heat, and summer and winter, and day and night shall not cease."
GENESIS 8:21–22

Prayer Thought for the Day

Prayer is a conversation with God. While it's not typical for God to speak out loud, He had a message in Genesis 8. The phrase you should pay attention to is the moment when God said, "I will not again curse the ground anymore for man's sake, for the imagination of man's heart is evil from his youth." God looked at everything that happened in the past and everything that was yet to come and knew that humans would continue to break His rules. A change of heart would require something more. That something was Jesus. He would deliver a new covenant (or contract). Those who came to this God conversation (prayer), confessing their need for Him, would be rescued.

Prayer Starter

Lord God, I'm grateful You don't start humanity over again every time there's rampant sin. I'm honored You provided a better way for people like me to be right with You. Help me to recognize my sin today and take a moment to turn away from things that break Your laws, such as. . .

DAY 4

GENESIS 11–14

Prayer Scripture

Abram said to the king of Sodom, "I have lifted up my hand to the LORD, the Most High God, the possessor of heaven and earth, that I will not take from a thread even to a shoe strap, and that I will not take anything that is yours, lest you should say, 'I have made Abram rich.'"
GENESIS 14:22–23

Prayer Thought for the Day

Abram received an incredible promise from God: He would become the father of nations. This was the start of an amazing journey for Abram. His name would be changed, and he would have offspring. That was a lot to look forward to. Maybe this is why it was easy for Abram to turn down the offer of riches from a human. Abram guided a rescue operation that led to the return of people, livestock, and riches. When the local king offered a financial reward, Abram turned it down. He wouldn't be remembered for being rewarded. Abram *would* be remembered for receiving God's promise because he believed it was worth the wait.

Prayer Starter

Father, being more interested in what You offer is more important than any other opportunity. May I always be encouraged to seek You in prayer before accepting opportunities that might leave You out. While I wait, give me the courage to. . .

DAY 5
GENESIS 15–18

Prayer Scripture

The Lord appeared to [Abraham] in the plains of Mamre. . . . And when he saw [the three men], he ran to meet them from the tent door, and bowed himself toward the ground, and said, "My Lord, if now I have found favor in Your sight, do not pass away."
Genesis 18:1–3

Prayer Thought for the Day

Abraham likely didn't have many guests on the plains of Mamre, but when God showed up, it was a celebration. Prayer became a conversation. Abraham invited Him to stay, and that's when he learned the specific timing of the birth of his son. Abraham had waited a long time for this promise. His wife, Sarah, seemed to have given up hope. But Abraham listened and enjoyed the company of the Promise Keeper. He didn't recognize his guest right away, but Abraham soon learned this was no ordinary visit.

You can meet with God anytime. There's no need to rush the visit. There's plenty of reason to remember prayer. Maybe you'll do it again soon.

Prayer Starter

Lord God, let me refuse to rush my time with You. Give me the wisdom to settle in for meaningful conversation with You. Speak to me through Your Word, and I'll speak from my heart. I need to share the things that concern me. You're listening now, so let me share. . .

DAY 6
GENESIS 19–21

Prayer Scripture

The LORD visited Sarah as He had said, and the LORD did to Sarah as He had spoken. For Sarah conceived and bore Abraham a son in his old age at the set time of which God had spoken to him. And Abraham called the name of his son who was born to him, whom Sarah bore to him, Isaac.
GENESIS 21:1–3

Prayer Thought for the Day

A year had passed since Abraham had been given the news that a son would be born to his wife Sarah. The sound of crying must have done some good to his aging heart. It certainly reaffirmed that when God said something, He did something. The promise of a son wasn't fulfilled overnight, and much had to happen before Isaac could be born—but once Abraham embraced the impossibility of having a child in his old age, God stepped in. Promises aren't delayed to annoy you but to prepare you for something amazing. Keep reading. Keep seeking. Keep praying.

Prayer Starter

Father, I don't always feel as if I'm where I need to be. Teach me what I need to learn. May I accept Your plans with gratitude and a changed heart ready for Your kept promise. So today I'll keep thinking about my future and the plans You have for me. While my dreams may not be Yours, I'm asking You to help me let You lead when I. . .

DAY 7
GENESIS 22–24

Prayer Scripture

[God] said, "Take now your son, your only son Isaac, whom you love, and get into the land of Moriah, and offer him there for a burnt offering on one of the mountains of which I will tell you." And Abraham rose up early in the morning and saddled his donkey and took two of his young men with him and Isaac his son.

Genesis 22:2–3

Prayer Thought for the Day

Think about how hard the struggle must have been for Abraham. He was asked to leave the family he'd been with most of his life. He was promised a son and had to wait more than two decades. Now, when the boy was still young and the hope inside was finally growing roots, God asked Abraham to take Isaac and sacrifice him on a mountain of God's choosing. This was an exceedingly hard request, but Abraham set out to do what God asked. God was doing no more or less than seeing if Abraham had truly learned to follow. He had. God chose and accepted an alternate sacrifice that day. His Son, Jesus, is the alternate sacrifice now.

Prayer Starter

Lord God, obedience is hard when I don't understand why, because what You ask is something that doesn't make sense. Give me the wisdom to remember that I don't have to understand everything to trust You enough to follow. Here are some of the things I struggle with. . .

DAY 8
GENESIS 25–27

Prayer Scripture

[God said,] "I will perform the oath that I swore to Abraham your father, and I will make your descendants to multiply as the stars of heaven and will give to your descendants all these countries. And in your descendants shall all the nations of the earth be blessed, because Abraham obeyed My voice and observed My charge, My commandments, My statutes, and My laws."
GENESIS 26:3–5

Prayer Thought for the Day

God confirmed the reason why He would be creating a nation from Abraham's family. It wasn't because future generations would always follow Him. It wasn't based on the perfection of Isaac or his sons, Jacob and Esau. God blessed this growing family simply because He made a promise to Abraham, and God keeps His promises. In a similar way, God would create a family from those who accepted His Son, Jesus. It wouldn't be because they were perfect but because of the promise of new life through Jesus.

Prayer Starter

Father, You made a promise. That promise was a blessing to Abraham, and a similar promise is a blessing to me. I can become a part of Your family because of Jesus. I'm so grateful for Your promise of rescue. It gives me the opportunity to. . .

DAY 9
GENESIS 28–29

Prayer Scripture

Jacob vowed a vow, saying, "If God will be with me and will take care of me in this way that I go, and will give me bread to eat and clothing to put on, so that I come again to my father's house in peace, then shall the LORD be my God."
GENESIS 28:20–21

Prayer Thought for the Day

God made a promise to Abraham's descendants, and the promise wasn't conditioned on anything other than His promise. That wasn't the case with Abraham's grandson Jacob. This descendant likely did what he felt was generous. He agreed to follow God—with a few conditions. If God walked with, fed, and clothed him when he didn't feel safe, *then* he would commit to calling God "Lord." Jacob had provisions for his allegiance to God, but it was a step in God's direction. You might also be hesitant. God makes promises to you even when you struggle to make a commitment to Him. God is always committed to seeking your good. Pray and thank Him for His kindness.

Prayer Starter

Lord God, Your commitment to love the people who live in this world is without condition. I may struggle with a commitment to follow You even when I have every reason to do so. Give me a heart that chooses to trust You with. . .

DAY 10
GENESIS 30–31

Prayer Scripture

"And the angel of God spoke to me in a dream, saying, 'Jacob.' And I said, 'Here I am.' And He said, 'Lift up now your eyes and see all the rams that leap on the cattle are striped, speckled, and gray-colored, for I have seen all that Laban does to you. I am the God of Bethel, where you anointed the pillar and where you vowed a vow to Me. Now arise, get out from this land, and return to the land of your family.'"
GENESIS 31:11–13

Prayer Thought for the Day

Jacob may have felt a bit like a vagabond. He left home when his brother, Esau, sought to kill him following the death of their father, Isaac. Jacob was now rushing to leave the land where he'd married and started raising his family. It wouldn't be his last move. This move was initiated by God and was designed to be obeyed without long-term consideration. Jacob was returning home, but there was an adventurous side trip waiting for him. A growing reliance on God was changing a man previously known for deception, and his conversations with God had an impact on Jacob's willingness to go where God was sending him.

Prayer Starter

Father, I want to believe that when You lead, following is always my best response. Help me to keep in touch with You so I can recognize Your voice, believe You love me, and. . .

DAY 11
GENESIS 32–34

Prayer Scripture

Jacob said, "O God of my father Abraham, and God of my father Isaac, the Lord who said to me, 'Return to your country, and to your family, and I will deal well with you,' I am not worthy of the least of all the mercies. . . . Deliver me, I ask You, from the hand of my brother, from the hand of Esau, for I fear him, lest he will come and strike me and the mothers with the children. And You said, 'I will surely do you good and make your descendants as the sand of the sea, which cannot be numbered for multitude.'"

Genesis 32:9–12

Prayer Thought for the Day

Jacob once accepted God with conditions. But he did come to rely on God more as each year passed. As he gained a God-directed change of address, Jacob learned that his brother Esau was coming to find him, and there were four hundred men with him. This news inspired fear, prayer, and a reminder that God had said a nation would come from Jacob's family. This promise was described as a multitude. In this troubling circumstance Jacob's response was a prayerful consultation with the great Promise Keeper.

Prayer Starter

Lord God, I'm often overwhelmed with things I don't know how to handle. I want to choose to let You handle them instead. Today I'm overwhelmed by. . .

DAY 12
GENESIS 35–36

Prayer Scripture

God appeared to Jacob again. . .and blessed him. And God said to him, "Your name is Jacob. Your name shall not be called Jacob anymore, but Israel shall be your name." And He called his name Israel. And God said to him, "I am God Almighty. Be fruitful and multiply. A nation and a company of nations shall be from you, and kings shall come out of your loins. And the land that I gave Abraham and Isaac, to you I will give it, and to your descendants after you I will give the land."

GENESIS 35:9–12

Prayer Thought for the Day

As Jacob's thinking became more aligned with God's plan, God determined it was time for a name change. This was something that happened with Abram (Abraham), and, with this change, Jacob would become the namesake of the future nation of Israel. God showed up and chose to bless this man who had come so far since his early days as a deceiver. Time spent with God had changed Jacob's heart and his family's future. There's a profound benefit in making time with God a priority. It will change your future.

Prayer Starter

Father, let me never see prayer as a burden. Give me a freedom to talk with You about anything. Even if my name never changes, please change my heart about. . .

DAY 13

GENESIS 37–39

Prayer Scripture

[Jacob said,] "It is my son's coat. An evil beast has devoured him. Joseph is without doubt torn in pieces." And Jacob tore his clothes and put sackcloth on his loins and mourned for his son many days. And all his sons and all his daughters rose up to comfort him, but he refused to be comforted.

Genesis 37:33–35

Prayer Thought for the Day

Maybe it was sons modeling the deception of their father, or perhaps it was simple jealousy, but the result was a band of brothers selling the second youngest of their clan to traders heading to Egypt. These brothers lied to their father, Jacob, by telling him that an animal had killed the son he favored. Imagine the grief in Jacob's next visit with God. Imagine the pain experienced for years, perhaps believing he could have done something to prevent a tragedy that never actually happened. Because God is near to the brokenhearted, He must have been very close to Jacob in the midst of everything he didn't know.

Prayer Starter

Lord God, when my internal hurt seems more than I can handle, may I remember You've been available to all the crushed and broken men with backstories that seem beyond revision. I need Your help today with. . .

DAY 14
GENESIS 40–41

Prayer Scripture

Pharaoh said to Joseph, "I have dreamed a dream, and there is none who can interpret it, and I have heard it said of you that you can understand a dream to interpret it." And Joseph answered Pharaoh, saying, "It is not in me. God shall give Pharaoh an answer of peace."
Genesis 41:15–16

Prayer Thought for the Day

While Jacob spent years grieving the loss of his son Joseph, the young man struggled through his own issues with deception, lies, and slavery. He'd been wrongfully accused and sat in a prison cell. He followed the God he learned about from an imperfect father, and that relationship with God sustained him through his own crushed and broken life.

But Pharaoh learned about Joseph. He summoned Joseph from the prison to the palace to help him understand a disturbing dream. Joseph made it clear that he served the only God who could answer such a difficult question. This led Joseph to a position that was second only to Pharaoh's. God had a plan.

Prayer Starter

Father, some struggles I face are of my own making. Others, I can't begin to understand. Give me the courage to do what I can for You in the place where I am. Help me to realize I don't need to know everything about why I'm here to know that You're good, and even in this You have a plan for. . .

DAY 15
GENESIS 42–43

Prayer Scripture

[Joseph's brothers] said to one another, "We are truly guilty concerning our brother, in that we saw the anguish of his soul when he begged us and we would not hear. Therefore this distress has come on us." And Reuben answered them, saying, "Did I not speak to you, saying, 'Do not sin against the child,' and you would not hear? Therefore, behold, also his blood is required." And they did not know that Joseph understood them, for he spoke to them by an interpreter. And he turned himself around from them and wept.

GENESIS 42:21–24

Prayer Thought for the Day

Joseph was eyewitness to an answered prayer. Many years had passed when suddenly the same brothers who sold him into slavery showed up hungry. They needed food, and Joseph was the man in charge of that commodity. What they felt was a miscommunication wasn't lost on a brother they didn't recognize. Joseph would later tell these frightened betrayers that God had used their worst decision to save many lives during the worst famine anyone had ever experienced. Joseph's ongoing connection with God led to forgiveness where bitterness usually thrives.

Prayer Starter

Lord God, being bitter is easy. Forgiveness is hard. I haven't always been treated well, and there are times I get angry remembering the circumstances that have never made sense. Please help me to forgive. . .

DAY 16
GENESIS 44–45

Prayer Scripture

"Hurry, and go up to my father, and say to him, 'This is what your son Joseph says: "God has made me lord of all Egypt. Come down to me. Do not delay. And you shall dwell in the land of Goshen, and you shall be near to me, you, and your children, and your children's children, and your flocks, and your herds, and all that you have. And there I will nourish you, for there are still five years of famine, lest you and your household and all that you have come to poverty."'"

GENESIS 45:9–11

Prayer Thought for the Day

Have you ever uttered a prayer that you struggled to believe God would answer? You wanted Him to, but it all seemed next to impossible. Sometimes God answers impossible prayers, and the recipient is left speechless. This was what happened to Jacob. Surviving the famine seemed impossible, and there were problems with an Egyptian leader who asked too many questions. But suddenly Jacob was confronted with a truth that had been hidden from him for years—Joseph was alive, and Pharaoh had invited the whole family to come to Egypt and live. It was all too much—or perhaps just enough.

Prayer Starter

Father, help me to be comfortable praying impossible prayers. May I refuse to believe that I bother You when I ask for something I have no reason to believe is possible. Let me boldly begin today. . .

DAY 17
GENESIS 46–48

Prayer Scripture

[Israel] blessed Joseph and said, "God, before whom my fathers Abraham and Isaac walked, the God who fed me all my life long to this day, the Angel who redeemed me from all evil, bless the boys. And let my name be named on them, and the name of my fathers Abraham and Isaac. And let them grow into a multitude in the midst of the earth."
Genesis 48:15–16

Prayer Thought for the Day

This part of Genesis 48 describes one who has been blessed blessing a new generation. Jacob was nearing death and insisted on blessing Joseph's two sons, Ephraim and Manasseh. These boys hadn't known their grandfather, had never seen the land in which he lived, and might have felt uncomfortable as he rested his hands on them. Jacob spoke words that described a good future for the boys. The result of Jacob's imperfect life spent praying to a good God was an extension of God's impact among the people. At that moment, Jacob was passing the faith baton to new family members, and it was good.

Prayer Starter

Lord God, let me not look at my prayer life as something entirely personal. I want to use my faith to impact my family so future generations might have the opportunity to know You. Today I pray for family members like...

DAY 18

GENESIS 49–50

Prayer Scripture

Joseph said to his brothers, "I will die, and God will surely visit you and bring you out of this land to the land that He swore to Abraham, to Isaac, and to Jacob."
GENESIS 50:24

Prayer Thought for the Day

For Joseph the move to Egypt had been permanent. Before he died, he reminded his family that one day God would arrange for them to return to the land He'd promised Abraham. After Joseph's passing, the people's connection with God, which had been well established, became more ceremonial than relational. Somehow, when few were paying attention, this growing family was transferred from the status of Egypt's guests to its servants and eventually to slaves. The Egyptians forgot about the famine and how Joseph made it possible for their families to survive. They forgot that Pharaoh made a home for Joseph's family. God's people drifted from their friendship with God. Perhaps prayer had become little more than a time-robbing throwback to a history no one recalled.

Things were changing, and hope seemed to make an exodus. But God had a purpose for those hard times.

Prayer Starter

Father, give me a memory that finds it easy to recall Your goodness even on hard days. I don't want my prayer life to feel like a duty that can be put off indefinitely. There are things I'll need help with and things I'll need to thank You for. Let me start. . .

DAY 19
EXODUS 1–3

Prayer Scripture

It came to pass in the process of time that the king of Egypt died. And the children of Israel sighed because of the bondage, and they cried. And their cry came up to God because of the bondage. And God heard their groaning, and God remembered His covenant with Abraham, with Isaac, and with Jacob.
EXODUS 2:23–24

Prayer Thought for the Day

Slavery was in full bloom. The aroma was unpleasant. The people of Israel remembered stories of how they came to Egypt as invited guests. Forced labor was unfair, unjust, and unwelcome. In their troubles, their prayers ascended to God as a cry. There seemed to be no one who could help them, and their inner groanings became outward weeping. When no one remembered the Israelites, the people suddenly remembered God, who was preparing a deliverer. His name was Moses. God had to show this man that he could do a job that was never a career choice.

You might think of yourself as one in bondage or one being prepared to do something big. Just don't forget to pray—you'll need help.

Prayer Starter

Lord God, I need a deliverer, and I'm in awe that You can use people like me to help others. I don't want to forget how You rescued me or that You'll rescue yet again. Sometimes things go well, or my heart is groaning under the pressure of life. Today I'm. . .

DAY 20
EXODUS 4–6

Prayer Scripture

Moses said to the LORD, "O my Lord, I am not eloquent, neither before now nor since You have spoken to Your servant. But I am slow of speech and of a slow tongue."
EXODUS 4:10

Prayer Thought for the Day

Prayer is a conversation between you and God. This usually looks like you speaking out loud or praying silently and God hearing you speak or think. God supplies His answers through the Bible or by speaking to your heart through His Spirit. That's a different kind of conversation than speaking to your mom, friend, or coworker. On the other hand, Moses prayed by having an actual conversation with God, which he could hear. One of Moses' more famous conversations with God was when he essentially told God, "You have the wrong man." He wasn't the only one to express himself that way, but God wasn't impressed with his excuse. Moses thought his lack of public speaking credentials disqualified him from rescuing more than a million people. Because God gives all good gifts, you have no real excuse to refuse to do the things He asks you to do. If He asks, you'll have everything you need to do what seems impossible.

Prayer Starter

Father, I think the reason You don't want me to stay in my comfort zone is because I'll never grow if I'm never challenged. Some of the ways You've challenged me include. . .

DAY 21
EXODUS 7–9

Prayer Scripture

Moses and Aaron went out from Pharaoh. And Moses cried to the Lord because of the frogs that He had brought against Pharaoh. And the Lord did according to the word of Moses. And the frogs died out of the houses, out of the villages, and out of the fields. And they gathered them together in heaps, and the land stank.
Exodus 8:12–14

Prayer Thought for the Day

The plan? Moses would lead the people out of Egypt and into freedom. God promised to go with Moses and give him the words to say. True to His word, God told Moses and his brother Aaron every bit of direction they needed to move the people closer to freedom. Repeatedly you'll read all the things God told Moses to do. Early on, speaking to a holy God might have seemed unnatural to Moses—he doesn't say much—but he was good at listening. And we read of one prayer for an end to a plague of frogs.

Perhaps you feel praying is unnatural, as Moses may have, but as God continues instructing and you keep listening, the next logical step is to respond.

Prayer Starter

Lord God, when it seems unnatural for me to speak to someone I can't see, I should remember that even Moses didn't see You while he was learning to pray. May I become comfortable enough to share what concerns me. Things like. . .

DAY 22
EXODUS 10–12

Prayer Scripture

"It shall come to pass, when your children shall say to you, 'What do you mean by this service?' that you shall say, 'It is the Passover sacrifice of the Lord, who passed over the houses of the children of Israel in Egypt when He smote the Egyptians and delivered our houses.'" And the people bowed their heads and worshipped.

Exodus 12:26–27

Prayer Thought for the Day

The very last plague had just begun in Egypt. This would be the one plague that would cause Pharaoh to send the Israelites away, but it would come at a terrible cost. It was also the beginning of an annual celebration for the Israelites called Passover, a time that is remembered as God's final answer to the liberation of slaves. It shouldn't be a surprise that when Jesus died for the liberation of sin slaves, it was also at the time of Passover. But, on a night that would move the people to the start of God's future for them, they did something rarely spoken of about the slaves—they bowed and worshipped. God's goodness deserves that kind of response.

Prayer Starter

Father, may I be grateful for Your wonderful unknown. I'm honored to follow in Your footsteps. You know more than I ever will and are with me every step into an adventure I've never been on. But there are times when I'm concerned because. . .

DAY 23

EXODUS 13–15

Prayer Scripture

Your right hand, O Lord, has become glorious in power. Your right hand, O Lord, has dashed the enemy in pieces. And in the greatness of Your excellency You have overthrown those who rose up against You.

Exodus 15:6–7

Prayer Thought for the Day

This passage in Exodus 15 is unique in that it's the first that used a more creative way to share a story. It's closely aligned with what many think of as a psalm and is often referred to as a "song of redemption." It was a celebration of freedom and a moment in which Moses found he could freely speak to God. What he seemed to focus on was marveling at God's incredible power and comprehensive plan. It was a recognition that God was big enough to stand above all who would seek to suggest He was nothing. Suddenly, after the great rescue of God's people from Egypt, Moses had an improved understanding of the Lord, who was less concerned about how well he spoke and more concerned with a man who knew *He* could.

Prayer Starter

Lord God, I have words that I won't say without encouragement. There are things that I struggle with that I don't want anyone to know. I'm listening to You. Give me the courage to join the conversation. I have a lot that I should share. . .

DAY 24
EXODUS 16–18

Prayer Scripture

The people thirsted there for water, and the people murmured against Moses and said, "For what reason have you brought us up out of Egypt, to kill us and our children and our cattle with thirst?" And Moses cried to the LORD, saying, "What shall I do to these people? They are almost ready to stone me."
EXODUS 17:3–4

Prayer Thought for the Day

As the story of Moses unfolds, God is still saying much more than Moses. God provided all kinds of directions and managed the hunger needs of the people. He dealt with issues of food greed. It seems frustration led Moses to finally pray. The people were thirsty, and they seemed to be getting violent about it. It feels a bit like a child on a road trip, whining at a parent, "Are we there yet?" Moses likely thought of the food God had given, the safety He provided, and the rescue from slavery, yet the others who witnessed these miracles were uptight about water. The people cried out and threatened him with flying stones. Moses prayed, and God once more provided for the needs of these complaining tribes. Moses learned who to go to in the midst of trouble. All he needed was trust in God.

Prayer Starter

Father, I don't want to wait until I'm frustrated to speak with You, but if I do, help me to remember that You're trustworthy to hear me when I. . .

DAY 25
EXODUS 19–20

Prayer Scripture

Mount Sinai was altogether covered in smoke because the Lord descended on it in fire. And its smoke ascended as the smoke of a furnace, and the whole mountain quaked greatly. And when the voice of the trumpet sounded long and became louder and louder, Moses spoke, and God answered him by a voice. And the Lord came down on Mount Sinai, on the top of the mount. And the Lord called Moses up to the top of the mount, and Moses went up.

Exodus 19:18–20

Prayer Thought for the Day

The friendship between God and Moses was increasing. God came down to Mount Sinai. The mountain was covered in smoke and fire. There was quaking and the sound of a trumpet. When the people were told to stay off the mountain, they suddenly had no issues with obedience. It's encouraging to read in Exodus 19 that after the noise became increasingly loud, *Moses* spoke and God answered. The timid Moses from the wilderness was being replaced with a bold leader who met God on the mountain. No matter where you are in your faith journey, there's hope for a vital friendship with God. Speak—He's listening.

Prayer Starter

Lord God, make me bold enough to come to You when the need is greatest. Because I have concerns, give me enough courage to. . .

DAY 26
EXODUS 21–23

Prayer Scripture

[God told Moses,] "You shall serve the LORD your God,
and He shall bless your bread and your water."
EXODUS 23:25

Prayer Thought for the Day

Because the people of Israel were going into a land—and because they had no experience governing themselves and because God loved them—there were laws they would need to follow. God was the author of their guiding document. These rules would impact the behavior of the people and have an impact on how they spoke to God. They could play the role of the grateful and express joy in the task of following God faithfully, or they could be dejected because they'd failed to live up to His standards while they asked for mercy. In view of fire and smoke, Moses heard the laws God said His people should follow. Moses listened to the penalties for not following and the promises for those who followed. Order was set in place in the midst of what appeared to be chaos.

God is in control, and He warns you about things to avoid and things to pursue. Pay attention, follow, and if you break a law, admit it. Ask God for mercy and forgiveness for wrong thinking and actions.

Prayer Starter

Father, I've broken the laws that You ask me to obey, and You made it very clear I can be forgiven. Today I admit I was wrong when I. . .

DAY 27
EXODUS 24–27

Prayer Scripture

The Lord spoke to Moses, saying: "Speak to the children of Israel, that they bring Me an offering. You shall take My offering from every man who gives it willingly with his heart."
Exodus 25:1–2

Prayer Thought for the Day

Moses was hearing God talk about all the things that would be needed for a tabernacle. This would be a meeting place for God and the people. It would require the crafting of the ark of the covenant, candlesticks, veils and curtains, an altar, and many other objects useful in honoring God in worship. This would be the first time there had ever been a location for the worship of God. It would be a large tentlike structure that could be moved because the people were still in the wilderness, and the meeting place needed to be portable. This structure would help solidify the idea that there was a God, the people needed to worship Him, and prayer was the way people talked to God. Being reminded that God will always be more than a story is important for those who want to make prayer a regular part of their day.

Prayer Starter

Lord God, thanks for reminding me that You make connections for people to recall the value of prayer. May my life show that prayer is valued time with You. Today I'm most concerned about. . .

DAY 28
EXODUS 28–29

Prayer Scripture

[God said,] "I will dwell among the children of Israel and will be their God. And they shall know that I am the LORD their God, who brought them forth out of the land of Egypt, that I may dwell among them. I am the LORD their God."
EXODUS 29:45–46

Prayer Thought for the Day

If the people of Israel were going to bring prayer into their everyday lives, they needed one very specific reminder—God promised to dwell with them and be their God. He wasn't going anywhere, and no other god was worth their attention. Of course this was a true declaration, but often ignored, overlooked, and reinterpreted. Questions arose that cast doubt on whether God really led them out of Egypt. If He did, was it really the best choice? Why didn't they get to choose whether they left Egypt? Who made Moses ruler over them anyway? Stubbornness was common in the questioning. It's common today.

God will be with His people. He brings you out of a failed past. He wants to be a very personal God. And still, He's questioned. If you're curious, ask Him genuinely and seek His Word regularly. Answers await.

Prayer Starter

Father, sometimes I wonder if it's all right for me to ask for answers. But if I really want to know, then I only need to ask *You* questions, like. . .

DAY 29

EXODUS 30–31

Prayer Scripture

When [God] had made an end of communing with [Moses] on Mount Sinai, He gave to Moses two tablets of testimony, tablets of stone, written with the finger of God.
Exodus 31:18

Prayer Thought for the Day

A powerful term is used in Exodus 31, and it shouldn't be overlooked. That term is *communing*. This is no longer a situation where God is doing all the talking with Moses, but there is a common conversation. Questions asked and answered. Concerns discussed and fears calmed. Friendship was growing. Trust was strong. You may remember that the first time God talked to Moses he was certain a mistake had been made. Now this same man had proven himself a friend of God. On a mountain in the wilderness, God and man were connected because of prayer. Not just one side talking, but this was genuine conversation. This communion might bring up ideas of a conversation around a fire or in a quiet place with no interruption. It's not duty; it's privilege. God offers the same opportunity to you today. . .forever.

Prayer Starter

Lord God, even when I don't think of prayer as a conversation with a close friend, it helps to think of Moses and the change that happened in him to know You as both deliverer and friend. When I think of You as a friend, I think. . .

DAY 30
EXODUS 32–33

Prayer Scripture

Moses returned to the LORD and said, "Oh, these people have sinned a great sin and have made themselves gods of gold. Yet now, if You will forgive their sin—and if not, I ask You, blot me out of Your book that You have written."
EXODUS 32:31–32

Prayer Thought for the Day

While Moses was communing with God and getting closer to the one who redeemed him from obscurity and the people from slavery, the people were as far away from the Lord as possible. Moses heard something that dismayed him. It was the singing, shouting, and dancing of people who were involved in a celebration—and God wasn't invited. The people had convinced Moses' brother, Aaron, to make an idol for them to worship. Yes, Moses had been on the mountain for a long time, but the people were only too willing to abandon God, their rescuer. Moses moved quickly to pray on behalf of people who continued to prove unfaithful. Moses explained briefly what the people had done, and he asked that they be forgiven. But he went further. If they couldn't be forgiven, would God please hold him responsible? This should give a hint about how much Moses had changed. God can make such changes in you.

Prayer Starter

Father, may I care enough about others that I pray for them. I will start by praying for. . .

DAY 31
EXODUS 34–35

Prayer Scripture

Moses hastened and bowed his head toward the earth and worshipped. And he said, "If now I have found grace in Your sight, O Lord, let my Lord, I ask You, go among us, for it is a stiff-necked people. And pardon our iniquity and our sin, and take us for Your inheritance."

Exodus 34:8–9

Prayer Thought for the Day

Moses finally felt comfortable asking for a personal favor from God. The people had offended God and broken His laws by following a non-god. Moses knew the promised land was absolutely the best promise the people would ever get, so his prayer was simple. He wanted God to consider whether he was viewed as favorable. If he was, would it be possible to take charge of this group of stiff-necked sinners, forgive them, and still give them the land of promise? That was an amazingly bold prayer for the once-timid leader.

When you find yourself struggling to ask God for what you really want, remember Moses. God can always say no, but giving Him a chance to say yes is wise.

Prayer Starter

Lord God, there are times when I hold back because it seems foolish to ask for what my heart really wants. If what I want is not something You've already said no to, then give me the courage to be bold enough to ask for. . .

DAY 32
EXODUS 36–38

Prayer Scripture

Moses gave command, and they caused it to be proclaimed throughout the camp, saying, "Let neither man nor woman do any more work for the offering of the sanctuary." So the people were restrained from bringing, for the goods they had were sufficient—too much—for all the work to make it.
Exodus 36:6–7

Prayer Thought for the Day

The prayer of Moses was answered. God continued to lead, and the people rallied to the cause of building the tabernacle and outfitting it with all that God had required. In fact, the people had brought more of their personal treasury than was needed, so they were asked to stop. It's not often that people are asked to cease being generous, but perhaps this overabundance was one way God was showing the people that He was still leading—as well as being evidence that they had chosen to recognize His leadership.

How has prayer changed your response to God?

Prayer Starter

Father, I'm grateful that there are people who pray for others and that You use those prayers to do something amazing in me, for me, and through me. Help me to remember those who have encouraged my faith. Thank You for…

DAY 33
EXODUS 39–40

Prayer Scripture

The children of Israel did all the work according to all that the LORD commanded Moses. And Moses saw all the work, and behold, they had done it; as the LORD had commanded, even so had they done it. And Moses blessed them.
EXODUS 39:42–43

Prayer Thought for the Day

There's power in a collective pursuit of God. Perhaps it began with the reprimand of God on the poor choices the people were making. Maybe it had to do with the development and outfitting of God's temple. It might have even been the fact that the people had a common objective, and this work project was useful in bringing them together. It certainly involved prayer, even if the only one praying was Moses. The work began and would later end at the command of God. The people were involved in following His command. It was proof that following God could be done. Their workday ended in a blessing. This was a good day in the wilderness.

When you become involved in a community of those who believe in God, you may find there's a work that you're connected to. Someone has prayed for an individual like you to help—your response comes next.

Prayer Starter

Lord God, becoming involved in something You're doing is nothing new, but it's something You use to help me grow. I see other people differently, and I want this work to succeed. Help me. . .

DAY 34
LEVITICUS 1–4

Prayer Scripture

The LORD spoke to Moses, saying, "Speak to the children of Israel, saying: 'If a soul sins through ignorance against any of the commandments of the LORD concerning things that ought not to be done, and goes against any of them, if the priest who is anointed sins according to the sin of the people, then let him bring to the LORD a young bull without blemish for a sin offering for his sin that he has sinned.'"

LEVITICUS 4:1–3

Prayer Thought for the Day

The Israelites made baby steps in following God. He took the time to share information about what a follower looks like. One of the common themes of this lawbook was that sin didn't need to permanently separate the follower from the God who led. The people were encouraged to stay connected to God, to return after they left, and then to follow once more. Prayer's the great connection to a very good God. The people saw God at work, witnessed miracles, and joined in the work. God had standards, and He made provisions to forgive when the people failed. You might think it's best to move away when you fail God, but His idea was always to have His family return to Him in prayer when failure occurred.

Prayer Starter

Father, I want to stay connected, but when I fail, I want to reconnect. Help me to admit that You're right when I'm wrong. In this moment, I admit that I...

DAY 35
LEVITICUS 5–7

Prayer Scripture

And the LORD spoke to Moses, saying. . .
LEVITICUS 6:24

Prayer Thought for the Day

Had any human heard directly from God as much as Moses? The law was delivered to him, and you've read over and over again that "the LORD spoke to Moses." God's people would need to know His mind on issues they'd face every day. Moses may have spoken to God in prayer more often than we read in Leviticus, but what he was listening to was more important than what he may have said. God spoke to this man about delivering the people from slavery, rescuing them from Egyptians, what the people would eat, how to build the temple, and how to manage daily affairs. God was comprehensive in His plans and deliberate in His instructions so that when the people engaged in prayer, they would know if they had broken His law—and if they did, they'd know what type of sacrifice was needed. There would come a time for praying, but this was a time for listening. God had something to say. He still does.

Prayer Starter

Lord God, help me to balance my friendship with You between what I want to say and what You have to say. May Your words bury themselves deep in my heart and change what I do and how I do it. Thank You for already teaching me. . .

DAY 36
LEVITICUS 8–10

Prayer Scripture

Moses did as the Lord commanded him. And the assembly was gathered together at the door of the tabernacle of the congregation. And Moses said to the congregation, "This is the thing that the Lord commanded to be done."
Leviticus 8:4–5

Prayer Thought for the Day

This was a break from God's instruction where Moses took all that he'd learned because he'd been communing with God and passed the instruction along. This might better be pictured as going to a leadership conference. You learn valuable things about being a leader, and then you go back to the workplace and put those new skills to work to make things better. Moses was the leader, God was the instructor, and this was a time when the living prayer experience resulted in doing what God asked to be done. Prayer isn't a replacement for action; it's a work that allows you to learn to do what you've never known how to do. It's not a moment of memorized prayer; it's a conversation—and it will benefit everyone you know.

Prayer Starter

Father, let's talk, and then I'll read. Let me learn so I can share. Let me share so others can know You. One of the first things I want others to know about You is. . .

DAY 37
LEVITICUS 11–12

Prayer Scripture

"For I am the Lord your God. Therefore you shall sanctify yourselves, and you shall be holy, for I am holy."
Leviticus 11:44

Prayer Thought for the Day

God provided the detailed information Moses needed for many common scenarios and events. Moses kept track of what God said. Then Leviticus 11:44 arrived to summarize the end goal of all the obedience required to follow His law. A paraphrase of this verse might be "I am the God worth following. So take My laws and use them to set yourself apart from those who will not follow. I am unique and I want you to be unique in the way you live, the choices you make, and the rules you live by."

Pray. Give God your personal status update about where you think you are in your friendship with Him, and where you want to be. Then ask Him to help you get to the place where others see godlike uniqueness in you.

Prayer Starter

Lord God, I don't always feel as if I'm set apart to be used by You in the way I think You want me to be. I don't want to stand on the sidelines, hoping You never call me up. If this were a sporting event, then "Put me in, coach." There are many areas in which I'll need help. My list includes. . .

DAY 38
LEVITICUS 13:1–14:32

Prayer Scripture

[God said,] "This shall be the law of the leper in the day of his cleansing. He shall be brought to the priest, and the priest shall go forth out of the camp, and the priest shall look. And behold, if the plague of leprosy is healed in the leper, then the priest shall command that two alive and clean birds, and cedar wood and scarlet and hyssop be taken for him who is to be cleansed."

Leviticus 14:2–4

Prayer Thought for the Day

To be diagnosed with leprosy meant a forced separation from family and friends. Those with this skin-wasting disease (or likely one of many different, but similar, skin diseases) had to live outside the city and call out, "Unclean!" if anyone came close. This disease meant drawing attention to yourself and never in a positive way. Some didn't return to their families, but a few received a new diagnosis of "clean," and it changed their future. A leper had two positive prayer options. The first was for healing. The second was gratitude when healing took place.

You can choose the same prayer options. Pray for healing of mental, emotional, or physical issues; then thank God for His help.

Prayer Starter

Father, there are times when I just feel—off. I may not have a diagnosis, but I'm struggling. I ask for Your help and thank You for walking with me as I deal with. . .

DAY 39

LEVITICUS 14:33–15:33

Prayer Scripture

"This is the law. . ."
Leviticus 14:54

Prayer Thought for the Day

God's laws continued to fill the scrolls of Leviticus. There would be a lot that the priests would need to know in order to help the people learn to do right. These priests would need to pray for guidance, understanding, and wisdom. The people would need to do the same. There would be questions about the law, and these words of scripture would be reviewed to gain a better understanding of what God wanted. Some of these laws dealt with the home and some with the people who lived inside those homes. These laws were important to God.

Part of your prayer life can be the questions you ask to bring light to subjects you don't understand. God doesn't want you to be confused—and you don't need to be. Your questions could include asking for the wisdom to know what to do, what not to do, and who is worth following.

Prayer Starter

Lord God, You have insight that I need about things I don't understand. You've helped so many others to learn the way You want things done. Help me to learn the things that I'll never understand without Your help. One of the things I've always wanted to know is. . .

DAY 40

LEVITICUS 16–17

Prayer Scripture

"Aaron shall lay both his hands on the head of the live goat and confess over it all the iniquities of the children of Israel, and all their transgressions, in all their sins, putting them on the head of the goat, and shall send it away into the wilderness by the hand of a fit man. And the goat shall bear all their iniquities on itself to a land not inhabited, and he shall release the goat in the wilderness."

Leviticus 16:21–22

Prayer Thought for the Day

As a priest, Aaron heard the sins of the people. There was one visual ceremony that's worth looking at, the observance of the scapegoat. Aaron would pray, confessing the sins of the people over the goat, which visually represented the sins of the people. The goat would leave the camp, taking the sin into the wilderness—never to be seen again. It was important that the people of Israel understood the meaning behind the scapegoat, because when Jesus came they'd see the final scapegoat who took on the sins of every human and removed them, never to be seen again.

Prayer is important in helping you realize the need for a scapegoat and express gratitude for the greatest gift you could ever receive.

Prayer Starter

Father, I thank You for sending Jesus as the scapegoat for every human's sin. If confession was the right decision for Aaron, let me admit my own sin. . .

DAY 41
LEVITICUS 18–20

Prayer Scripture

"I have said to you, 'You shall inherit their land, and I will give it to you to possess it, a land that flows with milk and honey.' I am the LORD your God. . . . And you shall be holy to Me, for I the LORD am holy and have set you apart from other people, that you should be Mine."
LEVITICUS 20:24, 26

Prayer Thought for the Day

God's conversation with Moses resulted in His instruction manual. Within these words, God took time to remind all who would pay attention that He hadn't forgotten the promise of a land ready to be claimed. The promise had been made. The promise would be kept. He reminded everyone that He was something other than the non-gods they would encounter. He was set apart from literally everything. This set-apart status was called holiness. This holy status was exactly what God wanted for His people, but they could never do that on their own. It would require a friendship—and God was all in. He was asking if the same was true for the people He'd rescued. Would they keep in touch through prayer? Will you?

Prayer Starter

Lord God, I want to pay attention to You. I want to be set apart to do the surprising work You have for me. Teach me how to be Your friend. I want to do more than. . .

DAY 42
LEVITICUS 21–23

Prayer Scripture

"You shall not offer to the LORD what is bruised or crushed or broken or cut; you shall not make any offering of it in your land."
LEVITICUS 22:24

Prayer Thought for the Day

For sacrifices, God expected the best and not the worst someone could bring. Should a conversation with God be less than your best? Should it be the prayer of a buddy, which contains no respect and honor for God? Prayer doesn't need to be made from a list of approved words. Sometimes you're fortunate if your grief allows much more than a groan. God understands when words are a struggle. Still, there's value in recognizing the importance of prayer, the majesty of the God you pray to, and the knowledge that He answers prayer. When you don't give prayer the respect it deserves, it'll become less important to you. It's hard to grow a friendship with someone you won't talk to.

Prayer Starter

Father, help me to balance my desire to pray with the freedom to pray about the things that mean the most to me. I don't want my prayer time to be something I do without thinking. Let this time be a meaningful conversation with my best friend. Teach me to pray meaningfully so it's easier to share. . .

DAY 43
LEVITICUS 24–25

Prayer Scripture

"You shall not oppress one another, but you shall fear your God. For I am the Lord your God."
Leviticus 25:17

Prayer Thought for the Day

An improved and ongoing connection with God leads to a greater willingness to connect with other humans. It's hard to love God, talk to Him, and still want the worst for other people. God's love is something that can transform hard hearts and harsh intent and convert it to a compassion that doesn't oppress. This kind of love seeks justice for those who live with oppression. The respect you show to God in prayer is a lesson in the respect you should offer those you encounter. You do this because the God who created you and gives you all you need to survive also wants a close and ongoing connection with you. If you really want to improve your prayer experience, then take the connection you're growing with God and make it visible in how you treat everyone you meet.

Prayer Starter

Lord God, I don't want to see prayer as a me-and-God-against-the-world connection. Help me to see prayer as a way to pass Your compassion on to those who need to know inhumanity shouldn't be the norm. Here are some ways I'd like to pass this message on to others. . .

DAY 44

LEVITICUS 26–27

Prayer Scripture

"You shall not make idols or a graven image. Nor shall you set up a standing image. Nor shall you set up any image of stone in your land to bow down to it, for I am the LORD your God."
LEVITICUS 26:1

Prayer Thought for the Day

Becoming a friend of God means admitting and then believing there's no other god besides Him. You can create a division within yourself if you split time between God and anything that would take His place. He's never been a part-time Savior. He takes the day shift and the night shift too. He's always available to listen. This happens because a man like you is talking. Nothing should stand between you and God. If you don't have time to pray, you may need to evaluate and identify what's standing between you and the God who listens and answers. Just know that if you're not connecting with God, He's never been the problem.

Prayer Starter

Father, it's easy to distract me. I can begin a prayer with You, and my mind wanders to every place but this conversation. Help me to stay focused by leaving distractions when I begin sharing today's life events with You. I want to get close, stay close, and. . .

DAY 45
NUMBERS 1–2

Prayer Scripture

The Lord spoke to Moses in the wilderness of
Sinai, in the tabernacle of the congregation. . .
after they had come out of the land of Egypt,
saying: "Take the sum of all the congregation of the
children of Israel, by their families, by the house of
their fathers, with the number of their names."
Numbers 1:1–2

Prayer Thought for the Day

Did God need to know the number of people in each of the tribes? This is a God who knows names before babies are born. He knows the number of hairs on your head. God even knows the intent of your heart. There may never be a stated reason for this counting (or census) of tribes, but maybe God wanted His people to remember there were others who, if they chose to believe, pray, and follow Him, would offer a difference to a world that seemed bent on non-god alternatives. If a people called by God would actually follow, then the impact on those around them would be noticed. Yet the people gave up praying, resisted believing, and set aside the idea of following—and other nations noticed their failure.

Prayer Starter

Lord God, I'm just one among the millions of individuals who understand the power of Your name, the hope in Your promises, and the richness of taking the time to pray to You. To You I'm not a number. To You I am. . .

DAY 46
NUMBERS 3–4

Prayer Scripture

Eleazar the son of Aaron the priest shall be chief over
the chief of the Levites and have the oversight of those
who take care of the needs of the sanctuary.
NUMBERS 3:32

Prayer Thought for the Day

The priests (the family of Levi) received housing assignments, work assignments, and all the details they would need to manage the work of the portable tabernacle. Leadership within the tabernacle wasn't the result of a deep personal knowledge, from birth, of the subject of God. There was a learning curve that would be part of their training over many years. Priests would learn God's laws, and they would pray for wisdom. In time, they would lead within the tabernacle. When someone asked why prayer was important, they would need answers, and the best answers came from their own personal experience coupled with the words God had already spoken.

You get to take on a similar role. Teach others the value of prayer because you've prayed and found the encouragement of God on the other side of amen.

Prayer Starter

Father, I'm blessed because You invite me to pray. I'm honored because I'll have a few answers for someone who asked. I'm humbled because You want to hear from me when. . .

DAY 47
NUMBERS 5–6

Prayer Scripture

The Lord spoke to Moses, saying, "Speak to the children of Israel: 'When a man or woman shall commit any sin that men commit, to do a trespass against the Lord, and that person is guilty, then they shall confess their sin that they have done.'"

Numbers 5:5–7

Prayer Thought for the Day

God gave the people more than six hundred laws. The priests were responsible for knowing the law and sharing what they knew. The people were responsible for following every single one of those laws. But if they failed to obey, their next response was to confess their lawbreaking tendency. This was owning their misdeed and knowing that the only remedy (at the time) was to be found at the tabernacle and at the direction of the priests.

Today, when you break God's laws, you confess your sin through prayer. Talk directly to God about everything associated with your guilty verdict. In this place forgiveness becomes possible. It's not in trying to do better. . .it's accepting that you can't but also that Jesus paid for your sin. Choose forgiveness and accept the help needed to stop repeatedly making this same choice.

Prayer Starter

Lord God, there's a lot I can learn from You. There are so many ways that I blow it when it comes to following You perfectly. Don't let me become discouraged as I own up to my role in lawbreaking choices like. . .

DAY 48
NUMBERS 7

Prayer Scripture

When Moses had gone into the tabernacle of the congregation to speak with Him, then he heard the voice of One speaking to him from above the mercy seat that was on the ark of testimony, from between the two cherubim. And He spoke to him.

Numbers 7:89

Prayer Thought for the Day

God spoke; Moses wrote down what He said. God spoke; Moses answered. God spoke; Moses obeyed. It seems like a simple formula, but it's what you might do today. It could be something you physically write down, it could be something you use technology to recall later, or it could be something that impacts your heart. What God speaks is both powerful and worth remembering. You'll learn something every time you read His Word. You'll also learn something every time you pray. You're visiting a part of scripture that seems like a burden because of the sheer number of laws God offered. Don't be overwhelmed. The intent of such a comprehensive set of rules is that no matter how hard you try you'll always need God's help. *Always.* The good news is the help you need is exactly the help He offers.

Prayer Starter

Father, speak and I'll listen. Teach and I'll learn. Help and I'll not be overwhelmed. I'll need the courage, strength, and wisdom to. . .

DAY 49
NUMBERS 8–10

Prayer Scripture

Moses said to them, "Stand still, and I will hear what
the LORD will command concerning you."
NUMBERS 9:8

Prayer Thought for the Day

The people of Israel had questions. Moses knew it was foolish to guess at an answer. He took the time to ask God for wisdom to know how to answer the people. The question they asked was about something God had addressed. God had told them about Passover, but they wanted to know if someone who was ritually unclean could celebrate the day. They still had questions, so God clarified His position, and it was recorded in Numbers 9.

It's possible that today you'll have questions that weren't specifically addressed in God's Word. You don't need to guess. Ask God for direction and study the words He already wrote. You'll find wisdom that can be applied to the question you have, and He'll help so that you can be convinced that what you're asking about is something to pursue or something to avoid. Guessing remains the least helpful option.

Prayer Starter

Lord God, You're the one with answers when I have questions. You're the one with wisdom when I'm confused. You know the way when I'm lost. Some questions I've had lately include. . .

DAY 50
NUMBERS 11–12

Prayer Scripture

Then Moses heard the people weep throughout their families, every man in the door of his tent. And the anger of the LORD was kindled greatly. Moses was also displeased. And Moses said to the LORD, "Why have You afflicted Your servant? And why have I not found favor in Your sight, that You have laid the burden of all these people on me?"
NUMBERS 11:10–11

Prayer Thought for the Day

The people sinned, and God wasn't happy because gratitude for the manna He gave them was less important to them than the desire to lodge a complaint. The people complained, and Moses seemed to wish that God had chosen someone else to lead them. Fed up, Moses asked God *why* questions that pointed to his feelings of being misused by the people. It was all just too much. But you'll notice that Moses didn't go to a human and pour out his complaint. No, Moses went to God in prayer. God didn't reprimand him for his meltdown; in fact, He helped the people. In doing so, God helped Moses. This human leader would struggle more than once with people who just couldn't seem to be satisfied with God's leadership.

Prayer Starter

Father, people can be frustrating. You know this more than anyone. I'm so glad You chose mercy and forgiveness first. When I'm frustrated, can You teach me how to deal with. . .

DAY 51
NUMBERS 13–14

Prayer Scripture

Joshua the son of Nun and Caleb the son of Jephunneh. . .spoke to all the company of the children of Israel, saying, "The land that we passed through to search is an exceedingly good land. If the LORD delights in us, then He will bring us into this land and give it to us, a land that flows with milk and honey. Only do not rebel against the LORD. Do not fear the people of the land."

NUMBERS 14:6–9

Prayer Thought for the Day

Twelve spies went into the promised land. Two returned to say, "The land is ours—why wait?" The other ten pointed to the strength of the people and the height of the men. It was as if they were saying the people would need to journey forty more years while they became comfortable with the label "Homeless." The majority apparently thought God wasn't big enough. Two put their trust in God's promise. They had developed a relationship with God and believed their prayers were being answered. But the virus of disbelief was spreading, and the people were afraid. The waiting continued.

Maybe you've allowed fear to prevent you from doing something you believe God's asking you to do. How long will you wait?

Prayer Starter

Lord God, it can be easier to refuse to step into the great unknown than to trust that I'll survive the experience. Help me trust You enough to. . .

DAY 52
NUMBERS 15–16

Prayer Scripture

Moses said to Korah, "Hear, I ask you, you sons of Levi:
Does it seem but a small thing to you that the God of Israel
has separated you from the congregation of Israel to bring you
near to Himself to do the service of the tabernacle of the LORD
and to stand before the congregation to minister to them?
And He has brought you near to Himself, and all your brothers,
the sons of Levi, with you, and you also seek the priesthood?"
NUMBERS 16:8–10

Prayer Thought for the Day

Korah had a bad case of envy. He wanted Moses' job, and he sought to point out that Moses was likely the reason the people still wandered in the wilderness. He believed Moses would be the reason they all died without a home. People were listening. But there's no mention of anyone asking God for wisdom to discover the truth. God continued to instruct the people through Moses, but that wasn't enough for Korah. This rebellious man had no idea what he was asking when he incited Moses' removal. Korah certainly didn't know the mind of God.

Prayer can keep emotions in check and actions on pause while we wait for God's answer to life's most stressful moments.

Prayer Starter

Father, help me to keep my emotions under Your control. I want to pray before I act or respond. I want to choose Your peace over my frustration when. . .

DAY 53
NUMBERS 17–19

Prayer Scripture

"You shall write Aaron's name on the rod of Levi. For one rod shall be for the head of the house of their fathers. And you shall lay them in the tabernacle of the congregation before the testimony, where I will meet with you. And it shall come to pass that the rod of the man whom I shall choose shall blossom, and I will make the murmurings of the children of Israel—which they murmur against you—to cease."
NUMBERS 17:3–5

Prayer Thought for the Day

Are complaints a prayer? Maybe not, but they get God's attention. Why? Maybe because you have so much to be thankful for. When you fail the gratitude test, it gets God's attention—but never in a good way. You can pray and tell God about the things He does that mean something to you—or you can complain without talking specifically to Him. In the case of Moses, complaints led God to prove once and for all that Moses would lead and Aaron would be in charge of the tabernacle. God will answer your complaint, but it may not be the way you want. "Be careful, little mouth, what you say."

Prayer Starter

Lord God, reserve my words for declarations of praise and keep complaints far from my everyday language. If I could honor You for just three good gifts today, that would include. . .

DAY 54
NUMBERS 20–21

Prayer Scripture

The people came to Moses and said, "We have sinned, for we have spoken against the LORD and against you. Pray to the LORD, that He take away the serpents from us." And Moses prayed for the people.

NUMBERS 21:7

Prayer Thought for the Day

There was a miracle taking place in the midst of a crisis. The people in the wilderness complained, rebelled, showed fear, and were about as uncooperative as anyone you've ever known. Day after day Moses endured their rebellion. Day after day God had to redirect their footsteps, but when snakes entered the picture and people were dying from their bites, the people universally asked Moses to do something they hadn't put much belief in. The people wanted Moses to pray. Moses didn't offer a lecture or ask for thirty days of good behavior before he prayed. Moses did something he knew helped—he prayed. And God listened. People were rescued from death. The people lived to complain another day. You can pray or complain, but God responds much better to the prayers of friends.

Prayer Starter

Father, I'd like to be considered Your friend, and I don't want to complain to get Your attention. I want to pray for others and for. . .

DAY 55
NUMBERS 22–24

Prayer Scripture

Balaam answered and said to the servants of Balak,
"If Balak were to give me his house full of silver and gold,
I could not go beyond the word of the LORD my God to do
less or more. Now therefore, I ask, you also remain here this
night, that I may know what more the LORD will say to me."
NUMBERS 22:18–19

Prayer Thought for the Day

Balaam was unlike most people. He was a prophet who recognized God but wasn't an Israelite. He didn't travel through the wilderness with them, and he could be influenced by the promise of money. The leader Balak sent word to Balaam that he'd like him to curse Israel. Balak promised a financial reward. That sounded good to this prophet, so he tried to pray a curse on Israel, but God said no. Balaam asked God repeatedly, and the answer on each occasion was no. God asked Balaam to bless Israel instead. The end was worse for Balak than if he'd just watched the Israelites wandering through the wilderness.

This is an early example of someone who wasn't an Israelite honoring God and praying to Him for answers, though he didn't always understand or appreciate the answer he got. That might just describe you.

Prayer Starter

Lord God, thank You for hearing my prayer and answering when I speak Your name. Thank You for blessing anyone You choose. Help me trust Your blessing even when I don't understand Your mercy when. . .

DAY 56
NUMBERS 25–27

Prayer Scripture

Among these there was not a man of those who Moses and Aaron the priest numbered when they numbered the children of Israel in the wilderness of Sinai. For the LORD had said of them, "They shall surely die in the wilderness." And there was not a man of them left, except Caleb the son of Jephunneh and Joshua the son of Nun.
NUMBERS 26:64–65

Prayer Thought for the Day

It had been nearly four decades since the people of Israel had been counted. It may have been a melancholy time for Moses as the people were counted once more. Men over the age of twenty when the journey started had passed away. Moses was told he wouldn't lead the people to the promised land. In this forty-year preparation there were so many heartaches for Moses, so many rebellious encounters, but so many answered prayers. The Israelites who'd learned wilderness living would have homes in a land of their own. The two spies from early in the journey were still alive. Joshua would lead the people in, and Caleb would claim his own piece of the promise. Prayers would be answered and promises kept. The wilderness wandering was almost over.

Prayer Starter

Father, sometimes an answered prayer reminds me of the hard journey it took to get there. It doesn't make me any less thrilled with Your answer, but I may take time to remember the journey. When I do, I'll. . .

DAY 57
NUMBERS 28–30

Prayer Scripture

Moses spoke to the leaders of the tribes concerning the children of Israel, saying, "This is the thing that the LORD has commanded: If a man vows a vow to the LORD, or swears an oath to bind his soul with a bond, he shall not break his word; he shall do according to all that proceeds out of his mouth."
NUMBERS 30:1–2

Prayer Thought for the Day

God made so many promises to the people of Israel, and these promises were coming true. It wouldn't be long before the people were finally home. Yet God had more to teach. Sometimes people who feel extremely generous will make promises they won't be able to keep. God had witnessed this before and wasn't interested in promoting promise breakers. God willingly accepted the vows of those who made them—but He always expected the vow maker to follow through. A vow signified that the promise made was because one person said it ("all that proceeds out of his mouth") and one Lord heard it (the God they prayed to). It's better to not promise God something than to break a promise.

Prayer Starter

Lord God, may I be careful when I make a promise to You. If I do make a promise, would You help me keep it? I'll need that help if I'm going to. . .

DAY 58
NUMBERS 31–32

Prayer Scripture

And all the gold of the offering that they offered up to the Lord, from the captains of thousands and from the captains of hundreds, was sixteen thousand seven hundred and fifty shekels. (For the men of war had taken spoil, every man for himself.) And Moses and Eleazar the priest took the gold from the captains of thousands and of hundreds and brought it into the tabernacle of the congregation for a memorial for the children of Israel before the Lord.

Numbers 31:52–54

Prayer Thought for the Day

In the decades of wilderness living, there was more than one nation that expressed hostility toward the people of Israel. When requests from Israel were made to move through specific areas, these requests were often denied. There were occasions when war was declared against Israel. This passage in Numbers 31 describes the end of one of those wars. A large amount of gold was amassed and offered to the Lord for use in the tabernacle. It would commemorate an answer to prayer. God went with them and brought victory.

Having something visual to remind you of God's goodness can be an important way to remember—and then continue walking with God.

Prayer Starter

Father, I need to remember those times when You showed up at times when a miracle was just what I needed. Thank You. Today I'll remember. . .

DAY 59
NUMBERS 33–34

Prayer Scripture

These are those whom the LORD commanded to divide the inheritance for the children of Israel in the land of Canaan.
NUMBERS 34:29

Prayer Thought for the Day

Good things happen when people pray. It's often the beginning of noticeable change. Significant historical movements began with prayer. They advanced with prayer. The impossible became possible with prayer. Having a history of prayer can change the history of a nation. On the threshold of the taking of the promised land, there was a period of time that brought an answer to the necessities the people required. The land was mapped out for the families that would live there, the inheritance was identified and passed along, and leaders were recognized. Would it be long before homes were built, businesses established, and roots tapped in the soil of their new home? If you're just starting a journey with Jesus, remember that not everything happens overnight. Sometimes you'll need time to prepare for the good things God has for you.

Prayer Starter

Lord God, no one likes to wait. Society makes it easy to get what I don't have before I can afford it. Give me wisdom in the wait. Thanks for preparing me for good things to come. Until then, I continue to pray for. . .

DAY 60
NUMBERS 35–36

Prayer Scripture

"Among the cities that you shall give to the Levites there shall be six cities for refuge, which you shall appoint for the manslayer, that he may flee there. And to them you shall add forty-two cities."
NUMBERS 35:6

Prayer Thought for the Day

It's worth noting that God sometimes answers prayers in advance of your need. Consider that God gave order to everything in the world you live in. The alternative is chaos that would constantly require His intervention. He gave rules to be followed so that people who may be oppressed had reason to hope. He gave boundaries to the oceans, seasons, day and night. And this forward-thinking God also provided a place where those who stood accused of manslaughter would have a place of refuge while the circumstances were sorted out. If you struggle with what you may feel are too many rules from God, then you need to know that if following the rules is the great expectation, then prayers for fairness have already been answered.

Prayer Starter

Father, I'm not sure I've thought of Your laws as a way for You to answer prayer before it ever needed to be spoken. Thanks for giving order to our world. Help me see Your expectations in a new way when I. . .

DAY 61
DEUTERONOMY 1–2

Prayer Scripture

"Then I said to you, 'Do not dread or be afraid of them. The LORD your God, who goes before you, He shall fight for you, according to all that He did for you in Egypt before your eyes, and in the wilderness where you have seen how the LORD your God bore you, as a man bears his son, all the way that you went until you came into this place.' Yet in this matter you did not believe the LORD your God."

DEUTERONOMY 1:29–32

Prayer Thought for the Day

Moses shares the outcome of the very early (but failed) opportunity to occupy the land God promised. This was the prayer of all who wandered in those early days of the journey. Yet the people couldn't manage the advice to live fearlessly. They struggled to believe God was going before them. They weren't sure God would work for their good. They were quick to forget what God had done for them. Moses concluded, "You did not believe the LORD your God." You might believe God has helped others while discounting the help He's offered you. You might believe all good experiences are coincidental, but God answers prayers. This means the ones *you* pray. Don't stop. Recognize His good. Thank Him.

Prayer Starter

Lord God, weakness fills me, but You have strength. I'm confused, but You have complete wisdom. My mind's forgetful compared to Your memory. Help me to thank You when. . .

DAY 62
DEUTERONOMY 3–4

Prayer Scripture

"Behold, I have taught you statutes and judgments, just as the Lord my God commanded me, that you should do them in the land that you are going to possess. Therefore keep and do them, for this is your wisdom and your understanding in the sight of the nations who shall hear all these statutes and say, 'Surely this great nation is a wise and understanding people.' For what great nation is there that has God so near to them as the Lord our God is in all things when we call on Him?"
Deuteronomy 4:5–7

Prayer Thought for the Day

Prayer would be part of the testimony other nations would witness when they encountered the Israelites. The miracles were noticed beyond their camp. The journey was long. Even when the faithful were few, there were still people calling out to God to prepare everyone for the home God already provided—one described as "a land flowing with milk and honey." It was a prosperous land, unlike the wilderness that sustained them with God's help. Some had forgotten the work God had already done. This was a call to remember—to be grateful and to embrace a renewed satisfaction in a very good God.

Prayer Starter

Father, may I always remember that when people look at me they either recognize You—or they don't. Help me be Your ambassador when. . .

DAY 63
DEUTERONOMY 5–7

Prayer Scripture

"Therefore you shall be careful to do as the Lord your God has commanded you. You shall not turn aside to the right hand or to the left. You shall walk in all the ways that the Lord your God has commanded you, that you may live and that it may be well with you, and that you may prolong your days in the land that you shall possess."
Deuteronomy 5:32–33

Prayer Thought for the Day

God had been described to a wayward people as "merciful." They were repeatedly reminded that the path God offered was paved with the expectation of obedience and that their choices would impact not only their future but the future of their children and grandchildren. It could also affect length of life and the terms of their admittance to the new land God offered Israel. God didn't want the people to look for loopholes, to walk just outside the path, or to convince others to do the same. The "walk" meant an ongoing connection, and that connection was made possible through the gift of prayer. You have a similar opportunity to obey, follow, and connect with God. Each of those opportunities is made understandable through prayer.

Prayer Starter

Lord God, prayer needs to be more to me than an emergency call on difficult days. It's the conversation of friends and advice that brings life to every single day. Help me to realize that when I pray I. . .

DAY 64
DEUTERONOMY 8–11

Prayer Scripture

[Moses said,] "Therefore you shall keep the commandments of the LORD your God, to walk in His ways and to fear Him. . . . When you have eaten and are full, then you shall bless the LORD your God for the good land that He has given you."
DEUTERONOMY 8:6, 10

Prayer Thought for the Day

God continued to do for the people of Israel what they couldn't do on their own. The journey to a promise was coming closer to reality, and a reminder was in order. God said this before. You've read it before. You might even be wondering why the people needed so many reminders to keep His commandments, walk in the direction He led, and show Him the utmost respect. The people seemed to have short-term memory issues. They often allowed themselves to believe that the reason for success was because they were part of the solution. They certainly could be part of the way God worked, but God was the one who continually supplied solutions.

You should do what God asked the people to do by blessing (in prayer) the Lord for what only He can do.

Prayer Starter

Father, I'm blessed because You're a blessing. I have because You gave. I can hope because You keep Your promises. I want to show You honor by remembering Your goodness that. . .

DAY 65

DEUTERONOMY 12–14

Prayer Scripture

[God said,] "Whatever I command you, be careful to do it. You shall not add to it or take away from it."
Deuteronomy 12:32

Prayer Thought for the Day

People have been notorious for adding to or taking away from what God said. Some, in the name of trying to help God out, added rules that God never did. Others said that not all of His rules were important and that some could be ignored. You may think this is a modern trend, but it was happening before God's people ever arrived in their new homeland. When Jesus walked the earth, there were men who thought it made sense to make prayer a sideshow for others to admire. They used big words, spoke loudly, and made disparaging remarks about other people in their prayers. This was not the conversation God had in mind when He asked His people to call on Him in prayer.

You never need to try to make following God a journey to enhance your own fame. Just pay attention to what He actually said.

Prayer Starter

Lord God, I need to be careful that my personal convictions about You don't find me trying to force other people to conform to something You never commanded. I should never ignore Your Word either. When I walk with You, help me. . .

DAY 66
DEUTERONOMY 15–17

Prayer Scripture

"And it shall be, when he sits on the throne of his kingdom, that he shall write for himself a copy of this law in a book, from what is before the priests the Levites. And it shall be with him, and he shall read in it all the days of his life, that he may learn to fear the LORD his God, to keep all the words of this law and these statutes, to do them."

DEUTERONOMY 17:18–19

Prayer Thought for the Day

God was the King of Israel. He supplied the laws and dealt with offenders. A day was coming when people would demand a human king. So He gave rules for future kings. A king would need to be as familiar with the law as the priests. This law was to inform all decisions the king would make. This future king would need to show God absolute respect, learn from Him, and encourage everyone to obey God. The king would need to be a spiritual leader of the nation. You'll soon be introduced to a variety of kings; some followed this command, while others didn't. Prayer is always a helpful way to keep these kings (and you) exposed to truth.

Prayer Starter

Father, if I'm called to be a leader, help me to know more about You and what You want so I can lead with Your truth by. . .

DAY 67

DEUTERONOMY 18–20

Prayer Scripture

[God said,] "I will raise up for them a Prophet like you from among their brothers, and will put My words in His mouth, and He shall speak to them all that I shall command Him."
DEUTERONOMY 18:18

Prayer Thought for the Day

Most scholars believe Deuteronomy 18:18 is a reference to the future coming of Jesus. This prophecy from Moses was an encouragement the people might not have entirely understood when Moses spoke of this man's arrival. This brief introduction to the arrival of God's Son would be discussed by other prophets and became a point of prayer as people longed for the day when God would have future-shaping words to say through this prophet (Jesus).

You have the benefit of discovering all of biblical history through the pages of the Bible. The people you read about were living through what they didn't know and struggled to understand. Perhaps you can identify with their struggle. But God doesn't leave you in the dark—just read, pray, and repeat. You'll learn something new every time you do.

Prayer Starter

Lord God, it's amazing to think that You once spoke words to humans just like me, and those words were written down to encourage me. Some of the words I've been thinking about include. . .

DAY 68
DEUTERONOMY 21–23

Prayer Scripture

"You shall keep and perform what has gone out of your lips, even a freewill offering, as you have vowed to the LORD your God, which you have promised with your mouth."
DEUTERONOMY 23:23

Prayer Thought for the Day

It could be the result of too much coffee, but there are times when you might make an impulse promise. It may seem the right thing to do, but you live to regret the promise. You might even come to believe no one can really hold you to it. You've learned a few things along the way and now consider it wise to reevaluate your position. God's wisdom is to carefully consider your promises so you never have to fail to keep them. God said that if you spoke the words, then you keep your promise. You do what you vowed to do. This isn't the first time you've read about vows. Maybe this subject is important in a society that walks back on almost everything said, if it no longer seems convenient to do what was promised. Before you make a promise, ask God for wisdom to know if this is something you really can do—or if it's even something He wants you to do.

Prayer Starter

Father, words are pretty important. You used them to speak the world into existence. My words can sometimes get me in trouble. May I ask for help before I promise to. . .

DAY 69
DEUTERONOMY 24–26

Prayer Scripture

"You shall speak and say before the Lord your God, . . .
'The Egyptians mistreated us, and afflicted us, and laid hard labor on us. And when we cried to the Lord God of our fathers, the Lord heard our voice and looked on our affliction and our labor and our oppression. And the Lord brought us forth out of Egypt with a mighty hand and with an outstretched arm. . . . And He has brought us into this place and has given us this land, even a land that flows with milk and honey. . . .' And you shall rejoice in every good thing that the Lord your God has given to you and to your house."

Deuteronomy 26:5–9, 11

Prayer Thought for the Day

The people were urged to approach God in prayer. The words *speak*, *say*, and *rejoice* are all part of prayer. Again the people were urged to never forget. By remembering the goodness of God, they'd have ample reason to understand how amazing it was for freedom to be found in the future. The people were reminded that, because God heard their cries of oppression, He responded with a rescue plan never seen before.

Today, speak, say, and rejoice in the story of your life.

Prayer Starter

Lord God, I speak words of honor about the good You have done for me. I say I'll follow because this will be how I learn. I rejoice because. . .

DAY 70

DEUTERONOMY 27–28

Prayer Scripture

"Because you did not serve the LORD your God with joyfulness and with gladness of heart, for the abundance of all things, therefore you shall serve your enemies that the LORD shall send against you, in hunger and in thirst and in nakedness and in want of all things. And He shall put a yoke of iron on your neck."
DEUTERONOMY 28:47–48

Prayer Thought for the Day

This was a prophecy no one wanted to hear. Deuteronomy 28 talks about how the sin of the people would result in devastating loss, profound grief, and renewed slavery. It was even spoken of in present tense, when speaking of serving Israel's enemies, as if it was something Moses was sure would happen. The book of Deuteronomy is essentially the sermons of Moses. Some parts provided historic information, others warning. This was a prophecy about the accumulated sin of a future generation. The people were warned that future family members would be as bad in decision-making as their parents were in the wilderness. God doesn't wink when you don't pray, as if it's not that important. He doesn't overlook sin simply because Jesus paid the price. He never once suggested that your actions no longer matter. He didn't in Deuteronomy 28, and He doesn't now.

Prayer Starter

Father, I believe You give me life to enjoy. I believe You give laws to protect. I believe You give warnings to pay attention to. I believe You gave me prayer to. . .

DAY 71

DEUTERONOMY 29–31

Prayer Scripture

"You stand this day, all of you, before the LORD your God. . .
that you should enter into covenant with the LORD your God
and into His oath that the LORD your God makes with you this
day, that He may establish you today as a people for Himself,
and that He may be to you a God, as He has said to you and as
He has sworn to your fathers, to Abraham, to Isaac, and to Jacob."
DEUTERONOMY 29:10, 12–13

Prayer Thought for the Day

The people were together. In this moment of collective agreement, they were entering a covenant with God. They would be leaving their wilderness wanderings and starting a new life. This was a solemn occasion and a time of celebration. God chose to rescue the Israelites, and the people struggled to follow their rescuer. On this day, when their future seemed so close, they were ready to sign on to a plan they'd rejected decades earlier. The fear that claimed their parents was altered because of the mercy of God. Prayers were being answered. They were going home.

Prayer Starter

Lord God, I'd like to say I'm more likely to follow You than the people I've just read about, but I sometimes treat Your rules as suggestions and Your desire to be friends as an option to consider. Help me to. . .

DAY 72

DEUTERONOMY 32–34

Prayer Scripture

[Moses said,] "Set your hearts to all the words that I testify among you this day, which you shall command your children to be careful to do—all the words of this law. For it is not a vain thing for you, because it is your life, and through this thing you shall prolong your days in the land that you are crossing over the Jordan to possess."
DEUTERONOMY 32:46–47

Prayer Thought for the Day

Anything less than a journey with God is no real journey to a forever life. This was the message Moses passed along to the people. There were laws to remember before they were followed. There was a God who orchestrated a freedom they'd never experienced. There was a conversation that was always waiting for their participation. God spoke and He waited for a human voice to respond. God said there were things that would proclaim to all generations that there was a God who rescues. These words needed no revisions. God didn't change His mind. He knew all that had happened, was happening, and would happen. His commands weren't subject to committee review. Pray and ask God to help you learn what you need to know to make this journey a joy.

Prayer Starter

Father, may the words in Your great book bring me to a place of understanding and a willingness to follow. May these prayer words lead me to. . .

DAY 73
JOSHUA 1–2

Prayer Scripture

"Be strong and very courageous, that you may observe to do according to all the law that Moses My servant commanded you. Do not turn from it to the right hand or to the left, that you may prosper wherever you go. This Book of the Law shall not depart out of your mouth, but you shall meditate on it day and night, that you may observe to do according to all that is written in it, for then you shall make your way prosperous, and then you shall have good success."
Joshua 1:7–8

Prayer Thought for the Day

If the history of the Israelites had a fence, then they'd arrived at the very thing that sought to keep them out. To move past the fence, they needed to believe God's promise. They needed to do internal battle with their everyday apprehension. This struggle was enhanced because Moses was no longer leading. His second in command, Joshua, was now in charge. He essentially asked the people to believe, trust, and follow God when he declared that the winning strategy was to be strong and courageous. Success depended less on skill and more on prayerful trust in God. The people would need to literally become prayer warriors.

Prayer Starter

Lord God, I walk forward into wars I may not choose but can't avoid. I don't want to pursue victory without You. I can't be strong enough or courageous enough to win without...

DAY 74
JOSHUA 3–5

Prayer Scripture

On that day the Lord magnified Joshua in the sight of all Israel. And they feared him, as they feared Moses, all the days of his life.
Joshua 4:14

Prayer Thought for the Day

Among the sojourners, only Joshua and Caleb remembered walking through the Red Sea on dry ground. It likely made quite an impression on people who'd never seen something like it and never thought they would. But, in a case that feels a little ironic, one of the ways the people had left slavery became a spotlight focused on freedom. Their new leader, Joshua, and twelve men from the various tribes of Israel stepped into the overflowing water of the Jordan River, and a God-orchestrated and invisible dam stopped the water from flowing. It continued to stack upriver, the ground dried, and the people made a safe passage into the land gifted by God to rebellious people. This was the power of communion between God and man. There was much work to be done; the first step was a safe passage through a dry riverbed. The new human leader was accepted, and new adventures continued after the river was allowed to flow once more.

Prayer Starter

Father, be my leader and let me follow. Give me reminders and help me remember You've done marvelous things in my life, like. . .

DAY 75
JOSHUA 6–8

Prayer Scripture

Joshua tore his clothes and fell to the earth on his face before the ark of the LORD until the evening. . . . Joshua said, "Alas, O Lord GOD, why have You brought this people across the Jordan at all, to deliver us into the hand of the Amorites, to destroy us? If only we had been content and dwelled on the other side of the Jordan! O Lord, what shall I say when Israel turns their backs before their enemies! For the Canaanites and all the inhabitants of the land shall hear of it, and shall surround us, and cut off our name from the earth. And what will You do to Your great name?"
JOSHUA 7:6–9

Prayer Thought for the Day

Joshua and the soldiers prepared to battle the people of Ai. It should have been easy. The people of Ai were few, and the people of Israel understood that God had given them this land. But this battle didn't end in Israel's favor. Everything hinged on the actions of the man named Achan, who quietly but deliberately disobeyed God. Joshua expressed despair. The fearful warriors had lost the battle. Joshua prayed a grieving prayer, and God revealed Achan's sin.

Prayer Starter

Lord God, I don't want my choice to rebel to stand in the way of the good You want to do. Help me to admit my wayward steps and accept Your mercy so I can. . .

DAY 76
JOSHUA 9–10

Prayer Scripture

The men took of their provisions and did not ask
for counsel from the mouth of the LORD.
JOSHUA 9:14

Prayer Thought for the Day

There's a downside to assumptions. Some nearby residents, knowing that Israel was taking over their area, came up with a plan. They would dress as weary travelers. The people would understand that challenge. They would say that when they left home their clothes and shoes were new, but now they looked very old and worn. The story was convincing, and the leaders of Israel believed it. These Israelite leaders didn't pray, asking God for wisdom to know for sure. They made agreements with the fake travelers that didn't line up with what God had said about the need to fully take over the land.

While you may never feel the need to ask God for wisdom about a prospective tenant, there are so many things you can ask God to help you with. The problem will always come if you assume you already know the answers. You may believe it's best not to trouble God with something meaningless. You might believe the answer is logical. God may have an answer that doesn't make sense to you, but it's always the right answer. Use prayer to avoid assumptions.

Prayer Starter

Father, help me to remember that nothing is too small for requesting Your guidance. I don't want to assume something that will only cause me trouble when. . .

DAY 77
JOSHUA 11–13

Prayer Scripture

As the LORD commanded Moses His servant, so Moses commanded Joshua, and so Joshua did. He left nothing undone of all that the LORD commanded Moses.

JOSHUA 11:15

Prayer Thought for the Day

If you made the trip through the first five books of the Bible, then you know that God spoke to Moses a lot. There were rules, regulations, and declarations that were written for you to read and for all people to follow. Joshua 11:15 is a bold proclamation. The man who followed in Moses' footsteps had the same commitment to God's rules. If God said it, Joshua was committed to doing it. This would be important to the people of Israel because they'd proven over and over again that they needed a leader who actually did what he asked the people to do. The people wouldn't always have this example. There were those that led without prayer, example, or belief.

Of course the greatest example isn't a human at all. God also does everything He asks you to do. So when you don't have an example to follow in your faith walk, follow Him. Even if you have an example—*follow Him.*

Prayer Starter

Lord God, I can pray because You spoke. I can listen because You give understanding. I can be an example because You've been my example. Help me. . .

DAY 78
JOSHUA 14–16

Prayer Scripture

"I was forty years old when Moses the servant of the LORD sent me from Kadesh-barnea to spy out the land, and I brought him back word as it was in my heart. Nevertheless my brothers who went up with me made the heart of the people melt, but I wholly followed the LORD my God."
JOSHUA 14:7–8

Prayer Thought for the Day

Caleb lived almost the first half of his life as a slave in Egypt, but he followed Moses out of Egypt. He believed God had a new home where freedom was normal. He spied out the land that would become his home in old age. He and Joshua were the only two spies who really believed the land was theirs. Yet Caleb couldn't enter the land immediately. He had to wait decades before claiming his mountain home. Like Joshua, Caleb chose to follow when others walked away. His life was marked by obedience and a growing friendship with God. At the age of eighty-five, Caleb finally received his hillside. Caleb was strong enough to make a home for himself in a land he had always recognized as God's gift. Were there prayers of gratitude? Were there moments of rejoicing? Was Caleb overwhelmed?

Prayer Starter

Father, even when it's hard and it seems I've been faithful for too long, help me to choose to take this sweet life-walk with You. The direction You're leading me is. . .

DAY 79
JOSHUA 17–19

Prayer Scripture

When they had finished dividing the land for inheritance by their borders, the children of Israel gave an inheritance among them to Joshua the son of Nun. According to the word of the LORD they gave him the city that he asked for, even Timnath-serah in Mount Ephraim. And he built the city and dwelled in it.

JOSHUA 19:49–50

Prayer Thought for the Day

The promised land was divided among the tribes of Israel. But the two men who engaged in observation and reporting on this land forty years earlier received their own land, separate from the tribal lands. Caleb received his land in the mountains, and Joshua received land in Ephraim. Joshua built a city, and this place was his new home.

God rewards faithfulness but rarely on the same day that you're faithful. God's rewards can take a while. For Caleb and Joshua, it took forty years. Maybe you've wondered if reading the Bible, praying, and making wise choices are solid investment strategies. Looking at it this way removes the joy of a future promise. God has something great in store for His family, and they'll all see it when the promised land of heaven is finally considered home. The time is coming, so be patient.

Prayer Starter

Lord God, teach me to wait. Let me not become impatient. You make promises, and I believe that one day You'll. . .

DAY 80
JOSHUA 20–22

Prayer Scripture

The LORD gave to Israel all the land that He swore to give to their fathers, and they possessed it and dwelled in it. And the LORD gave them rest all around, according to all that He swore to their fathers. And not a man of all their enemies stood before them. The LORD delivered all their enemies into their hand. Not any good thing that the LORD had spoken to the house of Israel failed; all came to pass.

JOSHUA 21:43–45

Prayer Thought for the Day

It was as if Joshua were placing an exclamation point at the end of his long journey. God made a promise. He kept that promise. The people struggled. The people found rest. Enemies sought the Israelites. God delivered them. Everything—every single thing—He'd said came true. This was a story of cause and effect. It was a story of truth and consequences. It was a story of victory for people who had a horrible personal track record. God heard the prayers of slavery, sent a deliverer, and spent a very long time removing the fear of freedom. "Not any good thing that the LORD had spoken to the house of Israel failed." Read—and wonder.

Prayer Starter

Father, I want to remember Your exclamation point for my story. You never fail and Your promises are kept. Help me to remember every turning point that. . .

DAY 81

JOSHUA 23–24

Prayer Scripture

"Be very courageous to keep and to do all that is written in the Book of the Law of Moses, that you do not turn aside from it to the right hand or to the left, that you do not come among these nations, these that remain among you, or make mention of the name of their gods, or cause to swear by them, or serve them, or bow yourselves to them. But cling to the LORD your God, as you have done to this day."
JOSHUA 23:6–8

Prayer Thought for the Day

The people witnessed the final days of their second leader since leaving Egypt. As Joshua's strength declined he spoke to the people of their need for courage and strength. The people who wandered physically were also prone to wander spiritually. Joshua wouldn't always be there to remind them to make God their priority. It was time for the people to grow up or stay children in their walk with God. They needed to know that God had no interest in seeing the people He'd rescued jumping back into old habits. God's direction would be needed. They'd needed to pray for guidance long before they encountered Moses or Joshua.

Prayer Starter

Lord God, give me the desire to follow You even when I don't seem to be encouraged by another human. Give me a heart to read what You say and say what I struggle with, like. . .

DAY 82
JUDGES 1–3

Prayer Scripture

The children of Israel did evil in the sight of the Lord and served the Baals. And they abandoned the Lord God of their fathers, who had brought them out of the land of Egypt, and they followed other gods—gods of the people who were all around them. And they bowed down to them, and they provoked the Lord to anger. And they abandoned the Lord and served Baal and Ashtaroth. And the anger of the Lord burned against Israel. . . . Wherever they went, the hand of the Lord was against them for misfortune, as the Lord had said and as the Lord had sworn to them. And they were greatly distressed.

Judges 2:11–15

Prayer Thought for the Day

With no one to constantly remind them to pray and remember God's law, the people just—forgot. They returned to a failed spiritual policy. They followed other non-gods that could neither speak nor change history. They walked away, and God placed roadblocks to convince the people to turn back to Him. Few chose this option. Without God to pray to—without God to follow—the people were "greatly distressed." No matter how many warnings are issued, some people will still believe God's rules were not meant for them. Spiritual slavery had begun. Actual slavery was coming.

Prayer Starter

Father, I don't want to be someone who delays obedience. I don't want to experiment with other ideas that leave You out. I don't want to. . .

DAY 83

JUDGES 4–5

Prayer Scripture

So let all your enemies perish, O LORD, but let those who love Him be as the sun when it goes forth in its might. And the land had rest forty years.
JUDGES 5:31

Prayer Thought for the Day

During the era of judges, there were those who followed God, but to others, it seemed God's influence was limited. A prophetess by the name of Deborah had a message from God to give to the soldier Barak. Judges 4:6–7 records God's message to Barak: "Go and march toward Mount Tabor and take with you ten thousand men from the children of Naphtali and of the children of Zebulun. And I will draw to you Sisera, the captain of Jabin's army, with his chariots and his multitude at the river Kishon, and I will deliver him into your hand." It should have been easy for Barak to follow such a guaranteed outcome, but he chose to say that he wouldn't go unless Deborah went with him. Sisera would be defeated, but God chose to give the glory of Sisera's death to someone willing to obey.

Prayer can ease anxiety, erase doubt, and invite you to adventure. There's no record that Barak chose to pray. This was absolutely part of his problem.

Prayer Starter

Lord God, I don't want to skip steps. Make me wise enough to know that prayer will help me make decisions to walk with You into. . .

DAY 84
JUDGES 6–8

Prayer Scripture

When Gideon perceived that he was an angel of the Lord,
Gideon said, "Alas, O Lord God! For I have seen an angel
of the Lord face to face." And the Lord said to him,
"Peace be to you. Do not fear; you shall not die."
Judges 6:22–23

Prayer Thought for the Day

Gideon was a faithful mouse. That may sound harsh, but even he considered himself the least among the least. That may have been why, when God told him to destroy altars to Baal and lead a battle, he was absolutely convinced (like Moses before him) that God had the wrong man. Gideon took divine nurturing to come to the place where he would give up his mouse status. God was with Gideon, and good things happened when this man became willing to do what God asked. The prayer in Judges 6 shows his astonished dread because he'd been in the company of the angel of the Lord and thought death was the only reasonable outcome for such a visit. But when Gideon prayed, God answered and assured him that life was his. It wouldn't be long before Gideon left his family's grain mill and followed God's command.

Prayer Starter

Father, when You give me an assignment, You never want to hear me telling You what I can't do. You make me able to do when I become willing to obey. This is true when. . .

DAY 85
JUDGES 9

Prayer Scripture

A certain woman cast a piece of a millstone on Abimelech's head to break his skull. Then he hastily called to the young man, his armor-bearer, and said to him, "Draw your sword and slay me, that men do not say of me, 'A woman slew him.'" And his young man thrust him through, and he died.

JUDGES 9:53–54

Prayer Thought for the Day

Was there a king in Israel before Saul? That depends on who you ask. If you were to ask Abimelech, then yes, he was king of Israel—but it was a self-proclaimed title that didn't bear God's stamp of approval. This three-year reign was marked by chaos and national upheaval. Abimelech murdered his seventy brothers to avoid any challenge for the title. The people rebelled against his leadership, and he was killed while trying to take a city. Some things you won't read in this story include any indication that Abimelech prayed, acknowledged God, or sought to obey Him. Perhaps he simply noticed that other nations had kings and saw an opportunity. At this point in scripture, things would get much worse before they got better.

Whether it's in your personal life or society, you have likely witnessed a decline. Is it possible this has something to do with people who don't pray, acknowledge God, or obey Him?

Prayer Starter

Lord God, let me resist walking before You, as if my plan is better. Let me not walk alone, because I'll need Your guidance to. . .

DAY 86
JUDGES 10–12

Prayer Scripture

The children of Israel said to the LORD, "We have sinned. Do to us whatever seems good to You. Only deliver us this day, we ask You." And they put away the foreign gods from among them and served the LORD. And His soul was grieved for the misery of Israel.
JUDGES 10:15–16

Prayer Thought for the Day

As so many times before, the people participated in the great walkaway. Yet when bad days became the worst times, they finally remembered prayer. Compelled to admit they were wrong, they became willing to obey for a time. This was not a onetime lesson for them, and it will never be a onetime lesson for you. What's interesting to see is the compassion of God, who had every right to be angry with the people, but in Judges 10 He was sad because the people's choice had moved them to a place of incredible misery. If you wander from God and come back again, you shouldn't expect things to be as if you'd never sinned. There are always consequences, but God's mercy will restore what poor decisions have taken from you.

Prayer Starter

Father, wandering is easy, forsaking is common, and wrong choices are all in a day's work. Yet You can help me follow, be faithful, and choose wisely. I want that when I think I. . .

DAY 87

JUDGES 13–16

Prayer Scripture

Manoah entreated the LORD and said, "O my Lord, let the man of God whom You sent come again to us and teach us what we shall do for the child who shall be born." And God listened to the voice of Manoah.

JUDGES 13:8–9

Prayer Thought for the Day

The people were confronted by the Philistines for a very long time—about as long as Moses had led the people in the wilderness. Living in the midst of fresh oppression were a man and his wife. The two had seemingly given up hope of having children. That was before a visit from one of God's messenger angels who gave the unnamed woman instructions and left. Manoah needed clarification—so he prayed. He wanted the instruction manual for a son who was to be set apart for God. That boy, Samson, would be a very colorful figure in the history of Israel as resident strongman, but before his story of waywardness was a story of parents who just wanted to know more about raising a child. This wisdom was provided then and is offered now. No matter your season of life, God is willing to navigate, guide, and direct each footstep into your future.

Prayer Starter

Lord God, I've come to believe that life choices come through trial and error. You want me to believe they come from following directions. Help me call on You when. . .

DAY 88
JUDGES 17–19

Prayer Scripture

And the man Micah had a house of gods and made an ephod and teraphim and consecrated one of his sons, who became his priest. In those days there was no king in Israel, but every man did what was right in his own eyes.
JUDGES 17:5–6

Prayer Thought for the Day

The term "whatever" may be a twenty-first-century phrase associated with apathy, but the idea is nothing new. Take Micah for instance. This wasn't the minor prophet whose book appears late in the Old Testament. It was a man who thought it would be a good idea to create customized non-gods. But it wasn't enough to make this a personal decision; he asked his son to be the priest of his new religion. His mother supplied the finances and encouragement to make things up. Apparently Micah wanted a priest upgrade, because he found a Levite in the region and offered him money to become his priest. This man agreed to be a freelance priest. If this sounds a little messed up, the very last part of verse 6 gives a perfect reason for this rebellion: "Every man did what was right in his own eyes." The same thing happens today. People make all kinds of faith choices. The best choices never make up a false god.

Prayer Starter

Father, I want to do what's right in Your eyes. Help me to see things the way You see them when I look at. . .

DAY 89
JUDGES 20–21

Prayer Scripture

Now the men of Israel had sworn in Mizpah, saying, "Not any of us shall give his daughter to Benjamin as a wife." And the people came to the house of God and remained there before God until evening and lifted up their voices and wept greatly and said, "O LORD God of Israel, why has this come to pass in Israel, that today there should be one tribe lacking in Israel?"

JUDGES 21:1–3

Prayer Thought for the Day

Men from the tribe of Benjamin engaged in what was essentially gang rape. When it was discovered, the rest of Israel was outraged, and a civil war broke out. The majority of the men of Benjamin fought the rest of Israel. They lost. Originally there'd only been a demand of justice for the men who were involved, but the rest of the tribe of Benjamin chose to fight. In the end, only a few men from Benjamin remained alive. This concerned the other tribes enough that they prayed that God would restore this nearly extinct tribe. They did what they thought was best, and even then it resulted in more death and family separation. Sometimes bad decisions inspire even worse decisions, which lead to horrible ideas and a full sprint away from God.

Prayer Starter

Lord God, help me to stop poor decisions by rejecting them and accepting Your wisdom instead. Let me make this choice for myself and encourage others to. . .

DAY 90

RUTH 1–4

Prayer Scripture

Ruth said, "Do not entreat me to leave you or to return from following after you, for where you go, I will go, and where you lodge, I will lodge. Your people shall be my people, and your God my God. Where you die, I will die, and there I will be buried. May the Lord do so to me, and more also, if anything but death parts you and me."
Ruth 1:16–17

Prayer Thought for the Day

Ruth's promise was solemn. Her determination was evident. Her words were heard by God and rewarded. Ruth traveled with her mother-in-law, Naomi, to Bethlehem. Both of their husbands had died in Moab, and Naomi felt whatever happy moments remained to her would be back in Bethlehem, where she'd once lived. God rewarded this choice. Ruth would remarry in Israel and would have a son. Her great-grandson would become King David.

Naomi would hold her grandson. She was reminded that God also was saying to her, "Do not entreat me to leave you or to return from following after you, for where you go, I will go, and where you lodge, I will lodge." Ruth's prayer had been answered in many ways.

Consider that God's answer to your prayers may positively impact others.

Prayer Starter

Father, may my prayers be bigger than personal needs. May they invite others to Your guidebook so they can. . .

DAY 91
1 SAMUEL 1–3

Prayer Scripture

[Hannah] was in bitterness of soul and prayed to the Lord and wept greatly. And she vowed a vow and said, "O Lord of hosts, if You will indeed look on the affliction of Your handmaiden and remember me and not forget Your handmaiden, but will give to Your handmaiden a male child, then I will give him to the Lord all the days of his life."

1 Samuel 1:10–11

Prayer Thought for the Day

There were two women mentioned earlier who were barren, but God gave them children. Abraham's wife Sarah became the mother of Isaac, and Manoah's wife became the mother of Samson. Prayer was important to both stories. Now, Elkanah's wife, Hannah, was praying that God would give her a son. It might sound as if she was bargaining with God by giving Him something if He gave her a son, but it was actually a vow. Samuel would be a gift back to God. She was dedicating her son before she was even pregnant. Her prayer was answered. God would use Samuel to identify the first two kings of Israel, kings whom God chose.

Why might faith strengthen your willingness to pray big prayers, knowing you're asking a big God?

Prayer Starter

Lord God, thank You for sharing stories of unbelievable prayer moments. It helps to know that Your answers can amaze. One of the things I've always wanted to pray for is. . .

DAY 92
1 SAMUEL 4–6

Prayer Scripture

They sent and gathered together all the lords of the Philistines and said, "Send away the ark of the God of Israel, and let it go again to its own place so that it does not slay us and our people." For there was a deadly destruction throughout all the city; the hand of God was very heavy there. And the men who did not die were struck with the tumors, and the cry of the city went up to heaven.

1 Samuel 5:11–12

Prayer Thought for the Day

The people of Philistia may not have realized they were praying to God, but He heard their cries. They had taken the ark of the covenant, thinking this would give them an advantage over Israel—but the ark wasn't meant for them. When the ark came to rest among the Philistines, so did destructive outcomes. Their prayer was an admission that they were wrong and had no right to the spiritual symbol. They sent the ark on the way back home. There were still consequences to their failed decision making. This is a good look at what repentance (turning away from sin) looks like. Restoration can begin, but there may still be residual effects from the choices made.

Prayer Starter

Father, I thank You for Your mercy, but I know that when I break Your laws, there may be consequences. Give me grace in those moments when I face. . .

DAY 93
1 SAMUEL 7–9

Prayer Scripture

When the Philistines heard that the children of Israel had gathered together to Mizpah, the lords of the Philistines went up against Israel. And when the children of Israel heard it, they were afraid of the Philistines. And the children of Israel said to Samuel, "Do not cease to cry to the LORD our God for us, that He will save us out of the hand of the Philistines."

1 SAMUEL 7:7–8

Prayer Thought for the Day

The Philistines won many victories over Israel. They were a formidable military force that Israel would battle with for a very long time. Once, the people of Philistia cried out to a God they didn't know—but the Israelites *did* know God, and they pled with the prophet Samuel to pray for their safety in dealing with the Philistines. It was a good thing Israel remembered God, because they'd set up monuments to non-gods that they'd received warnings against. They tore down the monuments, and God stepped in to help. The Philistines weren't going to be an immediate threat. The rescue in this instance was linked to obedience and prayer. Don't be surprised if this is your experience today.

Prayer Starter

Lord God, the possibilities of finding new ways to disobey You are everywhere. May I become more interested in obedience and in talking to You about the things that tempt me, like. . .

DAY 94
1 SAMUEL 10–12

Prayer Scripture

"The Lord sent Jerubbaal and Bedan and Jephthah and Samuel and delivered you out of the hand of your enemies on every side, and you dwelled safely. And when you saw that Nahash the king of the children of Ammon came against you, you said to me, 'No, but a king shall reign over us,' when the Lord your God was your king."

1 Samuel 12:11–12

Prayer Thought for the Day

The words above are something like the Judges Hall of Fame. These four men (Jerubbaal was also known as Gideon) were used by God to provide a divine realignment opportunity for the people of Israel. These men took a stand for God. They prayed and acted on what God told them, but it wasn't enough for the people, who continued to demand a king. A flawed individual named Saul became the first king. More would follow. It was understood that God was the King of Israel, and the people were rejecting Him in favor of an earthly king. In the New Testament there was a similar experience when the people rejected the disciples and by doing so rejected God's Son. This also happens today. God doesn't choose to be rejected, but He's used to this decision.

You can make a different one.

Prayer Starter

Father, I want to be one who chooses You rather than rejects You. Give me the strength to follow even when I. . .

DAY 95
1 SAMUEL 13–14

Prayer Scripture

Saul said, "Let us go down after the Philistines by night and plunder them until the morning light, and let us not leave a man of them." And they said, "Do whatever seems good to you." Then the priest said, "Let us draw near to God here." And Saul asked counsel of God, "Shall I go down after the Philistines? Will You deliver them into the hand of Israel?" But He did not answer him that day.

1 Samuel 14:36–37

Prayer Thought for the Day

Having the role of a national leader had gone to King Saul's head but failed to impact his heart. The Philistine army continued to bother Israel, and Saul wanted to pursue them. The people seemed agreeable. Their adrenaline levels must have been high. Then the priest spoke, reminding the king to ask God if this was the right thing to do. The king asked, but God remained silent. Saul had been making things up as he went along. Sometimes his actions looked spiritual, but there was always darker motivation behind them. Though Saul didn't seem especially interested in following God, he wouldn't stop God from helping him. Chaos ensued in a kingdom where truth was whatever you believed.

Prayer Starter

Lord God, I don't want to be someone who just says acceptable words about You. I want to know what You ask, do what You say, and. . .

DAY 96
1 SAMUEL 15–16

Prayer Scripture

Samuel said, "Has the LORD as great delight in burnt offerings
and sacrifices as in obeying the voice of the LORD? Behold,
to obey is better than sacrifice and to listen than the fat of rams.
For rebellion is like the sin of witchcraft, and stubbornness is
like iniquity and idolatry. Because you have rejected the word
of the LORD He has also rejected you from being king."
1 SAMUEL 15:22–23

Prayer Thought for the Day

Saul was commanded by God to go to war against King Agag of the Amalekites and not spare his people or their possessions. Israel's king didn't follow God's directions. When confronted, he claimed that his plan was better because it allowed a great number of animals to be sacrificed to God. This wasn't what God asked for. The prophet Samuel confronted Saul, and, after all the king's excuses, Samuel said, "To obey is better than sacrifice and to listen than the fat of rams." Then Samuel shared the soul-crushing news that God was now rejecting him as king. Saul allowed himself to be pursued by fear, anxiety, and a liberal dose of paranoia. His choices didn't change.

Prayer Starter

Father, You're very specific when I'm looking for loopholes. You tell me the truth when I want to believe a lie. Give me a heart that pays attention to Your specifics. And when I do, help me. . .

DAY 97
1 SAMUEL 17–18

Prayer Scripture

David said to the Philistine, "You come to me with a sword and with a spear and with a shield. But I come to you in the name of the LORD of hosts, the God of the armies of Israel, whom you have defied. This day the LORD will deliver you into my hand. . .so that all the earth may know that there is a God in Israel. And all this assembly shall know that the LORD does not save with sword and spear. For the battle is the LORD's, and He will give you into our hands."
1 SAMUEL 17:45–47

Prayer Thought for the Day

Young David arrived in Israel's military camp, carrying a care package from home. His three oldest brothers were standing by, looking every bit like soldiers. Across the valley stood the giant, Goliath, taunting Israel. David wasn't sure who this guy was, but he was making fun of God. Offended, David asked for and received permission from King Saul to confront Goliath. David chose a sling, a stone. . .and God. David didn't walk across the valley without Him. And David defeated the giant.

Do you have giants in your life? Do they seem to taunt you? Who will you take with you when it's time to confront them?

Prayer Starter

Lord God, why do I try to face struggle alone? Walk with me when I face personal giants like. . .

DAY 98
1 SAMUEL 19–20

Prayer Scripture

Jonathan said to David, "Go in peace, since we have sworn, both of us, in the name of the LORD, saying, 'The LORD be between me and you, and between my descendants and your descendants forever.'" And he arose and departed, and Jonathan went into the city.

1 SAMUEL 20:42

Prayer Thought for the Day

King Saul was very pleased that David killed Goliath, but something happened that changed his high opinion of the young man. David became famous and Saul chose jealousy. It may have started with small thoughts of how to stop David, but it wasn't long before those thoughts grew murderous. Saul's son Jonathan, David's best friend, wanted to believe his dad had the best of intentions concerning his top warrior, but he eventually learned the king's true motive—murder. Jonathan met David and told him of the plot. Like David, Jonathan brought God with him. He told David that the connection in his friendship with David was God—not jealousy, anger, and plots. What relationships do you have that need the prayerful intervention of God?

Prayer Starter

Father, I want friendships that have You in the center. May my choice of friends always have You included. May my friends help me. . .

DAY 99
1 SAMUEL 21–23

Prayer Scripture

David knew that Saul secretly plotted evil against him, and he said to Abiathar the priest, "Bring the ephod here." Then David said, "O LORD God of Israel, Your servant has certainly heard that Saul seeks to come to Keilah to destroy the city for my sake. Will the men of Keilah deliver me into his hand? Will Saul come down, as Your servant has heard? O LORD God of Israel, I beseech You, tell Your servant." And the LORD said, "He will come down." Then David said, "Will the men of Keilah deliver me and my men into the hand of Saul?" And the LORD said, "They will deliver you up." Then David and his men, who were about six hundred, arose and departed.

1 SAMUEL 23:9–13

Prayer Thought for the Day

This is one of the rare instances when someone prayed to know the future and God told them. God told prophets about the future, and they warned people to repent. In this case, King Saul had been persistent in trying to find David and kill him. David prayed twice, and God confirmed Saul's intent. So David and his men fled—because David prayed. God can give insight into difficult issues. Pray as often as you need to.

Prayer Starter

Lord God, I should pray and keep praying, seek and keep seeking, and then wait for Your answer to questions like. . .

DAY 100
1 SAMUEL 24–25

Prayer Scripture

[Abigail said to David,] "I ask you, forgive the trespass of your handmaiden. For the LORD will certainly make for my lord a secure house, because my lord fights the battles of the LORD, and evil has not been found in you all your days. Yet a man has risen to pursue you and to seek your soul, but the soul of my lord shall be bound in the bundle of the living with the LORD. . . . And it shall come to pass, when the LORD has done to my lord according to all the good that He has spoken concerning you, and has appointed you ruler over Israel, that this shall be no grief to you, nor offense of heart to my lord. . . . Then remember your handmaiden."

1 SAMUEL 25:28–31

Prayer Thought for the Day

This isn't a prayer, but it reads like one. It's the appeal of one who is bold enough to make a request. Abigail's husband had purposefully offended the future king, and it could result in the death penalty. But Abigail pleaded for mercy as she poured her heart out to David. This is a good blueprint for your prayer life. Seek forgiveness, make your appeal, plead for mercy, and share your heart.

Prayer Starter

Father, from my mouth to Your heart, I admit I've been wrong, I request mercy because I need Your help—and here's why. . .

DAY 101
1 SAMUEL 26–28

Prayer Scripture

Samuel said, "Why then do you ask of me, since the LORD has departed from you and has become your enemy? . . . The LORD has torn the kingdom out of your hand and given it to your neighbor, even to David. Because you did not obey the voice of the LORD or execute His fierce wrath on Amalek, therefore the LORD has done this thing to you this day. Moreover, the LORD will also deliver Israel with you into the hand of the Philistines. And tomorrow you and your sons shall be with me. The LORD shall also deliver the army of Israel into the hand of the Philistines."

1 SAMUEL 28:16–19

Prayer Thought for the Day

This story reads like something from a tabloid. The prophet Samuel was dead, and King Saul was nervous. God was silent. Saul sought a medium, who conjured up the deceased Samuel to give the king an answer. Samuel confirmed that Saul's reign was over and said his life would end in battle. Three of his sons would die, and the Israelites would lose the battle with the Philistines. This was an unfortunate end to the story of a man who ran from God and may have deeply regretted his wandering. Prayer works best when you walk *with* God.

Prayer Starter

Lord God, I don't want to run, hide, or reject You. May I read Your words while I share my heart, so I can. . .

DAY 102
1 SAMUEL 29–31

Prayer Scripture

David said to Abiathar the priest, Ahimelech's son, "I ask you, bring the ephod here to me." And Abiathar brought the ephod there to David. And David inquired of the Lord, saying, "Shall I pursue this troop? Shall I overtake them?" And He answered him, "Pursue, for you shall surely overtake them and recover all without fail."

1 Samuel 30:7–8

Prayer Thought for the Day

David's family had been taken by the Philistines. His livestock was gone. The people who followed him suffered their own losses. They weren't happy with David. The future king sought God's direction. When he got the green light from God, David pursued the opposition and rescued what had been lost. The enemy had relaxed while celebrating, and David defeated them with just two hundred soldiers. Would it have been harder for David if he wasn't already friends with God?

You have the same opportunity David had. You can stay close to God, which means coming to God is your personal choice. You also could wait until you need Him to talk to Him and feel a little awkward with every request. He wants to hear from you either way, but a friendship with God will always make the moment of prayer comforting.

Prayer Starter

Father, choosing to be close to You is what I want to do. I don't want to wait to follow this friendship. When I'm in trouble, may I. . .

DAY 103
2 SAMUEL 1–2

Prayer Scripture

It came to pass after this that David inquired of the LORD, saying, "Shall I go up to any of the cities of Judah?" And the LORD said to him, "Go up."
2 SAMUEL 2:1

Prayer Thought for the Day

David had been anointed the second king of Israel. It should have been a welcome transition, following the death of Saul, but it wasn't. One of King Saul's close associates, Abner, determined David shouldn't have it easy. Abner would deny David the throne of Israel by installing Saul's son Ish-bosheth as the new king. David was welcomed as the king of Judah—a prayer had brought him there, and the people made him their king. Ish-bosheth was king of Israel for two years while David grew into his role as king of the southern region. The process of king making hadn't been an easy journey, but David was proving a dependable leader who prayed to a dependable God.

Your journey to God's plan for your life may be equally infused with struggle. Keep trusting God, because nothing can top His plan—and His timing is perfect even when it differs from your expectations.

Prayer Starter

Lord God, my prayers need to be believing prayers, and I must be willing to wait. Your plan for me is good, and my ambition needs to obey Your directions when I am. . .

DAY 104
2 SAMUEL 3–4

Prayer Scripture

"I am weak this day, though anointed king, and these men, the sons of Zeruiah, are too hard for me. The Lord shall reward the evildoer according to his wickedness."
2 Samuel 3:39

Prayer Thought for the Day

Weariness is common among all humanity. It was also true of Judah's king, David. There were people plotting deeds that would fuel local gossip to a firestorm, but they were never fans of the king. They'd kill friends of the kingdom or those who opposed the king, in hopes of finding the king agreeable and pleased with their dark deeds. David proved over and over again that he didn't desire revenge and that he welcomed new friends—but when Abner was killed, the king became weary. Yet David allowed God to temper his responses and prove that he held himself to a higher standard. The prayers of a righteous king not only transformed his heart but encouraged others to consider the wisdom of such decisions.

You're exposed to this kind of decision maker, and you can internalize the example or walk away. There is wisdom in continuing to read through God's Word and considering His position on prayer.

Prayer Starter

Father, I want to be a man who sees value in prayer, relationships, and forgiveness. When I'm weary, remind me that. . .

DAY 105

2 SAMUEL 5–7

Prayer Scripture

Then King David went in and sat before the Lord, and he said, "Who am I, O Lord God? And what is my house that You have brought me here? And yet this was a small thing in Your sight. . . . And now, O Lord God, the word that You have spoken concerning Your servant and concerning his house, establish it forever and do as You have said. . . . Therefore Your servant has found in his heart to pray this prayer to You."

2 Samuel 7:18–19, 25, 27

Prayer Thought for the Day

The passage above is an abbreviated look at King David's prayer. He remembered his role as a shepherd, the day Samuel anointed him king, and the defeat of the giant Goliath. He spent time with King Saul, who either saw value in him or despised him. He was accused and betrayed. He went into hiding and continued to fight the Philistines. But on this day David was praying because he would finally be king over both Judah and Israel. He came from nothing, and God made something from what little he had. David recognized a promise was being kept.

Have you thanked God for how far you've come as you look forward to what comes next?

Prayer Starter

Lord God, help me remember all I've endured. Help me to remember all You've given. Help me to consider where I go next. With Your help I'll. . .

DAY 106
2 SAMUEL 8-10

Prayer Scripture

It came to pass after this that the king of the children of Ammon died, and Hanun his son reigned in his place. Then David said, "I will show kindness to Hanun the son of Nahash, as his father showed kindness to me." And David sent by the hand of his servants to comfort him for his father.

2 SAMUEL 10:1–2

Prayer Thought for the Day

David had the heart of a warrior, but he also understood compassion. One story of his kindness was to a lame man named Mephibosheth. He was Jonathan's son, and David wanted to give this young man all the benefits of living in the palace—like eating at the king's table—for the sake of his dad, who had been David's close friend. A lesser-known story of David's kindness stems from a heart that longed for God and sought Him regularly in prayer. Nahash, the Ammonite king, had helped David. When he died, his son Hanun ascended to the throne. David sent gifts to the young king, but his kindness was considered treachery. Not only was the kindness rejected, but it led to yet another war.

Not everyone will understand or accept your kindness, but it remains one of the best ways to change an enemy to a friend.

Prayer Starter

Father, I don't want to be jaded by the ungratefulness of others. Help me to be kind to others even when they. . .

DAY 107

2 SAMUEL 11–12

Prayer Scripture

It came to pass one evening that David arose from his bed and walked on the roof of the king's house. And from the roof he saw a woman washing herself, and the woman was very beautiful to look at. And David sent and inquired after the woman. And one said, "Is this not Bathsheba, the daughter of Eliam, the wife of Uriah the Hittite?" And David sent messengers and took her, and she came in to him. And he lay with her.

2 Samuel 11:2–4

Prayer Thought for the Day

There was war, and King David wasn't with his men. He could have prayed for his soldiers, but David was distracted. Maybe he was bored. One evening David looked out from his roof and spotted a woman bathing. He could have averted his eyes and left the roof, but he stayed and watched. Later he brought her to the palace. He would become intimate with this married woman, wife of one of his own soldiers. This led David to orchestrate the death of her husband so he could marry Bathsheba. God could forgive, but there were consequences for David's sin.

When you refuse to pray, you deny yourself the help God offers the tempted. You face struggles alone, and no one has a great track record in making decisions without God's help.

Prayer Starter

Lord God, may I make You my focus. I need to look to You because to look anywhere else is to drift from. . .

DAY 108

2 SAMUEL 13–14

Prayer Scripture

Amnon lay down and pretended to be sick, and when the king had come to see him, Amnon said to the king, "I ask, let Tamar my sister come and make me a couple of cakes in my sight, that I may eat from her hand." Then David sent home to Tamar, saying, "Go now to your brother Amnon's house and prepare food for him." So Tamar went.

2 Samuel 13:6–8

Prayer Thought for the Day

David had to come to terms with his own adultery, but it wouldn't be the only sexual sin in his family. His son Amnon lusted for his half sister, Tamar, a full sibling to David's ambitious son Absalom. Tamar thought she was going to Amnon's place to take care of a sick relative, but he raped her. After this horrible act, Amnon completely rejected Tamar. This led her to isolation, and Amnon would eventually be killed under Absalom's order. Everyone involved was negatively impacted by Amnon's behavior. This is another case where prayer was never spoken and forgiveness was never requested or offered. Then vengeance caused bloodshed, followed by banishment for Absalom. When lawbreaking is your choice, dealing rightly with the situation is much better than considering new sin.

Prayer Starter

Father, when I sin, help me to deal with it correctly. You can forgive, but also please bring restoration. May I experience the regret that brings me to You so I can. . .

DAY 109

2 SAMUEL 15–16

Prayer Scripture

One told David, saying, "Ahithophel is among the conspirators with Absalom." And David said, "O LORD, I ask you, turn the counsel of Ahithophel into foolishness." And it came to pass that when David had come to the top of the mount, where he worshipped God, behold, Hushai the Archite came to meet him with his coat torn and dust on his head.

2 SAMUEL 15:31–32

Prayer Thought for the Day

In David's anger over Absalom's role in killing his son Amnon, he had banished Absalom for a time. Eventually the young man returned, but the king wouldn't see him. Absalom devised a new plot—if David wouldn't talk to him, then he would stage a coup and take over as king. He was successful at getting the people of Israel to notice him and, in time, he entered Jerusalem after David left. It was David's prayer that a wise man named Ahithophel, who stayed to help Absalom, would speak words that sounded foolish to Absalom. God answered the prayer, and David returned to Jerusalem as king once more. David's prayer wasn't for physical harm but for confusion.

You might pray that the truth of a situation would become known. You might ask that God simply makes things right.

Prayer Starter

Lord God, let me be careful about how I pray when circumstances seem unjust. May You be glorified in my response as You take care of. . .

DAY 110
2 SAMUEL 17–18

Prayer Scripture

The king was very moved and went up to the chamber over the gate and wept. And as he went, he said this, "O my son Absalom, my son, my son Absalom! I wish to God I had died instead of you, O Absalom, my son, my son!"
2 Samuel 18:33

Prayer Thought for the Day

Treachery runs deep in this story. While David would return as king, his son Absalom would be killed by Joab. For David, the struggle was that he'd clearly commanded that Absalom shouldn't be killed.

David responded like any man broken by the loss of a child. He wept for the son who had every intention of killing his own father so he could become king himself. David would have preferred his own death to the death of his son. This series of events was a bit like falling dominos, and the only one who could stop it was God.

You shouldn't wonder how one sin left unchallenged leads to even more sin and involves more people. You may have heard of breaking generational sin. This steady decline is an example of why that's needed. Contact God for the wisdom needed to stop it.

Prayer Starter

Father, help me stop sin in its tracks. I don't want my bad choices to continue to affect my family. Help me to endure the consequences and accept the grace needed to change the direction of. . .

DAY 111

2 SAMUEL 19–20

Prayer Scripture

Barzillai said to the king, "How long have I to live that I should go up with the king to Jerusalem? I am this day eighty years old. And can I discern between good and evil? Can your servant taste what I eat or what I drink? Can I hear any longer the voices of singing men and singing women? Why then should your servant be yet a burden to my lord the king? Your servant will go a little way over the Jordan with the king. And why should the king repay me with such a reward? Let your servant, I ask you, turn back again, that I may die in my own city and be buried by the grave of my father and of my mother. But behold your servant Chimham. Let him go over with my lord the king."

2 Samuel 19:34–37

Prayer Thought for the Day

Barzillai had been kind to King David. The king was being restored to his throne and was prepared to reward that kindness by bringing this aging man to stay with him in Jerusalem. Barzillai argued that he was too old to leave his home and suggested the honor be transferred to the man Chimham. The idea seemed to please the temporarily displaced king.

Prayer Starter

Lord God, give me a heart of kindness toward others. May Your kindness inspire kindness in me and then on to. . .

DAY 112
2 SAMUEL 21–22

Prayer Scripture

[God] delivered me from my strong enemy and from those who hated me, for they were too strong for me. They confronted me on the day of my calamity, but the LORD was my support.
2 SAMUEL 22:18–19

Prayer Thought for the Day

This was David's psalm of deliverance. He'd faced many foes and profound struggles, yet he could pray a prayer that admitted his weakness as well as the strength of his enemy. David knew where the ultimate strength came from, and he chose to rely on his supportive God. It's worthwhile to note that David ran through cycles of disappointment and triumph. He was a solid example, but he was imperfect. He didn't always make sense in the choices he made, but he consistently returned to the God who chose him early in life and proved that He was always capable of helping David in his worst moments. When people hate you, when they show themselves to be stronger than you, and when you don't know what to do, there's always reason to talk to the God who supports you.

Prayer Starter

Father, there are days I feel so beaten down I'm not sure how I'll face another day. But in this moment I can tell You all about it and I remember how You've helped me before—like the time when You. . .

DAY 113
2 SAMUEL 23–24

Prayer Scripture

David said to the Lord, "I have sinned greatly in what I have done, and now, I beg you, O Lord, take away the iniquity of Your servant, for I have done very foolishly."
2 Samuel 24:10

Prayer Thought for the Day

Do you ever get defensive about admitting you were wrong? Maybe you give excuses, discuss the circumstances that prevented obedience, or claim that no one follows *that* rule anymore. It can sound a bit like arguing with a parent, when you're seven. King David demonstrated a better way to respond when God's laws are broken. He admitted his failed choice and then asked God to forgive his foolish decision. No arguments. No excuses. No blame. David even knew there would be consequences for his choice, and he refused to run away or give up. Prayer expresses a willingness to admit failure and accept help. Prayer is part of the process of learning to see a good God and the good things He does for those who follow—and for those who ask.

Prayer Starter

Lord God, I don't want to look at prayer as groveling, but as a way to realign my footsteps so I can follow You once more when I admit. . .

DAY 114
1 KINGS 1–2

Prayer Scripture

Benaiah the son of Jehoiada answered the king and said, "Amen! May the LORD God of my lord the king say so too. As the LORD has been with my lord the king, even so may He be with Solomon and make his throne greater than the throne of my lord King David."
1 KINGS 1:36–37

Prayer Thought for the Day

When you read the word *amen*, you usually think of it as the appropriate ending of prayer. Yet when Benaiah spoke to King David just before Solomon was named the new king, this man *began* his words by saying "amen." So is this word also a beginning? One way the word is translated is "so be it." *Amen* might even make sense as "I want this to come to pass" or "God is trustworthy and can do what I can't." In 1 Kings 1 it is used by a man who knew King David and wanted to see success for the new king, Solomon. Think about the way people might use "amen" today. They may be stating agreement that what has been said was worth saying, and they want what was said to come true. In prayer and in daily life the use of "amen" makes sense when you know what it means.

Prayer Starter

Father, thank You for the joyous exclamation of "amen." I have plenty of things to agree with You about. Let me name some of my favorites. . .

DAY 115
1 KINGS 3–4

Prayer Scripture

[Solomon prayed,] "O Lord my God, You have made Your servant king in place of my father, David, and I am only a little child; I do not know how to go out or come in. And Your servant is in the midst of Your people whom You have chosen, a great people who cannot be numbered or counted because of their number. Therefore give Your servant an understanding heart to judge Your people, that I may discern between good and bad. For who is able to judge this great people of Yours?"

1 Kings 3:7–9

Prayer Thought for the Day

Of all the gifts Solomon could have requested, he concluded that if he didn't have wisdom, then he wouldn't be a very good leader. This was the prayer of an overwhelmed prince who knew that he needed something more if he was going to become a good king.

What if, after accepting God's great rescue, you chose the gift of wisdom as a special gift from God? It is a gift He's always willing to give.

Prayer Starter

Lord God, I'd be honored to accept Your wisdom. I would be thrilled to know what You teach. I want to understand the things I'm not sure of. Give me wisdom so I can. . .

DAY 116
1 KINGS 5–7

Prayer Scripture

So all the work that King Solomon had done for the house of the LORD was finished. And Solomon brought in the things that David, his father, had dedicated, even the silver and the gold and the vessels, and he put them among the treasures of the house of the LORD.
1 KINGS 7:51

Prayer Thought for the Day

God didn't allow David to build the temple. Before Solomon started building this permanent worship center, the people had known only the tentlike tabernacle that never required a single location. David set aside the materials to build the temple, and Solomon became the general contractor for this massive undertaking. This would be a place where people came to know more about God. It would be a place to deal with personal sin. There people would gather for worship with others who loved God. This place would be a house of prayer. The day came when the temple was finished and was dedicated to God's use.

Today you are a recipient of God's presence. Find joy in this gift.

Prayer Starter

Father, make my heart a temple. Spend time with me and help me understand the value of spending time with You. Some of the things I want to learn from You include. . .

DAY 117

1 KINGS 8–9

Prayer Scripture

[Solomon said,] "Have respect for the prayer of Your servant and his supplication, O LORD my God, and listen to the cry and to the prayer that Your servant prays before You today, that Your eyes may be open toward this house night and day, even toward the place of which You have said, 'My name shall be there,' that You may listen to the prayer that Your servant shall make toward this place. And listen to the supplication of Your servant and of Your people Israel when they pray toward this place. And hear in heaven, Your dwelling place, and when You hear, forgive."

1 KINGS 8:28–30

Prayer Thought for the Day

The new temple meant something to Solomon, who prayed to the God who would occupy the structure. This was the same God who occupied Solomon's heart—and the same God Solomon wanted to occupy the hearts of all Israel. Solomon asked God to pay special attention to the present and future cries of His people. Solomon knew forgiveness would be needed, so he prayed for that too. This was a realistic prayer with hope that this connection would usher in a greater allegiance among the people.

Pray a similar prayer for your home and those who live there. It will mean something to you, them, and the God who made you both.

Prayer Starter

Lord God, hear, watch, and forgive me. Make my house Your home and help me...

DAY 118
1 KINGS 10–11

Prayer Scripture

The LORD was angry with Solomon because his heart had turned from the LORD God of Israel, who had appeared to him twice, and had commanded him concerning this thing, that he should not go after other gods. But he did not keep what the LORD had commanded.
1 KINGS 11:9–10

Prayer Thought for the Day

Solomon arrived at a very strange place. He possessed all the wisdom he'd requested from God but used almost none of that wisdom for personal decision-making. He built the temple, dedicated the structure, and prayed for forgiveness before that sin. Yet the wisest man who ever lived drifted. He began to honor non-gods. His personal decisions were apathetic. He engaged in the great walkaway and found himself with little interest in returning. No prayer, no seeking the scriptures, and seemingly no remorse. Solomon was told the kingdom would fracture. He knew he was to blame. But God had used this king to collect words of wisdom in the book of Proverbs and to build a temple. War was rare during Solomon's lifetime. Sin is a slow drift. One of the first things to be abandoned is prayer, because it's a blatant way to tell God you don't need Him.

Prayer Starter

Father, I don't want to abandon prayer, and I don't want to drift. Keep me engaged in prayer and seeking Your way and wisdom for those moments when. . .

DAY 119

1 KINGS 12–13

Prayer Scripture

[King Jeroboam] answered and said to the man of God, "Entreat now the face of the LORD your God and pray for me, that my hand may be restored to me again." And the man of God implored the LORD, and the king's hand was restored to him again and became as it was before.

1 KINGS 13:6

Prayer Thought for the Day

As God had said, things fell apart after the death of Solomon. His son Rehoboam was elevated to the status of king but lacked leadership skills and offended the people. So the kingdom was divided; a man named Jeroboam became king of Israel. Rehoboam was reduced to being the king of Judah only. It seemed both kings had little use for God. New plots developed, and suspicion was rampant. Jeroboam was burning incense to a non-god when a man of God showed up. Jeroboam didn't like what was said, and God caused his arm to shrivel. Suddenly Jeroboam thought prayer was a great idea. He asked the man of God to pray.

God delights in people who believe in Him without seeing signs and wonders. He welcomes people who pray even when they aren't faced with disaster.

Prayer Starter

Lord God, may my personal disasters be just one of the reasons I speak to You. Good days and bad days are alike; I'll need You on both. Give me a heart that. . .

DAY 120
1 KINGS 14–15

Prayer Scripture

Jeroboam said to his wife, "Arise, I ask, and disguise yourself, that you not be known to be the wife of Jeroboam, and get to Shiloh. Behold, Ahijah the prophet is there, who told me that I should be king over this people. And take with you ten loaves and brittle biscuits and a jar of honey, and go to him. He shall tell you what shall become of the child."

1 Kings 14:2–3

Prayer Thought for the Day

This was another close encounter with prayer for King Jeroboam. In his first encounter he asked someone to pray for him. In this encounter he asked his wife to inquire of one who followed God. Jeroboam wanted to know more about his son's illness. The king even sent gifts as perhaps a bribe or reward for seeking God—something he could have done on his own. Ahijah the prophet knew Jeroboam's wife would be deceptive, so he called her out on the lie and said her husband's reign would come to an end.

By all means, encourage others to pray for you, but don't use that as a substitute for personal prayer. God wants you to speak to Him personally.

Prayer Starter

Father, praying can seem a little intimidating when I remember I'm speaking to the one true God. Whatever You want me to know, help me to accept it because I heard it from You. Make me brave enough to accept. . .

DAY 121
1 KINGS 16–17

Prayer Scripture

[Elijah] cried to the LORD and said, "O LORD my God, have You also brought evil on the widow with whom I am staying by slaying her son?" And he stretched himself over the child three times, and cried to the LORD, and said, "O LORD my God, I ask you, let this child's soul come into him again." And the LORD heard the voice of Elijah, and the soul of the child came into him again, and he revived.

1 KINGS 17:20–22

Prayer Thought for the Day

Elijah the prophet lived during a time of unfaithful kings. They didn't want God's direction, and they didn't want anyone telling them they were wrong. King Ahab spent kingdom resources trying to find Elijah, who said there'd be no rain for more than three years. Elijah was hidden by God and taken care of by a widow and her son. God had already saved the lives of these two, but when the son died, the widow was heartbroken. Elijah prayed, and life miraculously returned to the boy.

Prayer is effective in hard times, and God sometimes orchestrates the impossible on behalf of those who pray. You can pray impossible prayers. God might just say yes.

Prayer Starter

Lord God, when it seems no one is interested in following You, keep me walking in Your footsteps so that I can make a bold move in Your direction. I want to know with certainty that. . .

DAY 122

1 KINGS 18–19

Prayer Scripture

It came to pass, at the time of the offering of the evening sacrifice, that Elijah the prophet came near and said, "LORD God of Abraham, Isaac, and of Israel, let it be known this day that You are God in Israel and that I am Your servant, and that I have done all these things at Your word. Hear me, O LORD, hear me, that this people may know that You are the LORD God and that You have turned their hearts back again."
1 KINGS 18:36–37

Prayer Thought for the Day

The time had come for a good rain. The earth could use it, and the people were tired of being thirsty. King Ahab wasn't happy with the prophet who said it wouldn't rain, but now Elijah had come to challenge the non-gods Ahab followed. The religious leaders of Baal did their best to encourage their god to respond, but he couldn't—he wasn't real. Elijah prayed and everyone saw. God heard and responded. This is the experience of any who truly seek God, ask for help, and wait for His response. No other non-gods should ever be consulted.

Prayer Starter

Father, thank You for hearing my heart and working all things together for my good and Your glory. May I be patient while I wait for You. . .

DAY 123
1 KINGS 20–21

Prayer Scripture

It came to pass when Ahab heard those words, that he tore his clothes and put sackcloth on his body and fasted, and lay in sackcloth and went about quietly. And the word of the LORD came to Elijah the Tishbite, saying, "See how Ahab humbles himself before Me? Because He humbles himself before Me, I will not bring the evil in his days. But I will bring the evil on his house in his son's days."

1 KINGS 21:27–29

Prayer Thought for the Day

Ahab faced the worst-case scenario, and it broke him. He did the right things to demonstrate he had remorse—that he understood the motivation to change. In His mercy, God delayed the pronounced sentence for this king's failure. For a moment the king knew he was wrong and wished things were different. His actions became something like a prayer. He fasted, demonstrated regret, and temporarily set pride on the shelf. God's mercy was bigger than the many sins that got Ahab into this place of correction. God's mercy is that way.

When you pray to God, it's the words you speak as well as the intent of your heart that He notices. God knows the reality of what you say, vow, and think. Prayer will always be more than words.

Prayer Starter

Lord God, let me speak honestly. May I think and feel when I talk to You. The things I'm most concerned with today include. . .

DAY 124
1 KINGS 22

Prayer Scripture

The king of Israel said to Jehoshaphat, "There is still one man, Micaiah the son of Imlah, by whom we may inquire of the LORD. But I hate him, for he does not prophesy good concerning me, but evil." And Jehoshaphat said, "Let the king not say so." Then the king of Israel called an officer and said, "Bring Micaiah the son of Imlah here quickly."

1 KINGS 22:8–9

Prayer Thought for the Day

Ahab's life was spared, but old habits are hard to break. Not much had changed within his heart, and he followed his own plan. Ahab had arranged a military operation with Jehoshaphat, the king of Judah, who wanted a second opinion. Bypassing prayer in favor of human opinion, Ahab called in non-god prophets. Finally, very curious about a man of God who could help them, Jehoshaphat insisted on hearing from the Lord's prophet. But that opinion had to come from Micaiah. Ahab said this man never had anything good to say, but Micaiah spoke anyhow. Ahab was predictably unhappy with his response, but the prophet knew what would happen if the kings engaged in this battle. It wasn't good.

Seek godly counsel *and* pray for God's wisdom. You may find rescue from your unexpected struggle.

Prayer Starter

Father, I don't want to be so hardheaded that I keep You from guiding me to the best solution. When I pray, help me to be. . .

DAY 125
2 KINGS 1–3

Prayer Scripture

Moab rebelled against Israel after the death of Ahab. And Ahaziah fell down through a lattice in his upper chamber that was in Samaria and was sick, and he sent messengers and said to them, "Go, inquire of Baal-zebub, the god of Ekron, whether I shall recover from this disease." But the angel of the LORD said to Elijah the Tishbite, "Arise, go up to meet the messengers of the king of Samaria and say to them, 'Is it because there is no God in Israel that you are going to inquire of Baal-zebub, the god of Ekron?' Now therefore, this is what the LORD says, 'You shall not come down from that bed on which you have lain, but you shall surely die.'" And Elijah departed.

2 KINGS 1:1–4

Prayer Thought for the Day

Ahaziah learned nothing worthwhile from his father, Ahab. He fell through a lattice and was concerned about his health. There was no prayer or seeking answers from a prophet. He sent his staff to inquire about his prognosis from a regional non-god. Elijah was God's prophet who had proved to Ahaziah's father that God was real. Ahaziah either hadn't heard this news or chose to disbelieve it. He sought intelligence from a non-god. That decision led to his death.

Prayer Starter

Lord God, I've been guilty of looking for answers elsewhere before seeking You. Help me to remember that You have answers I can't get anywhere else. Teach me to. . .

DAY 126

2 KINGS 4–5

Prayer Scripture

Naaman came with his horses and with his chariot and stood at the door of the house of Elisha. And Elisha sent a messenger to him, saying, "Go and wash in the Jordan seven times. And your skin shall come back to you, and you shall be clean." But Naaman was angry and went away and said, "Behold, I thought, 'He will surely come out to me and stand and call on the name of the LORD his God and wave his hand over the place and heal the leper.'"

2 KINGS 5:9–11

Prayer Thought for the Day

Naaman wasn't from Israel, but on the advice of a servant girl he arrived in Israel, seeking healing for a skin disease known as leprosy. The king had sent the man to the prophet Elisha, and when Naaman came to see the prophet, Elisha sent out a servant who gave Naaman instructions. Naaman had assumed the prophet would come out and perform a magic trick and just heal him. This soldier was upset that he seemed ignored by the prophet. But because Elisha spoke to God, he knew and was convinced that if this man obeyed, he would be made clean. And he was.

The same is true today—men who pray to God are convinced He can make others clean.

Prayer Starter

Father, Your Son makes me clean. I believe. Help me to share what I know, because others will need. . .

DAY 127

2 KINGS 6–8

Prayer Scripture

It came to pass as the man of God had spoken to the king, saying, "Two measures of barley for a shekel and a measure of fine flour for a shekel shall be tomorrow about this time at the gate of Samaria." And that lord answered the man of God and said, "Now behold, if the LORD should make windows in heaven, might such a thing be?" And he said, "Behold, you shall see it with your eyes but shall not eat of it."

2 KINGS 7:18–19

Prayer Thought for the Day

Famine had come to the region, and conditions were very bad for everyone. People were paying whatever they had to buy what was usually thrown away. A few resorted to cannibalism. The king blamed the prophet Elisha. This man of God had been in contact with God, and what he was certain of was that within twenty-four hours food would be plentiful and everyone could afford it. The king refused to believe, but when God makes a promise, He keeps it.

You can believe and have access to all the good God promises, or you can refuse to believe and you *will* miss the miracle.

Prayer Starter

Lord God, sometimes the improbable is true, the impossible is real, and hope sends anxiety away. Help me to believe You and explain just why to all who'll listen to. . .

DAY 128
2 KINGS 9–10

Prayer Scripture

The LORD said to Jehu, "Because you have done well in executing what is right in My eyes and have done to the house of Ahab according to all that was in My heart, your children to the fourth generation shall sit on the throne of Israel." But Jehu took no heed to walk in the law of the LORD God of Israel with all his heart, for he did not depart from the sins of Jeroboam, who made Israel to sin.

2 KINGS 10:30–31

Prayer Thought for the Day

Sometimes people approach their friendship with God with the objective of doing everything they can to color outside the lines. They want God to offer a free pass or a wink, to view their sin with a short-term memory. This was the case with King Jehu. Of course, he wasn't alone. Second Kings is filled with stories of national leaders who never seemed to believe God meant them to follow His laws. There didn't seem to be any interest in praying to the God they ignored. God showed mercy for temporary turnings or kings who struggled to follow Him.

This is an easy place to find yourself, but it will never get you closer to God.

Prayer Starter

Father, I don't want to live between following You and doing what I want. I need You more than my desire for things like. . .

DAY 129
2 KINGS 11–13

Prayer Scripture

Jehoahaz pleaded with the LORD, and the LORD listened to him, for He saw the oppression of Israel because the king of Syria oppressed them. And the LORD gave Israel a savior, so that they went out from under the hand of the Syrians. And the children of Israel dwelled in their tents as before. Nevertheless they did not depart from the sins of the house of Jeroboam, who made Israel sin, but walked in them.

2 KINGS 13:4–6

Prayer Thought for the Day

Jehoahaz wasn't a perfect leader, but he prayed a prayer of profound purpose. He saw that the people of Israel were being oppressed by the king of Syria, and it moved him to this prayer that considered the needs of others before himself. God has always sought justice for the oppressed, so this would have been a prayer He was eager to answer. This was true even though God was fully aware that while the king was faithful, the people, delivered from oppression, wouldn't consider Him worth following wholeheartedly.

Prayer Starter

Lord God, give me a concentrated gaze. Help me to see the oppression of others and allow my time with You to cause me to share what I see and how You help them to. . .

DAY 130
2 KINGS 14–15

Prayer Scripture

In the second year of Pekah the son of Remaliah, king of Israel, Jotham the son of Uzziah, king of Judah, began to reign. He was twenty-five years old when he began to reign, and he reigned sixteen years in Jerusalem. And his mother's name was Jerusha the daughter of Zadok. And he did what was right in the sight of the LORD. He did according to all that his father, Uzziah, had done. However. . .

2 KINGS 15:32–35

Prayer Thought for the Day

Jotham was probably a lot like most people. He didn't exactly disbelieve God. He thought the house of worship was a fine thing. Prayer wasn't something he objected to. He even participated in these things—in moderation. Jotham was noted for doing the right thing—as well as some, better than many. He was a pretty solid example. You might have noticed the word *however*, however. This word is the beginning of a contrast that pointed out that there were sinful practices this king overlooked, excused, or thought were no big deal. Jotham wasn't all in—he was just mostly in. He lived with a "however." No one who believes in God should ever live with a "however."

Prayer Starter

Father, when I'm tempted to overlook my own sin, help me to remember King Jotham, who received the However Award. I need to admit when I'm wrong and make a new choice to follow You when You ask me to. . .

DAY 131
2 KINGS 16–17

Prayer Scripture

Then the king of Assyria commanded, saying, "Carry one of the priests there whom you brought from there, and let him go and dwell there. And let him teach them the custom of the God of the land." Then one of the priests whom they had carried away from Samaria came and dwelled in Bethel and taught them how they should fear the LORD.

2 KINGS 17:27–28

Prayer Thought for the Day

Assyria had invaded Israel and had taken many people out of the nation and into bondage. Then they sent people from other nations to populate Israel's cities. The new residents had no idea what the religious customs were, and very few Israelites who remained were following God. Then a strange situation developed. Lions came to town and attacked the people. It was determined that because the new residents didn't know God their lack of knowledge led to the lion attacks. So the king of Assyria (who himself probably wasn't following God) sent back a priest to try to teach the new people in town about God, prayer, and following Him. This foreign king saw value in teaching something the people of Israel had largely rejected. Sometimes God answers prayers that have yet to be prayed.

Prayer Starter

Lord God, You can use anyone or anything to accomplish Your plan. Help me to pray. I thank You for answering some prayers that have never been spoken about needs like. . .

DAY 132

2 KINGS 18–19

Prayer Scripture

[Hezekiah] trusted in the LORD God of Israel, so that after him there was none like him among all the kings of Judah, nor any who were before him. For he clung to the LORD and did not depart from following Him but kept His commandments.

2 KINGS 18:5–6

Prayer Thought for the Day

A glowing report like this one in 2 Kings 18 might make you want to know more about Hezekiah. He wasn't like King Jotham, who did most things right. He wasn't exactly like King David, known as a man after God's own heart. He wasn't like King Ahab, who rarely made a good choice. This passage says that no king before or after him was like him. Hezekiah trusted, clung to, and prayed to God. Hezekiah didn't give up following God. This king was in leadership during a time of decline. Nations were seeking to take land from the people of Israel. This king provided a very visual example that some might have remembered when they were in exile.

You have the opportunity to be a similar example to people who find themselves in an exile of their own. What do they see in you?

Prayer Starter

Father, I'm learning. I'm growing. I want to be someone who resembles You in the way I treat others and in the way I respond to. . .

DAY 133
2 KINGS 20–21

Prayer Scripture

Then [Hezekiah] turned his face to the wall and prayed to the LORD, saying, "I beseech You, O LORD, remember now how I have walked before You in truth and with a perfect heart and have done what is good in Your sight." And Hezekiah wept sorely.

2 KINGS 20:2–3

Prayer Thought for the Day

A good king was in a very bad place. The king had been very sick, and Isaiah the prophet came to tell him that this illness would end in death. This was hard for the king to accept. He may have expected a longer life or thought his work wasn't done. Hezekiah had a close connection with God, so he prayed. The prophet, Isaiah, would be asked by God to return to talk to the king and pass along this message: "I have heard your prayer. I have seen your tears. Behold, I will heal you" (verse 5). This wasn't a promise to all people everywhere and for all time, suggesting that God would heal you whenever you ask Him to. This was a personal answer to a personal request from a man who made prayer a priority.

Prayer Starter

Lord God, I want to remember that You're concerned about the things that concern me. I need to recall that You want me to ask and seek You in prayer. Give me the words to ask for Your help with. . .

DAY 134

2 KINGS 22:1–23:30

Prayer Scripture

It came to pass, when the king [Josiah] had heard the words of the Book of the Law, that he tore his clothes. . . , saying, "Go, inquire of the Lord for me and for the people and for all Judah concerning the words of this book that has been found, for great is the wrath of the Lord that is kindled against us because our fathers have not listened to the words of this book, to do according to all that is written concerning us."

2 Kings 22:11–13

Prayer Thought for the Day

Josiah was only eight when he became king. He made good decisions. He followed God. This young king encouraged the repair of the temple. In the midst of this renovation, workers found a copy of the scriptures, which hadn't been read, remembered, or obeyed. You can almost imagine the blood draining from this king's features when he discovered that all the choices he'd been making still fell short of what God required. He understood God's displeasure and asked the religious leaders to pray so that God could reveal what next steps should look like. This is always a perfect question in prayer.

Prayer Starter

Father, give me a heart that expresses sorrow when a wrong is discovered and joy in Your excellent forgiveness. Search my heart and allow me to admit that I. . .

DAY 135

2 KINGS 23:31–25:30

Prayer Scripture

The LORD sent against [Jehoiakim] bands of the Chaldeans and bands of the Syrians and bands of the Moabites and bands of the children of Ammon, and sent them against Judah to destroy it, according to the word of the LORD that He spoke by His servants the prophets. Surely this came on Judah at the commandment of the LORD, to remove them out of His sight for the sins of Manasseh, according to all that he did, and also for the innocent blood that he shed, for he filled Jerusalem with innocent blood, which the LORD would not pardon.

2 KINGS 24:2–4

Prayer Thought for the Day

The land of Israel had survived in much the same way a yo-yo might. It was up and down, up and down, and eventually they simply stayed down. There was no more strength to rise from the dark place they insisted on visiting. To get back up, there would need to be a divine reset. This wouldn't be the worldwide flood of Noah. This would be a national exile with only a remnant remaining in Israel. The temple would be burned and the people led away. Prayer would eventually be rediscovered. Hope would eventually return. Justice had arrived, and the people mourned.

Prayer Starter

Lord God, guide me away from the yo-yo of a spiritually mismanaged life. Realign my priorities and keep me close as I. . .

DAY 136

1 CHRONICLES 1–4

Prayer Scripture

Jabez was more honorable than his brothers, and his mother called his name Jabez, saying, "Because I bore him with sorrow." And Jabez called on the God of Israel, saying, "Oh that You would bless me indeed, and enlarge my territory, and that Your hand might be with me, and that You would keep me from evil, that it may not grieve me!" And God granted him what he requested.

1 Chronicles 4:9–10

Prayer Thought for the Day

Who was Jabez? God knows all the details of his life, but as far as the Bible is concerned, he was a man who prayed a big prayer. This part of 1 Chronicles 4 stands out because it's surrounded by genealogical data. God wanted you to read about this man. Jabez had five very specific requests. He wanted God's blessing, more territory, God's closeness, protection from evil, and a life without regret. What made this prayer stand out? Besides the fact that God said yes to his request, this prayer would have allowed Jabez to have an influence on others. Today people continue to visit this passage to read the very short story of a man who prayed a big prayer. . .and God agreed.

Prayer Starter

Father, You can always tell me no to any prayer I pray. Help me to think of others and then be bold enough to ask as Jabez did, so You have the chance to teach me that. . .

DAY 137
1 CHRONICLES 5–7

Prayer Scripture

These are those whom David set over the service of song in the house of the Lord, after the ark came to rest. And they ministered before the dwelling place of the tabernacle of the congregation with singing, until Solomon had built the house of the Lord in Jerusalem, and then they served in their office according to their order.
1 Chronicles 6:31–32

Prayer Thought for the Day

There are people in your church who contribute to the worship that others experience. In their rehearsals and in their free time, they pray. There's a weight that comes with leading a congregation in worship. It's a solemn responsibility, but there's great joy as well. David appointed his own worship team. They led worship in song. Some played instruments. Some sang. Some wrote songs for the people to sing. Many did all these things. A close friendship with God was essential to help lead people to a place where following God was the spiritual outcome of worship. This is more than simply causing people to feel emotions—this is recognizing the majesty of God and knowing you're undone by such a wonderful glimpse of God's goodness.

Prayer Starter

Lord God, thank You for people who see the value in worship and work hard to make worship a powerful connection to You. May I show gratitude to. . .

DAY 138
1 CHRONICLES 8–10

Prayer Scripture

Saul died for his transgression that he committed against the LORD, even against the word of the LORD, which he did not keep, and also for asking counsel from a medium, to inquire of her. And he did not inquire of the LORD; therefore He slew him and turned the kingdom to David the son of Jesse.
1 CHRONICLES 10:13–14

Prayer Thought for the Day

Saul. A leader. A king. A man who made things up. He wanted to know things and chose the wrong way to find out. The most condemning phrase might just be "And he did not inquire of the LORD." The God who knew everything and had every answer Saul could have asked for was not consulted. Saul wasn't a self-starter who could do his job without input from his boss; Saul was a king who needed God's leadership but chose to offer a stiff arm, hard heart, and alternate belief system. This might sound appealing, but reread how well this choice worked for Saul.

Prayer Starter

Father, let me not consider myself wise when I keep choosing to make foolish decisions. Help me to resist making up my own rules and then suggesting they're Your rules for me. Give me the strength to. . .

DAY 139
1 CHRONICLES 11–14

Prayer Scripture

Then all Israel gathered themselves to Hebron to
David, saying, "Behold, we are your bone and your flesh.
And moreover, in time past, even when Saul was king,
you were he who led out and brought in Israel."
1 Chronicles 11:1–2

Prayer Thought for the Day

This passage may seem very similar to many other passages about David during his time as king. These words bear a significant difference. "You. . .led out and brought in Israel." This is a picture of a shepherd. He set the path for the sheep and urged them to follow. This was a job that God was well acquainted with. It was a job He'd been doing from the beginning of time, yet the people had proven to be very stubborn sheep. They wandered frequently and had little use for the safety of the sheepfold. The people were saying that even when Saul was king it was David who offered the better example. It was David who led with prayer, worship, and honoring God. Seeing this kind of leadership in you will always give people something to consider.

Prayer Starter

Lord God, let me be a sheep that follows You so others can see You in me and make the choice to follow. Let me honor You in. . .

DAY 140
1 CHRONICLES 15–17

Prayer Scripture

Give thanks to the Lord; call upon His name; make known His deeds among the people. Sing to Him, sing psalms to Him; tell of all His wondrous works. Glory in His holy name; let the hearts of those who seek the Lord rejoice. Seek the Lord and His strength; seek His face continually. Remember His marvelous works that He has done, His wonders and the judgments of His mouth.

1 Chronicles 16:8–12

Prayer Thought for the Day

If people internalized this passage, how might it change everything about their life outlook? Begin with gratitude, make God's name famous by talking to Him regularly, tell other people what God has been up to in your life, and be someone willing to share answered prayer.

But wait—there's more: Honor Him, rejoice in everything He does, look for Him, and accept His strength. And the life-changing message isn't done. Remember the good things He's done, recall moments of wonder, and pay attention to His laws. This is an incredible review of right living for those who struggle to remember. It can be an incredible start to your today—the day God made—the day you can live to its fullest.

Prayer Starter

Father, may I recall Your wonder, be grateful, and never be ashamed of You. Change today when I. . .

DAY 141
1 CHRONICLES 18–21

Prayer Scripture

King David said to Ornan, "No, but I will truly buy it for the full price, for I will not take what is yours for the LORD, nor offer burnt offerings without cost." So David gave to Ornan six hundred shekels of gold by weight for the place. And David built there an altar to the LORD, and offered burnt offerings and peace offerings, and called on the LORD. And He answered him.

1 CHRONICLES 21:24–26

Prayer Thought for the Day

Ornan the Jebusite owned a threshing floor on Mount Moriah. He likely hadn't planned on selling the location where he made his living. David was king over Israel. He conducted a census and it was considered a sin. The sin may not have been in the counting but the pride that caused David to count the number of people he ruled over. When God sent the correction for sin, it directed King David to a place of worship, which leads us back to Ornan. This farmer offered the threshing floor to David as a place to make an offering to God and pray. David insisted on paying for it because he couldn't believe that it really was his offering if it was taken from someone else.

Prayer Starter

Lord God, let me be willing to do Your will, as You command it. Provide all I need to be able to do what You desire in my life. And if I can help someone to obey You, show me. . .

DAY 142
1 CHRONICLES 22–24

Prayer Scripture

David also commanded all the princes of Israel to help Solomon his son, saying, "Is not the LORD your God with you? And has He not given you rest on every side? For He has given the inhabitants of the land into my hand, and the land is subdued before the LORD and before His people. Now set your heart and your soul to seek the LORD your God. Therefore arise and build the sanctuary of the LORD God, to bring the ark of the covenant of the LORD and the holy vessels of God into the house that is to be built for the name of the LORD."

1 CHRONICLES 22:17–19

Prayer Thought for the Day

King David was commissioning the work of building the temple to his son Solomon. David believed God was with those who would take on this project. The nation was at a unique time of peace, and the leadership needed to make this project their focus as they pursued the prayer and closeness the temple would represent. This is something you can do for your family. Commission and commend them to the work of following God through prayer, closeness, and the belief in a future identified with God.

Prayer Starter

Father, I'd be honored if my friendship with You is noticed by others who also choose to become friends with You. Help them to. . .

DAY 143
1 CHRONICLES 25–27

Prayer Scripture

All these were under the direction of their father for song in the house of the LORD, with cymbals, lyres, and harps, for the service of the house of God, according to the king's order to Asaph, Jeduthun, and Heman. So the number of them, with their brothers who were instructed in the songs of the LORD, even all who were skillful, was two hundred eighty-eight.
1 CHRONICLES 25:6–7

Prayer Thought for the Day

Two hundred eighty-eight individuals all leaned into the role of developing an atmosphere of praise for an entire nation. There were harp, lyre, and cymbals to play, songs to write and sing, and a variety of workmen who prepared for times of worship. This was more than just the act of an artistic personality or the development of a hit song. There were shepherds, farmers, businessmen, priests, and carpenters who served the temple—and then there were 288 men who served the worship needs of all who came to the temple to pray, worship, and honor God. Anyone who lives and breathes can be included in the number of people who worship God.

Prayer Starter

Lord God, I want to thank You for the men and women who understand the heart of worship and allow me to join them in honoring You. Help me to choose worship so I can. . .

DAY 144

1 CHRONICLES 28–29

Prayer Scripture

David blessed the Lord before all the congregation. And David said: "Blessed are You, Lord God of Israel, our Father, forever and ever. Yours, O Lord, is the greatness and the power and the glory and the victory and the majesty, for all that is in heaven and on the earth is Yours. Yours is the kingdom, O Lord, and You are exalted as head above all. Both riches and honor come from You, and You reign over all. And in Your hand is power and might, and in Your hand it is to make great and to give strength to all."
1 Chronicles 29:10–12

Prayer Thought for the Day

You might feel defeated by admitting that everything that exists is God's and nothing that's been created was the result of your effort. King David was praying at the commission of the materials for the temple when he joyfully declared that God's greatness, power, glory, and majesty was recognizable because there was nothing seen or known that God didn't create. God made it all and owned it all, and He offered strength to all. It was important for David to let God know, in prayer, that he fully understood the incredible scope of the Lord's role as creator and sustainer of all life.

Prayer Starter

Father, give me an interest in remembering how incredible You are. If I forget, help me to recall stunning views, miracles, and memories that remind me that You. . .

DAY 145
2 CHRONICLES 1–4

Prayer Scripture

Solomon said to God, "You have shown great mercy to my father, David, and have made me to reign in his place. Now, O LORD God, let Your promise to my father, David, be established, for You have made me king over a people as numerous as the dust of the earth. Now give me wisdom and knowledge, that I may go out and come in before this people, for who can judge this people of Yours, who are so great?"

2 CHRONICLES 1:8–10

Prayer Thought for the Day

Solomon was responding to God's offer of a gift. Solomon began his prayer request by reminding God of a promise made to his father, David. Solomon would be Israel's new king—and he felt overwhelmed. The people were many, and their needs would grow during his reign as king. The only logical request for this overwhelming job was the wisdom to know how to deal with the people and wisely judge the injustices he encountered.

Believe it or not, God has promised us hard days. You've probably experienced them. Having the wisdom to survive hard days would be an impressive gift. Have you asked?

Prayer Starter

Lord God, help me to be honest enough to admit there are moments when I'm very overwhelmed—and I can stay that way for a very long time without Your help. Give me the wisdom to. . .

DAY 146
2 CHRONICLES 5–7

Prayer Scripture

[Solomon prayed,] "Will God indeed dwell with men on the earth? Behold, heaven and the heaven of heavens cannot contain You. How much less this house that I have built! Therefore, consider the prayer of Your servant and his supplication, O LORD my God, and listen to the cry and the prayer that Your servant prays before You, that Your eyes may be open on this house day and night, on the place where You have said that You would put Your name, to listen to the prayer that Your servant prays toward this place. Listen therefore to the supplications of Your servant and of Your people Israel, which they shall make toward this place. Hear from Your dwelling place, even from heaven, and when You hear, forgive."

2 CHRONICLES 6:18–21

Prayer Thought for the Day

The temple was dedicated with a memorable prayer from Solomon, Israel's newest king, who requested that God listen to the prayers of His people. Solomon, the wise king, gave a curious summary. When God listened, he wanted God to forgive. He knew there would be failures, and he wanted God, and the people listening, to know that he recognized this new temple was a place that represented God's forgiveness.

It was needed then and remains one of man's most profound needs today.

Prayer Starter

Father, when You hear my prayer, please forgive me. I've always needed to admit my sin so You can clean my record and I can. . .

DAY 147
2 CHRONICLES 8–9

Prayer Scripture

King Solomon surpassed all the kings of the earth in riches and wisdom. And all the kings of the earth sought the presence of Solomon, to hear his wisdom that God had put in his heart. And they brought, every man his present, a rate year by year: vessels of silver, and vessels of gold, and clothing, armor and spices, horses, and mules.

2 Chronicles 9:22–24

Prayer Thought for the Day

Solomon's request for wisdom in a prayer to a good God was answered in 2 Chronicles 9. If you were curious about what it looked like to have the request for wisdom granted, you've learned that no one was wiser or richer than Solomon. Other leaders asked for appointments to talk with him, because they could use his wisdom too. People kept arriving in Israel to bring Solomon all kinds of presents in honor of his wisdom gift. And all of this word-of-mouth honor was due to a prayer. When God answers prayer, a story is created that can be shared in ways that help others and honor God.

Prayer Starter

Lord God, when I pray, You answer. Remind me to share Your answers to prayer. It can encourage others and help them to see the value of a friendship with You. Some of the prayers that have been answered for me include. . .

DAY 148
2 CHRONICLES 10–13

Prayer Scripture

The Levites left their suburbs and their property and came to Judah and Jerusalem, for Jeroboam and his sons had cast them off from carrying out the priest's office to the LORD. And he ordained for himself priests for the high places and for the demons and for the calves that he had made. And after them, those out of all the tribes of Israel who had set their hearts to seek the LORD God of Israel came to Jerusalem to sacrifice to the LORD God of their fathers.

2 CHRONICLES 11:14–16

Prayer Thought for the Day

What happens when no one shows up to pray, and there's no worship even when the worship team is prepared? There's no one to hear the preacher, and the people have remained at home when it was time to gather. Those who taught, sang, and led discovered there was no one to teach, sing with, and lead. There was a reason. King Jeroboam transferred allegiance from God to demons. He essentially told those who led worship that their services were no longer required. With this eviction, the priests and worship leaders set out on a journey to Jerusalem to minister to others who still honored God. Israel was in decline, and Judah was strengthened—briefly.

Prayer Starter

Father, keep me in the company of those who worship You, those who pray to You, and those who learn from You. Help me to begin by. . .

DAY 149

2 CHRONICLES 14–18

Prayer Scripture

The Spirit of God came on Azariah the son of Oded. And he went out to meet Asa and said to him, "Hear me, Asa, and all Judah and Benjamin. The LORD is with you while you are with Him. And if you seek Him, He will be found by you, but if you abandon Him, He will abandon you. Now for a long time Israel was without the true God and without a teaching priest and without law. But when in their trouble they turned to the LORD God of Israel and sought Him, He was found by them."

2 CHRONICLES 15:1–4

Prayer Thought for the Day

God wasn't hiding, but the people weren't seeking. Not only were the people intent on doing what they wanted, but the temple was without a teaching priest, and no one remembered God's law. It was as if God was saying, "Follow Me," and the people were saying, "And who are You?" Azariah would make those introductions and promised that prayer would be critical to the discovery of a lifetime. It was clear the people were in trouble, so when they sought God, they found Him.

Seek God, since *you* can also find Him. You're encouraged to seek, find, and follow.

Prayer Starter

Lord God, let me be a seeker. May I know instinctively that You exist and are waiting for me to find You. Thanks for not hiding. Thanks for loving me enough to. . .

DAY 150
2 CHRONICLES 19–21

Prayer Scripture

[Jehoshaphat] said, "O LORD God of our fathers, are You not God in heaven? And do You not rule over all the kingdoms of the nations? And in Your hand is there not power and might, so that no one is able to withstand You? . . . And now, behold, the children of Ammon and Moab and Mount Seir—whom You would not let Israel invade when they came out of the land of Egypt, but they turned from them and did not destroy them. . . . O our God, will You not judge them? For we have no might against this great company that comes against us, nor do we know what to do. But our eyes are on You." And all Judah stood before the LORD, with their little ones, their wives, and their children.

2 CHRONICLES 20:6, 10, 12–13

Prayer Thought for the Day

This prayer was both bold and direct. God saved His people for a purpose, and this was a good day for fresh rescue. King Jehoshaphat asked for God's promise to be kept. He wasn't alone. Standing with him was the collective of citizens, young and old, weak and weaker, believers and seekers. They would praise the Lord before they saw prayer answered. The enemy would be defeated.

Pray, believing. Praise God's working. Be grateful; God can be trusted.

Prayer Starter

Father, let me add praise to my prayer and gratitude for Your answer. I'll struggle to trust, so help me. . .

DAY 151
2 CHRONICLES 22–24

Prayer Scripture

When they had finished it, they brought the rest of the money before the king and Jehoiada, with which vessels were made for the house of the LORD, vessels for ministering and for offering, and spoons and vessels of gold and silver. And they offered burnt offerings in the house of the LORD continually, all the days of Jehoiada.
2 CHRONICLES 24:14

Prayer Thought for the Day

Was the temple repaired because of the youngest king of Judah? Was it because of the great influencer, Jehoiada? No, the temple was fully repaired because a great God moved the hearts of people to give, workers to work, prayers to pray, and believers to trust. If the project relied on people, they would be reluctant to give. When it might have relied on workers, they were prone to weariness. When it relied on influencers, that influence wasn't enough. The prayer of believers to a God who revives and renews saw the work completed. You can be that person who prays, believing that God is in control. He has answers when all you can contribute are questions.

Prayer Starter

Lord God, may I honor those who help me in this journey, but never to the neglect of honoring You—who does literally everything to help me start, continue, and complete this journey. I want to be a praying believer who. . .

DAY 152
2 CHRONICLES 25–28

Prayer Scripture

[Jotham] built cities in the mountains of Judah, and he built fortresses and towers in the forests. He also fought with the king of the Ammonites and prevailed against them. And the same year the children of Ammon gave him one hundred talents of silver and ten thousand measures of wheat and ten thousand of barley. The children of Ammon paid this to him in both the second year and the third. So Jotham became mighty because he prepared his ways before the LORD his God.
2 CHRONICLES 27:4–6

Prayer Thought for the Day

This is a story of intentionality. It may seem simple, but the investment must have been long term. Jotham was a king who was elevated to his position in his mid-twenties, and he served sixteen years. He was decisive in battle and was given tribute from those who were defeated. He regularly received wealth and food from the vanquished armies. King Jotham's investment is found in the last nine words of this passage, "He prepared his ways before the LORD his God." How are you preparing?

Prayer Starter

Father, You do great work in my life. Help me to cooperate with You. Give me a heart for the investment of a life lived out for You. May people see progress when I. . .

DAY 153
2 CHRONICLES 29–30

Prayer Scripture

They gathered their brothers, and sanctified themselves,
and came, according to the commandment of the king, by the
words of the LORD, to cleanse the house of the LORD.
And the priests went into the inner part of the house of the
LORD to cleanse it and brought out all the uncleanness that
they found in the temple of the LORD into the courtyard of the
house of the LORD. And the Levites took it to carry it out.
2 CHRONICLES 29:15–16

Prayer Thought for the Day

The cleansing of a nation isn't easy, but it's necessary. It may seem solemn, but it's a conduit to a celebration. It's an exodus from all the filth and depravity of a life refusing the influence and correction of God. There were items within the temple designed to be pure, but they'd been neglected. Other things were allowed in that tainted what had been created for purity. The unclean materials would need to be removed before the temple could be fully useful for a God who was perfectly clean. Once cleaned, worship resumed, prayers were uttered, and trust was replanted in the soil of hope.

This is a picture of your life and the God who removes the unclean, unneeded, and unproductive things that hinder your relationship with Him.

Prayer Starter

Lord God, please remove what prevents You from feeling at home in my life. Some things I believe need to be removed include. . .

DAY 154
2 CHRONICLES 31–33

Prayer Scripture

The Lord spoke to Manasseh and to his people, but they would not listen. Therefore the Lord brought on them the captains of the army of the king of Assyria, who took Manasseh with hooks and bound him with shackles and carried him to Babylon. And when he was in distress, he implored the Lord his God and humbled himself greatly before the God of his fathers, and prayed to Him. And He was entreated by him and heard his supplication and brought him again to Jerusalem into his kingdom. Then Manasseh knew that the Lord was God.

2 Chronicles 33:10–13

Prayer Thought for the Day

God can get your attention. You just read the proof. God could have removed Manasseh from office, but He chose to help the king with a massive perspective shift. When Manasseh said (and continued to say) that God wasn't worth following, he was given a personal time-out in Assyria. When this king chose to admit God was right, he prayed to the only wise God. The Lord brought Manasseh home to lead a country in which the people needed to know their leader followed the only God qualified to lead. If Manasseh had any doubts about God, he received a truth reminder.

Prayer Starter

Father, I'm a living temple, and I need You to clean every area that doesn't match Your plan for my life. Make me willing to own a clean heart as You. . .

DAY 155
2 CHRONICLES 34–36

Prayer Scripture

The Lord God of their fathers sent to them by His messengers, rising up early and sending, because He had compassion on His people and on His dwelling place. But they mocked the messengers of God and despised His words and misused His prophets, until the wrath of the Lord arose against His people, until there was no remedy.
2 Chronicles 36:15–16

Prayer Thought for the Day

In these decades of the history of Israel, God offered multiple merciful second chances. Sometimes those chances were taken seriously. Sometimes they were ignored. Because God is also identified as a God of justice, there would come an end to what might have been wrongly perceived as God's willingness to overlook lawbreaking. The messenger-prophets were dispatched to share God's communication, which included course correction for the people to follow. The people chose to reject a message they despised, and they treated with contempt the prophets who shared the message. No one sought God's Word or prayed for guidance. The people just said, "No!"

God's justice arrived in the form of long-term exile, and no amount of "I'm sorry" would change His mind. Taking God's offer of compassionate mercy and allowing it to change actions is a better way to witness change.

Prayer Starter

Lord God, I thank You for more than one second chance. Help me to witness change in my own life as I accept Your compassion and follow You more. . .

DAY 156
EZRA 1–3

Prayer Scripture

Many of the priests and Levites and chiefs of the fathers, who were ancient men who had seen the first house, when the foundation of this house was laid before their eyes, wept with a loud voice. And many shouted aloud for joy, so that the people could not discern the noise of the shout of joy from the noise of the weeping of the people. For the people shouted with a loud shout, and the noise was heard far away.
Ezra 3:12–13

Prayer Thought for the Day

A remnant of people remembered how things once were. Sometimes those who are younger have little interest in hearing about the past. But this was an unexpected praise festival. No one thought something like this could happen to a nation in exile. The leader who now ruled over those forced from their homes sent some exiled Jews back to rebuild the temple. Young men praised God for this symbol of their nation. It offered hope. Older men wept, perhaps because they remembered the God they once worshipped and prayed to there. This was a blend of longing for what once was and for what could be.

Maybe you've found yourself in both places. Look to the God who can change outcomes.

Prayer Starter

Father, teach my heart to long for You—to know what You've done and what You'll do. I want to rely on You when I feel. . .

DAY 157
EZRA 4–6

Prayer Scripture

[King Darius said,] I make a decree as to what you shall do for the elders of these Jews for the building of this house of God: that from the king's goods. . .expenses shall immediately be given to these men, so that they are not hindered. And what they have need of. . .let it be given to them day by day without fail, that they may offer sacrifices of sweet aromas to the God of heaven and pray for the life of the king and of his sons.

Ezra 6:8–10

Prayer Thought for the Day

This letter served a practical purpose for the king who oversaw the exiles' actions. He'd heard various challenges to the temple rebuilding that had been ordered by his predecessor. But this new king, Darius, discovered the work had been commissioned and funds allocated—and those opposing the rebuilding were in the wrong. Darius wanted the temple to be operational in the same way it once was so that priests could "pray for the life of the king and his sons."

Everyone can use prayers—especially those who may not believe.

Prayer Starter

Lord God, thank You for moving in the hearts of others to do what is useful for reaching people like me and others who. . .

DAY 158
EZRA 7–8

Prayer Scripture

[Ezra prayed,] Blessed be the Lord God of our fathers, who has put such a thing as this in the king's heart, to beautify the house of the Lord that is in Jerusalem, and has extended mercy to me before the king and his counselors and before all the king's mighty princes. And I was strengthened as the hand of the Lord my God was upon me, and I gathered together out of Israel chief men to go up with me.

Ezra 7:27–28

Prayer Thought for the Day

The strongest dynasty on earth at the time had granted the people of Israel everything they needed to build a temple. This gift was considered a mercy from the hand of God. Yet there were individuals who consistently detracted from the effort. And all the money, with all the well wishes of the most influential man around, wasn't enough to make the rebuilding easy. So Ezra prayed because he was taking a group of influential men to Jerusalem to continue the effort that remained agonizingly slow.

When you pray, invite others to pray with you. When you're working with God, gather helpful friends.

Prayer Starter

Father, I need to be reminded that I shouldn't attempt to do life alone. Bring friends who will help me to. . .

DAY 159
EZRA 9–10

Prayer Scripture

[Ezra prayed,] O my God, I am ashamed. . . . For our iniquities have increased over our head and our guilt has grown up to the heavens. Since the days of our fathers we have been in great guilt to this day. And for our iniquities we, our kings, and our priests have been delivered into the hand of the kings of the lands, to the sword, to captivity, and to plunder, and to shamefacedness, as it is this day. . . . For we were slaves. Yet our God has not abandoned us in our bondage but has extended mercy to us in the sight of the kings of Persia, to revive us, to set up the house of our God, and to repair its desolations, and to give us a wall in Judah and in Jerusalem. . . . Behold, we are before You in our guilt, for we cannot stand before You because of this.

Ezra 9:6–7, 9, 15

Prayer Thought for the Day

God was being exalted through the rebuilding of His temple. Yet the people refused to see this as His blessing. They marched from personal slavery to spiritual slavery, and Ezra cried out to God, remembering His mercy and lamenting this national response. Ezra refused to try to find an excuse.

Prayer Starter

Lord God, break my heart about the things that break Your heart about me. Let me arrive condemned and leave forgiven for things that stand in the way of. . .

DAY 160
NEHEMIAH 1–3

Prayer Scripture

[Nehemiah prayed,] "O Lord, I beseech You, let Your ear now be attentive to the prayer of Your servant and to the prayer of Your servants, who desire to fear Your name. And give success to Your servant this day, I pray You, and grant him mercy in the sight of this man."
NEHEMIAH 1:11

Prayer Thought for the Day

Nehemiah would be treading ground that was potentially dangerous. He was the cupbearer for a foreign king. This wasn't just another job that he could lose and search for employment elsewhere. Nehemiah was a slave, and sharing his heart with the slave owner was generally discouraged. This is why this prayer was so important to him. Nehemiah was looking for an opportunity to share something very important, even though he knew it could be life threatening. The king could tell something was wrong, and he asked his servant about it. Not only was the king receptive to what Nehemiah had to share about the broken walls of Jerusalem, he was willing to fund the repairs.

Prayer can open doors that you never dreamed possible. When you face a frightening situation, pray. God's already with you.

Prayer Starter

Father, because I have a choice, I choose for You to come with me in all places where I go. Remove my fear, show me the way, and walk before me when I struggle to. . .

DAY 161
NEHEMIAH 4–6

Prayer Scripture

The wall was finished on the twenty-fifth day of the month of Elul, in fifty-two days. And it came to pass that when all our enemies heard of it, and all the nations who were around us saw these things, they were very downcast in their own eyes. For they perceived that this work was done by our God.

NEHEMIAH 6:15–16

Prayer Thought for the Day

In less than two months, Nehemiah the cupbearer and those who helped completed the rebuilding of the walls around Jerusalem. As with other rebuilding efforts in Jerusalem, they faced opposition. Some who could have been building were assigned to security detail. A significant group of people didn't want to see the walls rebuilt. The walls could mean Jerusalem might be seen as a legitimate city, that its past might have a link to the future, and that ultimately God answered the prayers of the people to see the project to completion. It must have been encouraging to know that people who didn't want the walls rebuilt came to the conclusion that this work was done by God.

Pray big prayers. God can say no, but, if He affirms your request, then it'll be easy to point to the truth that this work was done by God.

Prayer Starter

Lord God, I love to see answers to prayer that only You could do. I have seen this before and I thank You for. . .

DAY 162
NEHEMIAH 7–9

Prayer Scripture

Now in the twenty-fourth day of this month the children of Israel were assembled with fasting and with sackcloth and dust on them. And the descendants of Israel separated themselves from all foreigners and stood and confessed their sins and the iniquities of their fathers. And they stood up in their place and read from the Book of the Law of the LORD their God for one-fourth of the day, and for another fourth they confessed and worshipped the LORD their God.

NEHEMIAH 9:1–3

Prayer Thought for the Day

The people were learning things that God had commanded so many years before, but those things were mostly forgotten. They weren't shared around campfires or on family trips. They weren't discussed in the temple because, until recently, the temple wasn't fit to be used. The people were undone because they heard from God's Word that there were things they should be doing or should stop doing. It was important information to receive, but this was also a day of learning, praying, and admitting sin. There was so much to take in, but in that moment the people rejoiced because they could begin to understand the reason for their exile.

Prayer Starter

Father, may I refuse to be afraid of what I learn from You. May my heart receive this news with joy. May I accept Your gift of. . .

DAY 163

NEHEMIAH 10–11

Prayer Scripture

Now those who sealed were Nehemiah the governor, the son of Hacaliah, and Zidkijah, Seraiah, Azariah, Jeremiah, Pashhur, Amariah, Malchijah, Hattush, Shebaniah, Malluch, Harim, Meremoth, Obadiah, Daniel, Ginnethon, Baruch, Meshullam, Abijah, Mijamin, Maaziah, Bilgai, and Shemaiah. . . . And all those who had separated themselves from the people of the lands to the law of God, their wives, their sons, and their daughters, everyone having knowledge and having understanding, they joined with their brothers, their nobles, and entered into a curse and into an oath to walk in God's law, which was given by Moses, the servant of God, and to observe and do all the commandments of the LORD our Lord and His judgments and His statutes.

NEHEMIAH 10:1–8, 28–29

Prayer Thought for the Day

Every biblical name has a story you may never know, about a closer friendship with God. Every name here was just one of many who came to understand the God they'd heard about and the law to which they were recently introduced. This was another sign of exiles in recovery. These were people who were understanding the value of prayer, obedience, and wisdom.

You have the choice to be part of a similar movement toward recovery.

Prayer Starter

Lord God, perhaps someday my name will be shared as someone who learned about You and chose to walk with You. I pray that my life will impact others because. . .

DAY 164
NEHEMIAH 12–13

Prayer Scripture

Remember me, O my God, concerning this, and do not wipe out my good deeds that I have done for the house of my God and for its services. . . . Remember me, O my God, for good!
NEHEMIAH 13:14, 31

Prayer Thought for the Day

Nehemiah had engaged in a journey in prayer. He found favor with God and the king, and so many of the people who prepared the wall also learned the law and made the temple their spiritual home. Their vocal commitment to God made it seem as if Israel had turned a page in its national history. Nehemiah returned to the king, but in time he revisited Jerusalem, and the spiritual decline was evident. It seems Nehemiah felt that all his good intentions could be discounted or overlooked, based on the misdeeds of some who'd been left behind to care for the new construction. He may have felt like a failure. Nehemiah's prayer was essentially a plea for mercy for the people—for himself.

When it seems as if society around you has no recollection of God, remember Nehemiah and the work he did when others thought him foolish. Then? Continue.

Prayer Starter

Father, I need to pray for others, but I also need to remember that the only person I have any control over is me. Help me to make wise decisions with no regret so I can help others. . .

DAY 165

ESTHER 1–3

Prayer Scripture

The king took his ring from his hand and gave it to Haman the son of Hammedatha the Agagite, the Jews' enemy. And the king said to Haman, "The silver is given to you, the people also, to do with them as it seems good to you."

Esther 3:10–11

Prayer Thought for the Day

The Persian king Ahasuerus had a history of making decisions without knowledge. He exiled his wife. Then, to find a new queen, he held a beauty contest. In Esther 3, Ahasuerus essentially gave his second in command (a vindictive man named Haman) a blank check to do whatever he wanted about whatever it was that bothered him. The king didn't follow God, so there was no searching of the scriptures and no prayer for guidance. What the king didn't know was that Haman hated one man—Mordecai—and was willing to punish every one of his relatives. Now Haman had the king's approval. His bad decision was courtesy of the king's bad decision. Both decisions were the result of an unwillingness to ask God for help in understanding what a good decision looks like.

Similar bad decisions are made every day. You've either made one or one has been made that impacted your life.

Prayer Starter

Lord God, let me resist impulsive decisions. Give me the wisdom to seek You before I make decisions that affect. . .

DAY 166
ESTHER 4–6

Prayer Scripture

Then Esther asked them to return to Mordecai with this answer: "Go, gather together all the Jews who are present in Susa, and fast for me, and neither eat nor drink for three days, night or day. I and my maidservants also will fast likewise, and so I will go in to the king, which is not according to the law. And if I perish, I perish." So Mordecai went his way and did according to all that Esther had commanded him.

Esther 4:15–17

Prayer Thought for the Day

The king made a very bad decision, and Queen Esther would have to make a very hard decision that could end her life. Haman's hatred of Mordecai would spill over to the queen. She was related to Mordecai. Haman didn't know this. The only way to advance a case for survival would mean Esther would need to visit the king without an invitation. If the king rejected her, she would be killed. If she didn't make the visit, she would die because of the law her husband agreed to. She asked Mordecai to send out a request for fasting, which usually includes prayer. If Esther was going to meet the king, she would need support only God could provide.

Always invite others to pray with and for you. It makes a difference.

Prayer Starter

Father, thank You for the reminder that I'm not better alone. Help me to invite others to pray for me when. . .

DAY 167
ESTHER 7–10

Prayer Scripture

Esther the queen, the daughter of Abihail, and Mordecai the Jew wrote with all authority to confirm this second letter of Purim. And he sent the letters to all the Jews, to the one hundred and twenty-seven provinces of the kingdom of Ahasuerus, with words of peace and truth, to confirm these days of Purim in their appointed times, as Mordecai the Jew and Esther the queen had commanded them, and as they had decreed for themselves and for their descendants concerning the matters of their fasting and crying.

Esther 9:29–31

Prayer Thought for the Day

It was the start of the celebration of surviving a massacre. This was the new holiday of Purim, and Queen Esther and her relative Mordecai were living through the first celebration. They sought God's direction. Beyond the saving of life, this celebration reminded the Jews that fasting and crying out to God were keys to avoiding a plot to annihilate them. You can celebrate every day when you remember that God wants to be found by you. He wants to rescue you. He wants a close friendship with you.

Prayer Starter

Lord God, I may have never considered a celebration of my ability to connect with You. Help me to remember this celebration and seek ways to commemorate my connection with You by. . .

DAY 168
JOB 1–5

Prayer Scripture

"My sighing comes before I eat. And my roarings are poured out like the waters. For the thing that I greatly feared has come on me, and what I was afraid of has come to me. I was not in safety. Nor did I have rest. Nor was I quiet. Yet trouble came."
Job 3:24–26

Prayer Thought for the Day

Job did nothing to invite the difficulty he faced, yet he would face trouble. God trusted him with grief. Satan asked to test Job and God agreed. It would be a test Job didn't understand. Friends came to visit and could only pretend to understand. They chose lectures over compassion. They criticized instead of praying. In Job 3 you'll find that fear and anxiety were Job's choices before the test. All the things he was most worried about came true. Worrying hadn't helped him. Fear hadn't protected him. Anguish was a companion to his misery. "Yet trouble came." As much as Job knew about God, he'd learn more in the furnace of adverse circumstances.

Maybe you've been there. . .are there. . .will be there. . .and testing leaves you with questions. Learn how never giving up on God is vital in the center of struggle.

Prayer Starter

Father, thank You for the reminder that fear and anxiety never prevent anything bad from happening. Give me everything I need to face and survive struggle in every moment I. . .

DAY 169
JOB 6–10

Prayer Scripture

[Job said,] "Oh, that I might have my request, and that God would grant me the thing that I long for. Even that it would please God to destroy me, that He would let loose His hand and cut me off!"
Job 6:8–9

Prayer Thought for the Day

Job had been praying, and it was honest and filled with a dark request. Job was literally asking God to kill him. His grief had seeped into every part of his being, and there seemed to be nothing in the act of living that inspired the hope he needed. Job felt that an end to his existence would be preferable to the words from friends that didn't help and questions that remained unanswered. It can be easy to skip over these dark moments, because you may not want to consider the implications of such an intense moment. Job was suggesting that an end to his life was his request. There have been other instances in which well-loved characters in scripture reached their limit—but they hadn't reached the end of God's grace, strength, and compassion. Good news—you haven't either. Don't give up.

Prayer Starter

Lord God, it's good to know that people I read about in Your Word faced deep struggles. Their example gives me courage to trust You when I. . .

DAY 170
JOB 11–14

Prayer Scripture

"What you know, the same I know. I am not inferior to you. Surely I would speak to the Almighty. And I desire to reason with God. But you are forgers of lies. You are all physicians of no value. O that you would altogether remain silent! And it should be your wisdom."
Job 13:2–5

Prayer Thought for the Day

Job wanted a face-to-face meeting with God. He reviewed his past, his actions, and his faithful pursuit of God, and nothing about his current situation made sense. His friends seemed to develop a predictable pattern of condemnation. They thought about all the bad things Job must have done to invite such severe judgment from God. Then they told their "friend" that everything he was going through was his fault. He should blame no one but himself.

Job had had enough and he concluded that if they were physicians, they couldn't help anyone. If there were lies being told, these friends were experts at hand-crafted falsehoods. Job told them that the wisest choice they could make would be to keep their mouths closed.

Spend your time talking to God and invite only His perspective to alter your outlook.

Prayer Starter

Father, in moments of anger, allow me to resist a response until I spend quality time with You. Help me to share my heart without accusing You of wrongdoing. Calm me when I. . .

DAY 171
JOB 15–19

Prayer Scripture

[Job said,] "Behold, I cry out of wrong, but I am not heard. I cry aloud, but there is no judgment. He has fenced up my way that I cannot pass, and He has set darkness in my paths. He has stripped me of my glory and taken the crown from my head. He has destroyed me on every side, and I am gone. And He has removed my hope like a tree."

Job 19:7–10

Prayer Thought for the Day

Job was being tested by God and condemned by those who called him friend. He expressed his feelings in this passage. Job admitted that he cried out to God but was certain no one was listening. He prayed, but there was no remedy or justice for him. He felt that God set a wall in place that he couldn't go through or around. He sought light, but all was dark. He considered himself destroyed and without hope. These feelings are common to all humans at some point. Very bad circumstances can leave you feeling friendless, aimless, and hopeless. Please remember this: Feelings are deceitful, and they don't always represent the truth.

Prayer Starter

Lord God, I want to feel heard, but even when I don't feel that way, help me to remember that *You* listen. And Your timing is more perfect than my desperation. Give me hope when. . .

DAY 172

JOB 20–24

Prayer Scripture

"They say to God, 'Depart from us, for we do not desire the knowledge of Your ways. What is the Almighty, that we should serve Him? And what profit should we have if we pray to Him?' Behold, their good is not in their hand. The counsel of the wicked is far from me."

Job 21:14–16

Prayer Thought for the Day

Job had witnessed those who had no use for God. He'd seen them stiff-arm God and insist they had no use for His wisdom and no interest in understanding what they didn't know. People who were very vocal about their lack of interest in God combined with their intentionally poor choices seemed to be in a better place than Job. He had a growing question about what he might have done wrong, when the wicked possessed much. Had he rejected wisdom? The current view made no sense to Job, and the lack of answers likely made him claustrophobic. When you feel overwhelmed and unsure that you've done nothing that needs correction, you can, at the very least, pray that God would help you understand either where you've sinned or what He may want you to learn.

Prayer Starter

Father, this is a story of a crushed and bruised man, and it can make me anxious to think anyone needs to face this. But when I do, please help me remember. . .

DAY 173
JOB 25–31

Prayer Scripture

[Job prayed,] "I cry to You, and You do not hear me.
I stand up, and You do not regard me. You have
become cruel to me. With Your strong hand You
oppose Yourself against me. You lift me up to the wind.
You cause me to ride on it and dissolve my substance.
For I know that You will bring me to death."
Job 30:20–23

Prayer Thought for the Day

Job was standing on life's stage, trying to get God's attention and seeming to fail with every arm movement or wail of vulnerability. Job refused to curse God—but suddenly he suggested that this God he'd followed for so long was cruel. Job wasn't sure what he'd done, but the God who'd always been there for him suddenly seemed an oppositional force. Like wheat in the wind, Job was being sifted, and there wasn't much left. At first he wanted to die, but suddenly Job felt certain God would kill him. These words were spoken to God and to three friends who would quickly reprimand Job for speaking dark words.

Sometimes the very raw anguish is too hard for you to handle and for others to hear—but those same words can be a part of your prayer to God. Don't accuse, just let Him know about life from your perspective.

Prayer Starter

Lord God, if it's true that You'll take my burdens, then let me share my struggle. . .

DAY 174
JOB 32–37

Prayer Scripture

Elihu also proceeded and said, "Bear with me a little, and I will show you that I have yet to speak on God's behalf. I will bring my knowledge from afar and will ascribe righteousness to my Maker. For truly my words shall not be false. He who is perfect in knowledge is with you."
Job 36:1–4

Prayer Thought for the Day

What you will read from Job's "friends" are words spoken to Job as if they were speaking to an errant schoolboy. You won't read much about any of them praying to God, seeking the wisdom needed to comfort Job. There was an arrogance in the Job 36 words of Elihu. You can almost sense the condescension when he said, "Bear with me a little." He went so far as to say he spoke for God. He couldn't envision that his words were false. Job was left with the declaration from Elihu that he was in the company of someone with perfect knowledge. This would be correct if God had said it. But Elihu wasn't God.

Refuse to speak for God before you speak to God.

Prayer Starter

Father, it's easy to verbally dump words that sound good but may not reflect Your heart. May I seek You before I say. . .

DAY 175
JOB 38–42

Prayer Scripture

After the LORD had spoken these words to Job, the LORD said to Eliphaz the Temanite, "My wrath is kindled against you and against your two friends. For you have not spoken of Me the thing that is right, as my servant Job has. Therefore, now take for yourselves seven bulls and seven rams and go to my servant Job and offer up for yourselves a burnt offering. And my servant Job shall pray for you. For I will accept him, lest I deal with you according to your folly, in that you have not spoken of Me the thing that is right, like My servant Job."

JOB 42:7–8

Prayer Thought for the Day

It's rare that God won't accept the prayer that someone prayed to Him, but in the case of Eliphaz, God said Job would need to pray, and He would accept the prayer of this righteous man. God dealt with Job's friends who believed their word was equal to anything God had to say. In the end, Job was honored, and God blessed him in a way that would have been a surprise to the three friends who could only speak about something they took no time to understand.

Prayer Starter

Lord God, give me a heart of compassion. Help me to use words to pray before they ever accuse. If I'm a friend to anyone, let me bring them to You with a heart that feels their pain so that my words will. . .

DAY 176
PSALMS 1–10

Prayer Scripture

As for me, I will come into Your house in the multitude of Your mercy, and in Your fear I will worship toward Your holy temple. Lead me, O LORD, in Your righteousness because of my enemies. Make Your way straight before my face.
PSALM 5:7–8

Prayer Thought for the Day

King David lived a colorful life filled with highs and lows. He was a warrior, a leader, a poet, and a follower of God. Most of the time he worked to combine everything that he was with everything God is. This Psalm 5 example is a part of a larger prayer from David. Job would have likely agreed with his thoughts. The highlights are that God shows mercy and that His righteousness is worth more than anything an enemy could do to him. God makes the way forward straight, and He's absolutely worthy of every moment of worship. You have choices when it comes to prayer. You can complain about circumstances that are out of your control, or you can honor God for the daily work He does every day of your life.

Prayer Starter

Father, may I spend time thinking about the good things You've done today that have meant something to me. More than remembering, let me be grateful. I'll start with thanking You for. . .

DAY 177
PSALMS 11–18

Prayer Scripture

Help, LORD, for the godly man ceases, for the faithful are lacking from among the children of men. They speak lies, every one with his neighbor. They speak with flattering lips and with a double heart.

PSALM 12:1–2

Prayer Thought for the Day

You can almost imagine David writing this after spending time observing life around him. Godly men were giving up. It was fashionable for lies to be shared like free samples at the grocery store. The people flattered others but were hypocrites because they didn't mean the nice things they said. David was eyewitness to the games people played, and everything about this high-stakes game was a matter of acting. Nothing was real. Nothing was genuine. Nothing was authentic. David noticed the hypocrisy and spoke of the real, genuine, and authentic God who offered mercy instead of flattery and who told the truth while lies dripped from the lips of the majority. If you could choose the way people treat you, would you choose lies or truth, authenticity or flattery?

Prayer Starter

Lord God, help me to speak truth and help me to be real with everyone I meet. Give me a longing for a life that's not defined by pretending. When I meet others, help me to say words that. . .

DAY 178

PSALMS 19–27

Prayer Scripture

The judgments of the Lord are true and righteous altogether.
More to be desired are they than gold, yes, than much fine gold;
sweeter also than honey and the honeycomb. Moreover Your servant
is warned by them, and in keeping them there is great reward.
Who can understand his errors? Cleanse me from secret faults.
Psalm 19:9–12

Prayer Thought for the Day

Psalm 19 is just one of many magnificent songs written by King David. This particular psalm revolves around the preservative effect of God's law. It's worth more than gold and sweeter than honey. It's a warning alarm and a mechanism of reward. There's no fault in God, and He can forgive the faults of mankind. See? Nothing but good news here. Not everyone felt the same way about God. They committed "errors," needed forgiveness, and still stayed away. This psalm is a reminder that following God is a good thing, understanding His warning is a good thing, and returning to Him is a good thing.

You have access to all of these good things. Take the time to explore.

Prayer Starter

Father, may I want to take advantage of all the good things found in Your Word. May I be encouraged as I seek to understand the value of obedience in. . .

DAY 179

PSALMS 28–34

Prayer Scripture

In You, O Lord, I put my trust. Let me never be ashamed.
Deliver me in Your righteousness. Bow down Your ear to
me. Deliver me speedily. Be my strong rock, a house of
defense to save me. For You are my rock and my fortress.
Therefore for Your name's sake, lead me and guide me.
Pull me out of the net that they have laid secretly for me,
for You are my strength. Into Your hand I commit my
spirit. You have redeemed me, O Lord God of truth.
Psalm 31:1–5

Prayer Thought for the Day

If you are looking for a treasure chest of material you can use to inform and inspire prayer, then the book of Psalms is a premier prayer book. You can take the Psalm 31 passage above and use it as a prayer. Customize it and make it your own. Spend time with each sentence. What does it mean to be delivered speedily? What does it mean that God is a rock and fortress? Why do you want Him to lead and guide you? How is God your strength? More than praying the same words, spend time thinking about what these verses mean.

Prayer Starter

Lord God, in You I put my trust. Let me never be ashamed. Deliver me speedily. Be my defense. Lead and guide as I. . .

DAY 180
PSALMS 35–39

Prayer Scripture

Plead my cause, O Lord, with those who contend with me. Fight against those who fight against me. Take hold of shield and buckler, and stand up for my help. Draw out also the spear, and stop the way of those who persecute me. Say to my soul, "I am your salvation." Let those who seek after my soul be confounded and put to shame; let those who devise my hurt be turned back and brought to confusion.

Psalm 35:1–4

Prayer Thought for the Day

King David found himself in a place where he was considered an enemy, and people would fight against him unjustly and unwisely. Why was it unwise to fight against David? As they do today, people assumed more than they should. This prayer is all about God defending the innocent. One of the ways David asked for help was by God speaking the truth about him into the life of one who was seeking to harm him. David prayed for an enemy to know the truth so the persecution could cease. This is a good reason to pray for those who hurt you. By knowing the truth, maybe they will stop.

Prayer Starter

Father, there are people who don't treat me very well. I want them to know the truth, and I'm asking You to help them learn what I could never tell them. Calm me and help me. . .

DAY 181

PSALMS 40-47

Prayer Scripture

As the deer pants for the water brooks, so my soul pants for You, O God. My soul thirsts for God, for the living God. When shall I come and appear before God? My tears have been my food day and night, while they continually say to me, "Where is your God?" When I remember these things, I pour out my soul within me. For I had gone with the multitude; I went with them to the house of God, with the voice of joy and praise, with a multitude who kept a holy day. Why are you cast down, O my soul? And why are you restless in me? Hope in God, for I shall yet praise Him for the help of His presence.

Psalm 42:1–5

Prayer Thought for the Day

David wanted God to know he had more than a casual interest in following Him. Deer go to great lengths to find the refreshment of water. This was the picture King David used to describe the desperate need he had to follow God. His internal dialogue was filled with personal struggle, intentional praise, and hope in this God whom David considered as important as water.

Prayer Starter

Lord God, I want You to be as important to me as the food I eat, the air I breathe, and the water I drink. You are necessary for life. May the things that I say and the things that I do be. . .

DAY 182
PSALMS 48-55

Prayer Scripture

Have mercy on me, O God, according to Your loving-kindness; according to the multitude of Your tender mercies, blot out my transgressions. Wash me thoroughly from my iniquity, and cleanse me from my sin. For I acknowledge my transgressions, and my sin is ever before me. Against You, You only, have I sinned, and done this evil in Your sight.

PSALM 51:1–4

Prayer Thought for the Day

The prophet Nathan confronted King David about his adultery with a married woman. You may remember reading about Bathsheba earlier in this book. What you didn't read then was this psalm that the king wrote in response to his guilt. He described how he wanted to reengage with God in light of his sin. David asked for mercy and loving-kindness. He wanted forgiveness. David wanted to be clean. The king apparently kept reliving the choice to break God's law, and it couldn't be put out of his mind. A key point in his prayer is that he admitted he was wrong. All the things God longs to hear from those who break His laws are part of this prayer.

Prayer Starter

Father, my mind reminds me of my sin, and You remind me I can be forgiven. I want to be clean. You can do that. I have broken Your laws, and I admit I was wrong. Turn my heart. . .

DAY 183
PSALMS 56–65

Prayer Scripture

Be merciful to me, O God, be merciful to me, for my soul trusts in You. Yes, in the shadow of Your wings I will make my refuge, until these calamities have passed. I will cry to God Most High, to God who performs all things for me. He shall send from heaven and save me from the reproach of him who would swallow me up. *Selah*. God shall send forth His mercy and His truth.

Psalm 57:1–3

Prayer Thought for the Day

Before David was king, he was chased by Saul. The first king of Israel wanted to kill the man who would become the next king. Saul was anxious and didn't want to lose his kingdom to a man whose greatest early skill set was that of a shepherd. Of course, David killed the giant, Goliath, but in Saul's mind David didn't deserve the kingdom. David responded in prayer by asking for God's mercy, declaring his trust and need for God's refuge. David could have staged a coup, but he trusted in God's timing and waited.

Are you considering a solution and believing that God needs to make it happen as soon as possible? Maybe waiting, as David did, will help you prepare for the future God has planned for you.

Prayer Starter

Lord God, let me be patient as I wait with You for Your best answer to the life challenges I face. When I'm impatient, help me remember that You. . .

DAY 184
PSALMS 66–71

Prayer Scripture

My lips shall greatly rejoice when I sing to You, and my soul, which You have redeemed. My tongue also shall speak of Your righteousness all day long, for those who seek to harm me are confounded; they are brought to shame.
Psalm 71:23–24

Prayer Thought for the Day

The acknowledgment of redemption can be a powerful part of your prayer experience. To be redeemed is to be bought back from the bank of condemnation so your existence can be deposited in God's freedom bank. Redemption is a key component of praise. . .and praise is a key component of prayer. . .and prayer is a key component of the life of someone who believes in God. This would be someone who wants to live a life of right decisions based on God's definition. And this news is too good to keep to yourself. Simply put, you've been rescued. God's freedom removed your guilty verdict. Prayer is a life conversation with the God who gave you life after the choice of sin.

Rejoice! This news is amazing.

Prayer Starter

Father, the act of redemption is a rescue bringing freedom to a slave who makes bad decisions. Thank You for showing me that You paid the price to make me free from. . .

DAY 185
PSALMS 72–77

Prayer Scripture

[Asaph prayed,] Surely You set them in slippery places; You cast them down into destruction. How they are brought into desolation, as in a moment! They are utterly consumed with terrors. As a dream when one awakes, so, O Lord, when You awake, You shall despise their image.

Psalm 73:18–20

Prayer Thought for the Day

Asaph worked in the temple, writing holy music for the people to hear and sing. He's responsible for some of the psalms you read. In Psalm 73 he gave voice to something you've probably experienced. He seemed to compare the life of one who follows God against the life of those who don't acknowledge or follow God. It seemed the life of those who chose to break God's laws could be easy and prosperous, while those who believe in God live in struggle. Asaph needed to consider timing. While he struggled to make sense of this comparison, he wasn't originally considering the long-term consequences. This is important because you'll likely compare too. You need to know this has been done before and Asaph's conclusion, "You shall despise their image," is worth considering.

Prayer Starter

Lord God, when I think it would be better not to follow You, remind me that at the end of this life I get to spend forever with You. May this good news inspire me to. . .

DAY 186
PSALMS 78–82

Prayer Scripture

O Lord God of hosts, how long will You be angry with the prayer of Your people? You feed them with the bread of tears and give them tears to drink in great measure. You make us a strife to our neighbors, and our enemies laugh among themselves. Restore us again, O God of hosts, and cause Your face to shine, and we shall be saved.

Psalm 80:4–7

Prayer Thought for the Day

God's justice can feel a little like being abandoned. It's important to remember that God is with you, even when justice is the new normal. The well-respected worship leader Asaph wrote this psalm, and it seemed he was recalling the exodus from Egypt and the struggle the people faced—mostly because of the poor choices they continued to make. Yet this prayer suggests that in the tears, the spite of neighbors, and the laughter of enemies, there's a request for mercy and a very real need for rescue.

The struggles you face today are a recurring theme of human existence. In every moment of personal wandering, there's always the underlying desire to find God.

Prayer Starter

Father, when it feels as if every circumstance and person stands opposed to me, may I remember that You want me to look for and find You so I can. . .

DAY 187
PSALMS 83–89

Prayer Scripture

A day in Your courts is better than a thousand. I would rather be a doorkeeper in the house of my God than dwell in the tents of wickedness. For the LORD God is a sun and shield. The LORD will give grace and glory; no good thing will He withhold from those who walk uprightly. O LORD of hosts, blessed is the man who trusts in You.

PSALM 84:10–12

Prayer Thought for the Day

Experiencing a closeness with God is such a powerful connection. When you're immersed in a sold-out friendship with God, you discover that even in the hardest of times there's a sense that no other life option provides the overwhelming wonder of following God with your entire being. The other option described by this unnamed psalmist is dwelling in tents occupied by the wicked. In that place there's no light, protection, grace, or trust. In the end, the one who's blessed is the one who trusts God and spends time with Him. There are so many ways you can include God in your daily experience. Don't leave Him out. Don't walk away from the place where He is. Don't withhold what God has freely given to you.

Prayer Starter

Lord God, walk with me, and I'll walk with You. Spend time with me, and I'll spend time with You. Give me wisdom so I can understand that. . .

DAY 188

PSALMS 90–99

Prayer Scripture

Teach us to number our days, that we may apply our hearts to wisdom. . . . O satisfy us early with Your mercy, that we may rejoice and be glad all our days. Make us glad according to the days in which You have afflicted us, and the years in which we have seen evil. Let Your work appear to Your servants, and Your glory to their children. And let the beauty of the LORD our God be on us, and establish the work of our hands for us. Yes, establish the work of our hands.

PSALM 90:12, 14–17

Prayer Thought for the Day

Moses weaves a prayer of longing tinged with regret and of planning colored by detours. Those who read Moses' words and apply them to their personal prayers to a good God would recognize mercy and joy as well as melancholy and memories of days remembered. Some might recall the stories of men, women, and children living years in the wilderness waiting for their home. Others might remember difficult years and waiting for their forever home with God. As is often the case, you're left to consider where you are and what you're experiencing and how God is working to establish you and the things you do for Him.

Prayer Starter

Father, where You move, take me with You. Make Your steps clear enough for me to see so following You will become something I trust. You're here to help me when I. . .

DAY 189

PSALMS 100–105

Prayer Scripture

Bless the LORD, O my soul. O LORD my God, You are very great; You are clothed with honor and majesty, who covers Yourself with light as with a garment, who stretches out the heavens like a curtain, who lays the beams of His chambers in the waters, who makes the clouds His chariot, who walks on the wings of the wind.

PSALM 104:1–3

Prayer Thought for the Day

King David, to whom this psalm is often attributed, used the majesty of nature to make the very solid conclusion that God's greatness was responsible. If light could be worn as a favorite coat, then that coat was created and worn by God. This same God stretched out the heavens. He could build a home in the ocean depths, if He wanted. God could ride clouds and walk on wind. It's easy to conclude that God is bigger than a storm, the ocean, the universe. And somehow this big God doing big things loves to spend time with *you*. This is one of the life-expanding reasons to pray the kind of prayer found in Psalm 104.

Prayer Starter

Lord God, You amaze me. Your creation inspires me. Your help encourages me. Thank You for all You do for me, share with me, and promise me. Keep me focused on You so I can. . .

DAY 190
PSALMS 106–109

Prayer Scripture

Deal with me, O God the Lord, for Your name's sake; because Your mercy is good, deliver me. For I am poor and needy, and my heart is wounded within me. I am gone like the shadow when it declines. I am tossed up and down like the locust. My knees are weak through fasting, and my flesh lacks fatness. I also became a reproach to them; when they looked on me, they shook their heads. Help me, O Lord my God. O save me according to Your mercy, that they may know that this is Your hand, that You, Lord, have done it.

Psalm 109:21–27

Prayer Thought for the Day

David admits it—he's a mess. The struggle bus arrived, and he carried an all-access pass. In the aftermath of all that life delivered, David simply asked God to deal with him. God's mercy was preferred to the mess. God's riches were preferred to David's loss. God's help was preferred to his need. David required rescue, and he was ready to schedule a praise parade. God's hand could move him beyond the mess—and it was just what David needed. When life's mess is overwhelming, take this prayer and ask God to deal with you.

Prayer Starter

Father, there are times when it seems everything I try to do ends in failure. Sometimes my worst choices are my first choices. Take the struggle I'm in and. . .

DAY 191
PSALMS 110–118

Prayer Scripture

Not to us, O Lord, not to us, but to Your name
give glory, for Your mercy, and for Your truth's sake.
Why should the nations say, "Where now is their God?"
Psalm 115:1–2

Prayer Thought for the Day

No one knows who wrote this psalm, but many scholars feel it was written sometime after the exile. Our anonymous but perceptive psalmist recognized that no glory was due God's people. Their good deeds were not the focus of greatness, and they could take no credit for all He had done. Their works were designed only to glorify God, and they made it clear that the silver and gold idols that surrounding peoples worshipped were the valueless creation of humans (verses 4–8).

Further on, the unknown psalmist called on Israel's people to trust in God, not the non-gods of the nations around them. They could believe that God would be faithful to them as they consistently gave glory to Him. And when the unbelieving nations saw God's glory, they could begin to see His power.

If you give glory to God, others may begin to see Him more clearly. Make sure you aren't taking glory to yourself that rightly belongs to Him.

Prayer Starter

Lord God, I want to give You the glory so that everyone can see what it means to know and serve You. Forgive me if I have stolen Your glory, and help me. . .

DAY 192
PSALM 119

Prayer Scripture

You are my portion, O Lord. I have said that I would keep Your words. I entreated Your favor with my whole heart; be merciful to me according to Your word. I thought about my ways and turned my feet to Your testimonies. I hastened and did not delay to keep Your commandments. The bands of the wicked have robbed me, but I have not forgotten Your law. At midnight I will rise to give thanks to You because of Your righteous judgments. I am a companion of all those who fear You and of those who keep Your precepts.
Psalm 119:57–63

Prayer Thought for the Day

This is a very visual prayer. The psalmist is walking back to the place where viewing God's goodness was most impressive. God's Word informed actions, revealed sin, and improved the psalmist's response time. When it came to prayer, the psalmist was all in. His obedience was immediate. His trust in God wasn't swayed by the injustice of people around him.

You can have trust in God that doesn't listen to opinion polls or current trends. God hasn't changed. He still loves you and wants a friendship with you that never ends.

Prayer Starter

Father, help me to trust You enough to refuse any doubt when others suggest You aren't trustworthy. Help me to turn to You and follow Your commands so I can. . .

DAY 193

PSALMS 120–134

Prayer Scripture

LORD, my heart is not haughty, nor my eyes lofty, nor do I exercise myself in great matters or in things too high for me. Surely I have behaved and quieted myself, like a child who is weaned by his mother; my soul is even like a weaned child.

PSALM 131:1–2

Prayer Thought for the Day

The psalmist admits that he has grown up. He might not be an adult in the faith yet, but he knows more than to assume he has all the answers. No haughty heart in this man. There is no biographical press release designed to impress all who would read or listen. He doesn't interrupt with strong opinions, and he recognizes wisdom in remaining silent. This is a prayer that essentially tells God to speak, because the psalmist sees value in listening. He isn't interested in outguessing God or trying to use predictive texts to finish God's thoughts. This is the prayer of the humble, wise, and contemplative. This passage is in the book of Psalms because someone like you needed to read it.

Prayer Starter

Lord God, let me speak, then let me listen. Let me share and then receive. Let me be grown up enough to know I can learn a lot from You about. . .

DAY 194
PSALMS 135–142

Prayer Scripture

Where shall I go from Your Spirit? Or where shall I flee from Your presence? If I ascend up into heaven, You are there. If I make my bed in hell, behold, You are there. If I take the wings of the morning and dwell in the uttermost parts of the sea, even there Your hand shall lead me and Your right hand shall hold me. If I say, "Surely the darkness shall cover me, even the night shall be light around me," yes, the darkness does not hide from You, but the night shines as the day. The darkness and the light are both alike to You. For You have possessed my inward parts. You have covered me in my mother's womb. I will praise You, for I am fearfully and wonderfully made.

Psalm 139:7–14

Prayer Thought for the Day

You can't go where God doesn't exist. You aren't so emotionally damaged that God can't rescue and heal you. You can't hide from Him or run too far away for Him to lose you. Your dark thoughts don't hold a candle to the light that He brings with Him. God knew you before you were born and made you wonderfully well. This prayer recognizes God's closeness and love—for you.

Prayer Starter

Father, I thank You for bringing light to see, love to feel, and Your presence to experience, so I never have to be alone. Walk with me when I. . .

DAY 195
PSALMS 143–150

Prayer Scripture

All Your works shall praise You, O Lord, and Your saints shall bless You. They shall speak of the glory of Your kingdom and tell of Your power, to make known to the sons of men His mighty acts and the glorious majesty of His kingdom. Your kingdom is an everlasting kingdom, and Your dominion endures throughout all generations.

Psalm 145:10–13

Prayer Thought for the Day

There's something very affirming about reading the prayers, praises, and proclamations found in the book of Psalms. You leave this part of the journey with a psalm from David, who's praying a prayer of collective worship to God. He's speaking for a congregation of people who've chosen praise over complaint, blessing over accusation, and God's everlasting dominion over the disinterest of the uncommitted. Taken together, these individuals were blessing God and sharing the real-life stories of His glory, power, and majesty. This was a committed celebration, and all were invited to the experience. Find those who honor God, and join together to make it a regular celebration.

Prayer Starter

Lord God, I don't want to overlook any of the praise that You deserve or take credit for what only You could do. Make my heart the transfer station for all the glory that You deserve because. . .

DAY 196
PROVERBS 1–5

Prayer Scripture

I have taught you in the way of wisdom; I have led you in right paths. When you go, your steps shall not be hindered, and when you run, you shall not stumble. Take firm hold of instruction; do not let her go. Keep her, for she is your life. Do not enter into the path of the wicked, and do not go in the way of evil men. Avoid it; do not pass by it; turn from it and pass away.
PROVERBS 4:11–15

Prayer Thought for the Day

God teaches, and He leads. If you learn and then follow, something amazing happens. You move from what hasn't worked to the only thing that will. There are instructions, but you must read them. There are commands, and you need to choose to follow them. There are several paths, but only one follows God. Spending time exploring alternate paths wastes your time and decreases your interest in the only things that will move you from failure to success—not as you understand success, but how God designed success. Embrace it, spend time with it, and never leave it. Failure is easier for a reason: Things of real value take effort.

Prayer Starter

Father, when You lead, I'll pray. I need to trust Your definition of success and agree it's worth the pursuit. Give me passion tempered with patience in my pursuit of. . .

DAY 197

PROVERBS 6–9

Prayer Scripture

Give instruction to a wise man, and he will be wiser yet; teach a just man, and he will increase in learning. The fear of the LORD is the beginning of wisdom, and the knowledge of the holy is understanding. For by me your days shall be multiplied and the years of your life shall be increased.

PROVERBS 9:9–11

Prayer Thought for the Day

Prayer always begins with wisdom. Why? Prayer won't take place when people feel they know more than most and can handle more than others. The self-sufficient often struggle to pray because to do so admits there's a need. Self-sufficiency prides itself on not needing help—even God's. If you really want to learn to pray, then respect God; admit He's all-sufficient, while you're not; and admit you want the gift of understanding. Wisdom needs to embrace prayer. Wisdom isn't the conclusion that you no longer need anyone; it's knowing that without God wisdom is little more than practical experience. For someone who believes there's a God, this will never be enough.

Prayer Starter

Lord God, I need the wisdom required to pray, knowing beyond a doubt that I need Your help. Let me set self-sufficiency aside so I can recognize Your sufficiency. Some of the things I struggle to handle today include. . .

DAY 198
PROVERBS 10–14

Prayer Scripture

Whoever loves instruction loves knowledge, but he who hates correction is senseless. A good man obtains favor from the LORD, but He will condemn a man of wicked schemes. A man shall not be established by wickedness, but the root of the righteous shall not be moved.
PROVERBS 12:1–3

Prayer Thought for the Day

Someone who prays is on a path to a place called "Settled." They are in pursuit of calm assurance, bold conviction, and enduring trust in God. It makes sense that others, who hate correction, involve themselves in wicked schemes—and aren't typically involved in the act of prayer. This would mean a need to admit that God's more important than they are and that His life instructions mean more than their own ideas. He's worth following.

Prayer suggests that you believe these things are true about God. And it's why many people refuse to pray. You have a choice today: Become settled, assured, and then trust the God who encourages you to pray. Or you can choose all those other things that have never worked before.

Prayer Starter

Father, I don't want to be someone who believes I have no need for You. I don't want to entertain the idea that I'm more important than You. Calm my spirit and bring me close as I pray for. . .

DAY 199
PROVERBS 15–19

Prayer Scripture

The sacrifice of the wicked is an abomination to the
LORD, but the prayer of the upright is His delight.
The way of the wicked is an abomination to the LORD,
but He loves him who follows after righteousness.
PROVERBS 15:8–9

Prayer Thought for the Day

There have always been individuals who seem to feel better about life if they can pay respect to a religion but never let faith change their hearts. God says this is a disgrace. This perspective isn't meaningless, but it doesn't mean anything good. Those who truly follow God pray to Him—and *that* makes Him happy. "The sacrifice of the wicked," a contradiction in terms that demonstrates obvious hypocrisy, is abominable to God.

It seems the cooperation of those involved in right living (the followers of God's truth) is what He's always sought among humanity. You don't need to wear a mask with God. He sees who you are all the time, so pretending is the act of lying to God. Follow or admit you aren't following. These are the only conclusions God accepts.

Prayer Starter

Lord God, install in me a heart that sincerely wants to follow You and honor You in ways that are real and life changing. May I make a choice that. . .

DAY 200
PROVERBS 20–23

Prayer Scripture

The king's heart is in the hand of the LORD, like the rivers of water; He turns it wherever He wishes. Every way of a man is right in his own eyes, but the LORD ponders the hearts.
PROVERBS 21:1–2

Prayer Thought for the Day

There's a good reason for complete honesty with God. That reason has everything to do with God's ability to examine your thoughts, intentions, and feelings. He knows you even better than you know yourself. Being dishonest with God is a nearly laughable notion. Maybe you can attempt to be dishonest with yourself, but not with God. This is the same God who directs mankind to move in the direction He wishes. That doesn't mean you have no choice, but God can influence your willingness. He does the same thing with world leaders.

Pray with absolute honesty. This will save you time, effort, and frustration. Pray, seeking clarity. This will help you with yesterday's efforts, today's decisions, and tomorrow's plans. Pray seeking connection. This will help you recognize God as rescuer, counselor, and friend.

Prayer Starter

Father, accept, guide, and forgive me. I'll need Your help to know what to do, where to go, and how to respond to all I experience in life. When I pray to You, help me to be honest enough to. . .

DAY 201
PROVERBS 24–28

Prayer Scripture

Do not boast about tomorrow, for you do not know what a day may bring forth. Let another man praise you, and not your own mouth—a stranger, and not your own lips.
Proverbs 27:1–2

Prayer Thought for the Day

God made promises about what He would do in the future. He can do that—He's God. When *you* make too many promises about the future, it sounds as if you're bragging, and there are just so many things that can change that you don't know anything about. It makes no sense to discuss all aspects of your future as if you had perfect certainty about what's going to happen. The choice to brag isn't just arrogant; it's a very quick way to set yourself up for ridicule when you fail. You don't need to come to God with a list of your successes, as if you wish to prove that God's lucky to have you on His side. Let Him and other people come to recognize what you can do without ever pleading your own case. God has a plan for your life—that's what people should notice.

Prayer Starter

Lord God, help me to be comfortable enough with Your plans that I don't feel the need to brag about what I can do. Help me to pay enough attention to You that I go where You. . .

DAY 202
PROVERBS 29–31

Prayer Scripture

Remove far from me deception and lies; give me neither poverty nor riches; feed me with food suitable for me, lest I be full and deny You and say, "Who is the LORD?" or lest I be poor and steal and take the name of my God in vain.
PROVERBS 30:8–9

Prayer Thought for the Day

You've just witnessed a solid and wise prayer. This prayer in the form of a proverb suggests two powerful requests that have great value to the one praying. It asks for honesty in personal conduct and contentment in what's owned. Agur, who wrote these words, wanted to have enough of what he needed to live on, because the alternative was a temptation to take. A poor man can become desperate, a rich man can become greedy, and Agur just didn't want money to be a stumbling block between himself and God. This man simply wanted enough to keep his mind free to consider the wisdom, value, and love of a very good God.

Prayer Starter

Father, whether it's money, a career, or personal interests, help me to resist allowing any of these things to stand in the way of my friendship with You. Help me to remove barriers like. . .

DAY 203
ECCLESIASTES 1–6

Prayer Scripture

I returned and considered all the oppressions that are done under the sun. And I saw the tears of those who were oppressed, and they had no comforter. And there was power on the side of their oppressors, but they had no comforter.
Ecclesiastes 4:1

Prayer Thought for the Day

Pray for the mistreated. Look for an opportunity to help them.

King Solomon wrote this biblical book that includes a lot of thoughts on wisdom. Solomon witnessed mistreatment and observed the emotional struggle of the mistreated. He even observed that those who were mistreating them seemed to be getting away with it. The mistreated had no one to comfort or help them.

You may have witnessed something similar and likely felt anger, frustration, or maybe even helplessness. That's why prayer is a great first option. Let God know that this means something to you. Give Him the burden and then help if you can. You may not be asked to help. However, you're always asked to bring God to your struggle.

Prayer Starter

Lord God, it can be so frustrating to see people mistreated. Sometimes I don't think there's much I can do. But I can pray and allow You to bring comfort and justice to situations like. . .

DAY 204
ECCLESIASTES 7–12

Prayer Scripture

There is not a just man on earth who does good and does not sin. Also do not take heed to all words that are spoken, lest you hear your servant curse you. For often also your own heart knows that you yourself likewise have cursed others.
ECCLESIASTES 7:20–22

Prayer Thought for the Day

Eavesdropping is common. Getting all kinds of judgy is also common. You overhear someone saying something that is unfair or unkind—and it's about you—then anger, frustration, and a dose of seething bubble to the surface. You wonder what gives them the right to say such things. Would they say what they said to you personally? Probably not. Before you make a passive-aggressive social media post to or about that person, draft a letter to the editor, or defriend them in real life, you should pray. When praying, remember times when you've done the same thing. It may be the perfect opportunity to overlook an offense and forgive a flaw. You've needed that same flaw to be forgiven by God.

Prayer Starter

Father, thank You for giving me the opportunity to forgive instead of hanging on to hurt and bitterness. I'm grateful You chose mercy. Help me to make the same choice when. . .

DAY 205
SONG OF SOLOMON 1–8

Prayer Scripture

Set me as a seal on your heart, as a seal on your arm. For love is strong as death; jealousy is cruel as the grave. Its coals are coals of fire that have a most powerful flame. Many waters cannot quench love, nor can the floods drown it. If a man would give all the wealth of his house for love, it would be utterly condemned.

Song of Solomon 8:6–7

Prayer Thought for the Day

Is there room for prayer when it comes to marriage? Prayers for and with your family are key ways to share faith. This relationship can be a demonstration of the selfless acts that love offers. This passage in Song of Solomon 8 is from the perspective of the groom, who declares that love has a powerful flame that's difficult to quench. Marriage comes with physical, emotional, and spiritual components. When a relationship is built solely on the physical or emotional, it will struggle—because what should be sacrificial love is redefined as attraction. Pray for your marriage before you say, "I do," and pray afterward because you'll be working together to be companions. That requires teamwork.

Prayer Starter

Lord God, let me remember to pray for marriages. Whether it's mine or others, let me be compassionate enough to pray that teams are created from two very individual people. May they learn from You and. . .

DAY 206
ISAIAH 1–4

Prayer Scripture

O house of Jacob, come, and let us walk in the light of the Lord.
Isaiah 2:5

Prayer Thought for the Day

You're entering a section of scripture dedicated to warning God's people of promised judgment. Messenger-prophets like Isaiah were given the less-than-desired task of letting people know that exile was coming, and telling them how to deal with exile once it arrived. Even amid this promise of impending displacement, Isaiah had an interesting invitation: "Come, house of Jacob, and let us walk in the light of the Lord." This was addressed to lawbreakers—rebellious and defiant people. Those hearing this were on their way to a corrective time-out, yet the prophet was suggesting that at that moment they should resist waiting to return to God and immediately rediscover the clarity of God's light in the steps they took. This was both a declaration and likely a theme of prayer for Isaiah.

It can be your prayer too. Modify it if you like: "Let *me* walk in the light of the Lord." You can get started today.

Prayer Starter

Father, I don't want to wait to follow You. I don't want to keep walking away before I return. I don't want to be corrected before I follow. Give me the courage to follow and the strength to. . .

DAY 207

ISAIAH 5–7

Prayer Scripture

I heard the voice of the Lord, saying, "Whom shall I send, and who will go for Us?" Then I said, "Here I am. Send me." And He said, "Go, and tell this people, 'Hear, indeed, but do not understand, and see, indeed, but do not perceive.' Make the heart of this people fat, and make their ears heavy, and shut their eyes, lest they see with their eyes, and hear with their ears, and understand with their hearts, and convert and be healed."

Isaiah 6:8–10

Prayer Thought for the Day

Pharaoh was unwilling to listen and understand the need for God's people to be released from slavery. His heart was hardened while he made horrible decisions. God's conversation with Isaiah seems similar to this. Isaiah would give the Israelites warnings, but the people dismissed them with very little consideration. Knowing this would be a failed effort, Isaiah answered God's question about who would go by praying, "Here I am. Send me." The prophet immersed himself in the message. If followed, it would be the gift of hope. But Isaiah knew the warnings would be ignored.

Some people may refuse God's warnings, and some will redirect their journey movements. Maybe it's time to redirect your life too.

Prayer Starter

Lord God, why is it so easy to ignore Your warnings? Why is it so hard to redirect my steps? Help me to pay attention to You so I can deal with. . .

DAY 208
ISAIAH 8–10

Prayer Scripture

For a Child is born to us, a Son is given to us, and the government shall be on His shoulder. And His name shall be called Wonderful, Counselor, the Mighty God, the Everlasting Father, the Prince of Peace.
Isaiah 9:6

Prayer Thought for the Day

As warnings were given—and while the people actively rejected them—there was a piece of good news they wouldn't understand. In the middle of a forced exile for the Israelites' lawbreaking, a passage in Isaiah 9 talks about Jesus. For all these men, women, and children cast out of the land God promised, there was a better future. . .and it was for *all* of mankind. One of the primary prayer points for humanity is the request for forgiveness, because people have suffered with poor decision-making since the beginning. This preview of coming attractions let the people know that Jesus would come and bring a new agreement. This coming event would finally make it possible for mankind to be right with God—so *you* could be right with God.

Prayer Starter

Father, because I need forgiveness, I find value in knowing that in one of the hardest moments in a nation's history, You told those living through struggles that something future changing was coming. May I be quick to thank You for. . .

DAY 209
ISAIAH 11–14

Prayer Scripture

In that day you shall say: "O Lord, I will praise You. Though You were angry with me, Your anger is turned away and You comfort me. Behold, God is my salvation. I will trust and not be afraid, 'for the Lord Jehovah is my strength and my song. He also has become my salvation.'"
Isaiah 12:1–2

Prayer Thought for the Day

This is a prayer in the middle of correction. It touches on a time when the lesson God was teaching was acknowledged, internalized, and resulted in a new perspective. This perspective taught gratitude even before God's promised blessing came true. There will come a time of salvation and singing. There will be moments of comfort and trust. There was a future even when the present seemed far from ideal.

A prayer like this is important to note because you need to remember that even correction has a graduation day. Correction can be one of the greatest tools to encourage a close relationship. Punishment wants only to exact a penalty for an infraction. Correction seeks to restore relationships. That's what God was doing in Isaiah. It's what He may be doing in your life today.

Prayer Starter

Lord God, I'm grateful that You think enough of me to help me discover a closeness with You that I've always needed. Help me to return—and when I do, may I. . .

DAY 210
ISAIAH 15–19

Prayer Scripture

Gladness is taken away, and joy from the plentiful field,
and in the vineyards there shall be no singing, nor shall there
be shouting. The treaders shall not tread out wine in their
presses. I have made their grape harvest shouting to cease.
Isaiah 16:10

Prayer Thought for the Day

The concept of being grateful amid trouble will fight with a decrease in happiness. Joy may seem stripped like a field in the face of a hailstorm. Harvesttime will be a reminder of profound loss. For the Jews, normal work satisfaction was replaced with sorrow.

It can seem as if the worst situation known to man has become an uninvited and very bossy roommate who enjoys creating chaos. If you're in the middle of such a situation, pray for a better internal housemate, and ask God to help you through every hard moment that must take place between today and your reunion with the act of smiling. Invite others to join you in prayer—and then? Believe that God walks with you in this journey beyond this place of dark shadows and a megaphone of sorrow.

Prayer Starter

Father, there are days I believe I can't handle another difficulty, but You never asked me to. You can walk with me even when I'm struggling because of my own decisions. Help me to believe in that better day when. . .

DAY 211

ISAIAH 20–23

Prayer Scripture

For it is a day of trouble and of trampling and of perplexity by
the Lord God of hosts in the Valley of Vision—breaking down
the walls and of crying to the mountains. . . . And behold,
joy and gladness, slaying oxen and killing sheep, eating meat and
drinking wine: "Let us eat and drink, for tomorrow we shall die."
Isaiah 22:5, 13

Prayer Thought for the Day

This was a time when giving up was a trend and weeping made scheduled visits; giving in to fatalistic thinking seemed sensible. The people sought a diversion that would cheer some withered part of their lives, believing death would ultimately find them. This wasn't a stable place or a highlight-reel moment in the history of Israel. Without hope, this was a depressing place.

Sometimes it's in this place where you take the time to deeply consider who you are, what you've done, and what you should do. No one likes this place. Most will avoid this place. But God can be found—even in this place.

Prayer Starter

Lord God, when I'm at my lowest point and there's nothing that encourages me in the circumstances I face, make Yourself known to me. When You do, help me to notice You and accept Your encouragement so I can. . .

DAY 212
ISAIAH 24–27

Prayer Scripture

O LORD, You are my God. I will exalt You. I will praise Your name, for You have done wonderful things. Your plans of old are faithfulness and truth. For You have made a city into a heap, a ruin of a fortified city. A palace of foreigners is no longer a city. It shall never be rebuilt. Therefore the strong people shall glorify You. The city of the terrifying nations shall fear You. For You have been a strength to the poor, a strength to the needy in his distress, a refuge from the storm, a shadow from the heat, when the blast of the terrifying ones is like a storm against the wall.

ISAIAH 25:1–4

Prayer Thought for the Day

Isaiah 25 might seem a confusing prayer. God is praised. His works are considered wonderful. Then comes the front-page news. The city was in ruins, and there were no immediate plans to rebuild. Where was the praise coming from in this struggle? God's strength was found by the poor and needy. He was a refuge in these everyday storms and a shelter from the heat of affliction. This is another great reminder to use your prayers to praise a God who's bigger than anything you're going through.

Prayer Starter

Father, give me the reassurance I need to remember that my struggle isn't beyond Your ability. Help me to praise You when. . .

DAY 213
ISAIAH 28–31

Prayer Scripture

Therefore this is what the Lord God says: "Behold, I lay in Zion a stone for a foundation, a tested stone, a precious cornerstone, a sure foundation. He who believes in it shall not make haste. I will also lay judgment to the line and righteousness to the plumb. And the hail shall sweep away the refuge of lies, and the waters shall overflow the hiding place."

Isaiah 28:16–17

Prayer Thought for the Day

This is another message from God about the arrival of His Son, Jesus. No one who first heard these words would see the fulfillment of this prophecy. This passage indicates that even those who believed would need to wait. That was the good news, with more to come, but it didn't sound that way. God promised judgment, a righteous plumb line, and a massive proverbial storm to sweep the human heart of pesky lies. This was a divine reset that people could survive. It was a time of purging, cleansing, and purifying. People would need to get close to God and trust this process. No one looks forward to correction, though it may be necessary.

Prayer Starter

Lord God, help me to allow You to diagnose what's wrong in me and then make the changes I need to move me toward You. Help me to trust You enough to. . .

DAY 214

ISAIAH 32–35

Prayer Scripture

O Lord, be gracious to us. We have waited for You.
Be their arm every morning, our salvation also in the
time of trouble. At the noise of a tumult the people fled.
At the lifting up of Yourself the nations were scattered.
Isaiah 33:2–3

Prayer Thought for the Day

One man, praying, saw firsthand that no one can stand before God when justice is His decision. No one is innocent. In this time of trouble, it was a sensible prayer to ask God to be gracious to those who wait expectantly for Him. They were in trouble, and they needed strength and rescue. This is a fresh visit to the plains of fear, because instead of focusing on being afraid, this prayer gives evidence of a decision to honor God, acknowledge trouble, and invite His help. You don't need to be afraid of God. He invites you to come close and ask Him for help. He longs to be close to you. In moments when you're being corrected, lean into the end result of God's internal renovation. There are better days just beyond the course correction.

Prayer Starter

Father, give me the grace to endure the alterations taking place inside so I can deal with the struggles occurring outside. Live within me and help me to. . .

DAY 215

ISAIAH 36–39

Prayer Scripture

King Hezekiah. . .tore his clothes and covered himself with sackcloth and went into the house of the LORD. And he sent Eliakim, who was over the household, and Shebna the scribe, and the elders of the priests, covered with sackcloth, to Isaiah the prophet, the son of Amoz. And they said to him, "This is what Hezekiah says: 'This day is a day of trouble, and of rebuke, and of blasphemy, for the children have come to the birth, and there is no strength to bring them forth. It may be that the LORD your God will hear the words of Rabshakeh, whom his master, the king of Assyria, has sent to dishonor the living God, and will rebuke the words that the LORD your God has heard. Therefore lift up your prayer for the remnant that is left.'"

ISAIAH 37:1–4

Prayer Thought for the Day

King Hezekiah encountered a man called Rabshakeh, a servant of the king of Assyria, who declared that his army would be coming—and no one could stand against it. Fear was familiar and overwhelming to God's people. Their king wanted to know what he should do. He sent trusted men to visit the prophet Isaiah and ask him to plead with God on behalf of His very nervous people. The king believed in both the power of prayer and the God Isaiah prayed to.

Prayer Starter

Lord God, when I pray, I need to believe that You exist and will hear my concerns. Help me to believe that. . .

DAY 216
ISAIAH 40–42

Prayer Scripture

"'Do not fear, for I am with you. Do not be dismayed, for I am your God. I will strengthen you. Yes, I will help you. Yes, I will uphold you with the right hand of My righteousness.' Behold, all those who were incensed against you shall be ashamed and confounded. They shall be as nothing, and those who contend with you shall perish. You shall seek them and shall not find them—even those who contended with you. Those who war against you shall be as nothing and as a thing of emptiness. For I, the LORD your God, will hold your right hand, saying to you, 'Do not fear. I will help you.'"

ISAIAH 41:10–13

Prayer Thought for the Day

The prayers were desperate and came from discouraged humanity. When God answered, it was the encouragement people needed. No fear or dread was required. God would be their strength, He would hold them up, and He would put their enemy in its place. Like a father with a young child, God said He would take their hands and walk them out of their struggle. He's never stopped this level of care.

Prayer Starter

Father, there are many days when I need reassurance. Remind me that I don't need to walk alone and without comfort. I need to know that You fight my battles—and victory is always the outcome. Help me to trust You with. . .

DAY 217
ISAIAH 43–45

Prayer Scripture

"I am the Lord, and there is no one else. There is no God besides Me. I girded you, though you have not known Me, that they may know from the rising of the sun, and from the west, that there is no one besides Me. I am the Lord, and there is no one else. I form the light and create darkness. I make peace and create disaster. I, the Lord, do all these things."
Isaiah 45:5–7

Prayer Thought for the Day

God wanted the people to get the bigger picture of who He was. He can be found in life's messiest moments as well as the days recalled for being the best of times. When the sun rises and sets, God exists and sustains life. When it's light or dark, God stands ready to deal with struggle. You may remember Job and how God was within the struggle that Job didn't understand. No matter how he felt, the truth was that God didn't abandon Job. Men throughout the Bible wrestled with a variety of issues, and God was found to be the architect of good even when most thought things would end very differently.

Prayer Starter

Lord God, there's no one like You. You have no challenger that even comes close. Help me to remember that even when things seem chaotic, You're in control. You can. . .

DAY 218
ISAIAH 46–48

Prayer Scripture

[God said,] "I have declared the former things from the beginning, and they went forth out of My mouth, and I proclaimed them. Suddenly I did them, and they came to pass. Because I know that you are obstinate, and your neck is an iron sinew, and your brow brass, even from the beginning I have declared it to you. Before it came to pass I proclaimed it to you."
Isaiah 48:3–5

Prayer Thought for the Day

For some who prayed seeking relief from oppression, God had an answer. That answer was essentially, "I am simply keeping My promise. I told you what I would do. I was ignored." There are some powerful visuals in Isaiah 48—a neck of iron and a brow of brass. Hard, unyielding, and unwilling to admit wrong. You can make personal decisions, but God can give you reasons to make the best decisions. Sometimes that will be consequences for poor choices. There's a practical reason why God's plans are always best: Because He's all knowing, God knows how everything turns out. His plan is perfect because His plan is always based on what He knows to be the best outcome. It's never been to make life hard on you.

Prayer Starter

Father, I don't want to be hard-hearted. I don't want to miss Your plan. I do want to make the wise choice by seeking Your plan, which will always be. . .

DAY 219
ISAIAH 49–51

Prayer Scripture

Sing, O heavens. And be joyful, O earth. And break forth into singing, O mountains. For the LORD has comforted His people and will have mercy on His afflicted.
ISAIAH 49:13

Prayer Thought for the Day

Does it sound peculiar to say that all creation celebrates God's goodness? What God makes is something He holds together, was created for a purpose, and exists to be enjoyed. In Isaiah 49 we—at the very least—have a word picture of a colossal celebration involving this world and everything around it. The mountains add their own bit of harmony, and a praise fest is happening even when it's not recognized by humanity. Why is this a good image to consider? Because you get to use words to express praise and worship in the form of prayer. You can use the eyes of creation to recognize the good that God does and then celebrate what you've witnessed. When you see someone finding comfort in tragedy, praise God. When someone enduring affliction experiences mercy, it's time to cheer God and His goodness. Don't wait—stop delaying—let the words you speak share praise to a God even creation recognizes.

Prayer Starter

Lord God, if I would just take the time to notice, I would see Your goodness not only in my life but in the lives of people around me. If I think about what I've seen just this week, I would praise You for. . .

DAY 220
ISAIAH 52–56

Prayer Scripture

We all like sheep have gone astray. We have turned, each one, to his own way, and the LORD has laid on Him the iniquity of us all. He was oppressed and He was afflicted, yet He did not open His mouth. He was brought as a lamb to the slaughter, and as a sheep before its shearers is mute, so He did not open His mouth.

ISAIAH 53:6–7

Prayer Thought for the Day

You likely remember that Isaiah was a prophet. He gave warnings, and he spoke of things that would happen someday. The Isaiah 53 passage was one of those future moments. It probably didn't make much sense to those who heard these words. The future moment was the sacrifice of Jesus. The waywardness of mankind would continue, and God's justice would still need to be satisfied. Men, women, and children would turn their backs on God, and Jesus would be punished for the lawbreaking of all mankind. Jesus would be oppressed, afflicted, and killed without retaliating.

Because of His sacrifice, you have the ability to pray so boldly to a God who planned His great rescue long before Jesus was born in Bethlehem.

Prayer Starter

Father, I'm so glad that I can understand what a gift it was when You told Isaiah that Your Son was coming. Thanks for the gift that allows me to pray. Thank You for. . .

DAY 221

ISAIAH 57–59

Prayer Scripture

Behold, the LORD's hand is not shortened, that it cannot save, nor is His ear heavy, that it cannot hear, but your iniquities have separated you from your God, and your sins have hidden His face from you, that He will not hear. . . . No one calls for justice; no one pleads for truth. They trust in vanity and speak lies. They conceive evil and bring forth iniquity.

ISAIAH 59:1–2, 4

Prayer Thought for the Day

If God is described as a God who never leaves, forsakes, abandons, or denies knowing you, then how is it possible for Isaiah 59 to say that there's a separation and a hiding of His face? The explanation is probably best understood by asking another question: Who left, forsook, abandoned, or denied? If it wasn't God, there's only one possible explanation. Your sin is the choice that separates you from God. You're playing a dangerous game of soul keep-away. How can He hear words you aren't praying? How can He tell you the truth when you won't listen? He can only do these things when you do your part.

Prayer Starter

Lord God, I don't want to ignore You, but I have. I want to make the right choices, but I've resisted listening to Your truth. Help me to pay attention to everything You say so I can. . .

DAY 222
ISAIAH 60–63

Prayer Scripture

I will greatly rejoice in the LORD. My soul shall be joyful in my God, for He has clothed me with the garments of salvation; He has covered me with the robe of righteousness, as a bridegroom decks himself with ornaments and as a bride adorns herself with her jewels. For as the earth brings forth its bud and as the garden causes the things that are sown in it to spring up, so the Lord GOD will cause righteousness and praise to spring up before all the nations.

ISAIAH 61:10–11

Prayer Thought for the Day

Did you know that people can begin to recognize God when they see Him in how you respond? If you respond with bitterness, anger, and resentment, then finding God in your response seems unlikely. But when you rejoice, find joy, and share God's goodness with people looking for this wonderful resource, it can become a chance to wear God's righteousness robe, His salvation ensemble, and the jewels that adorn those who belong to God. Let others see this special wardrobe so that it becomes possible for them to pray to the same God you model through rejoicing and praise.

Prayer Starter

Father, how I respond to life events either attracts people to You or makes You seem harsh and bitter. Help me to represent You well when I. . .

DAY 223
ISAIAH 64–66

Prayer Scripture

O Lord, You are our Father. We are the clay, and You our potter. And we all are the work of Your hand.
Isaiah 64:8

Prayer Thought for the Day

If you've ever watched a potter shape clay on a wheel, you know that that clay can go from a lump to a beautiful vessel in a very short time. But if that potter is unhappy with what he sees, if he detects bubbles in the rim or if he's not happy with the shape, he'll make something new with it by collapsing the existing clay vessel and starting over. This is a picture of the God who doesn't make mistakes but also doesn't leave you with self-inflicted flaws that need to be removed. You're the work of God's hand. You also make choices that create those imperfections that the Potter needs to deal with. God will continue to reshape you so you can find reason to praise Him. He's making sure you don't stay the way you once were.

Prayer Starter

Lord God, may I be willing to let You remove the imperfections from my life. May I give You permission to reshape me. May I want to be something different than what I once was. Help me to understand what You do and why You do it, as clay in Your hands, so I can. . .

DAY 224
JEREMIAH 1–3

Prayer Scripture

[Jeremiah] said, "Ah, Lord GOD! Behold, I cannot speak, for I am a child." But the LORD said to me, "Do not say, 'I am a child,' for you shall go to all to whom I shall send you, and whatever I command you, you shall speak.". . . Then the LORD put out His hand and touched my mouth. And the LORD said to me, "Behold, I have put My words in your mouth."

JEREMIAH 1:6–7, 9

Prayer Thought for the Day

Jeremiah joined a long line of men who were not sold on the idea of doing what God asked ("I cannot speak"). Every one of them had reasons why they were unfit for assignment. God, in His incredible wisdom replied, "You shall speak." Then God gave Jeremiah the words he needed to share. He became a man who seemed incapable of saying much beyond what God wanted him to say. Those words weren't always comforting or what you might think of as encouraging, but Jeremiah became a reliable messenger. Whether you're young or old, shy or outgoing, a longtime student of God's Word or new to the faith, He is seeking your willingness. You don't need to rely on excuses. If God asks, it's because He knows you can do the job with His help.

Prayer Starter

Father, I don't need reasons not to follow You, but I'll need the courage to take each step with You. Make me willing when You. . .

DAY 225
JEREMIAH 4–6

Prayer Scripture

O Lord, are Your eyes not on the truth? You have struck them, but they have not grieved. You have consumed them, but they have refused to receive correction. They have made their faces harder than a rock; they have refused to return.

Jeremiah 5:3

Prayer Thought for the Day

Think about this prayer. Does it sound as if Jeremiah was asking, "Hey, God, do You really know what You're doing?" The truth according to this prophet was that the people were being corrected but it changed nothing. God's people agreed together to do the great walkaway. They hardened their hearts, their faces, and their resolve. There was no interest in turning back, and the prophet was concerned that God wasn't paying attention. Of course, he didn't need to be concerned. God knew. He had a plan. If people listened, then this prophet's job would be over. Maybe Jeremiah wanted that. Never be concerned that God is unaware. Pray, believing that, at the right time, the answer will come.

Prayer Starter

Lord God, I can pray because You answer prayers. You don't always agree to my requests, and sometimes You make me wait. Help me to be patient when Your answer isn't immediate. Help me to trust You when. . .

DAY 226
JEREMIAH 7–9

Prayer Scripture

"And they bend their tongues like their bows for lies. But they are not valiant for the truth on the earth. For they proceed from evil to evil, and they do not know Me," says the Lord.
Jeremiah 9:3

Prayer Thought for the Day

Today's verse presents a scenario that almost seems dystopian. People have done what they wanted to do and they haven't wanted to change. They finished one evil act and were on the lookout for something even more devious. They had no interest in God, and they didn't want to be introduced. They metaphorically twisted their tongues into the shape of a bow and shot lies like arrows. God noticed and shared His observations with Jeremiah. These observations were mirrored in the way Jeremiah saw the world around him. This was a difficult time in history, populated by people who had so little interest in God that they'd pursue anything else before they would give God a fair hearing. They needed to pray but chose to break a new set of laws instead.

Pray that God would make Himself known to those who chase evil while running away from Him.

Prayer Starter

Father, it often seems that society isn't getting any better. People treat others shamefully. Many have no interest in knowing You. May they be introduced to You. May they discover the goodness they have resisted. May they. . .

DAY 227
JEREMIAH 10–12

Prayer Scripture

[Jeremiah prayed,] "You are righteous, O Lord, when I plead with You. Yet let me talk with You about Your judgments. Why does the way of the wicked prosper? Why are all those who deal very treacherously happy? You have planted them; yes, they have taken root. They grow; yes, they produce fruit. You are near in their mouth and far from their minds."

Jeremiah 12:1–2

Prayer Thought for the Day

The prophet Jeremiah acknowledged the righteousness of God, but he continued to struggle with everything he observed—and he wanted to report his findings. The wicked were getting rich, the treacherous were happy, and the fellowship of the unfaithful was growing. They might talk about God in a positive way, but there was no consideration of His laws. They were emboldened by seeing that their bad behavior seemed to receive absolutely no negative consequences. This is what Jeremiah observed—this was the subject of his prayer. It's easy to conclude that God's plan is simply allowing evil to thrive, but what if all of this is because God's kindness can bring about the greatest change?

Prayer Starter

Lord God, I want to be more concerned about how You transform my heart and less demanding about how You transform others. This is what You want, so let me. . .

DAY 228
JEREMIAH 13–15

Prayer Scripture

[Jeremiah prayed,] O Lord. . .we have sinned against You. O, the Hope of Israel, its Savior in time of trouble, why should You be like a foreigner in the land, and like a traveling man who turns aside to stay for a night? Why should you be like a man astonished, like a mighty man who cannot save? Yet You, O Lord, are in the midst of us, and we are called by Your name. Do not leave us.
Jeremiah 14:7–9

Prayer Thought for the Day

Desperation had been growing within Jeremiah. He shared everything God told him to say. He was often ignored. Sometimes he cried. When Jeremiah had a moment to talk to God, he recognized national sin. He admitted that God was his nation's only hope and Savior. Then the prophet had questions. He wanted to know why God seemed like a foreigner passing through an abandoned land. Jeremiah wanted to know why God didn't seem to be doing anything. Then, after all the frustration, the prophet spoke: He pleaded with God not to abandon them.

Even when you have questions about what God is doing, never forget to recognize the hope that's still yours by believing in God.

Prayer Starter

Father, help me to remember Your faithfulness before I question Your presence. Help me to long for Your presence and seek You when. . .

DAY 229
JEREMIAH 16–19

Prayer Scripture

O Lord, my strength and my fortress, and my refuge in the day of affliction, the Gentiles shall come to You from the ends of the earth, and shall say, "Surely our fathers have inherited lies, vanity, and things in which there is no profit."
Jeremiah 16:19

Prayer Thought for the Day

This must have been a surprising prayer. A prophet from Israel was praying because he was learning from God about something unexpected. For the most part the people of Israel felt that God was for them and not for Gentiles, the non-Jewish population. This prayer was from the perspective of a prophet who worked closely with God. What Jeremiah shared in his prayer was that there would be a time when Gentiles from everywhere would admit they'd been living a lie and there was no profit in the non-gods their people served. This good news would come true. This would be realized. This would prove God was for all people, everywhere. This news showed up because "God so loved the world that He gave His. . .Son" (John 3:16).

Prayer Starter

Lord God, thank You for sharing Your love with all mankind. I'm speaking to You because You came for all. May I never think that others aren't the right choice for Your love. Give me a heart that. . .

DAY 230
JEREMIAH 20–22

Prayer Scripture

[Jeremiah prayed,] O Lord. . .I am ridiculed daily—everyone mocks me. For since I spoke, I cried out. I cried, "Violence and plunder!" because the word of the Lord was made a reproach to me and a mockery daily. Then I said, "I will not make mention of Him or speak in His name anymore." But His word was in my heart like a burning fire shut up in my bones, and I was weary with holding it in, and I could not stay.

Jeremiah 20:7–9

Prayer Thought for the Day

Jeremiah was a prophet who became overwhelmed with the enormous scope of his agreement to speak for God. He shared what God had to say, knowing he'd be bruised, accused, and confused. Jeremiah apparently made a promise to himself that he was going to stop telling people what God was saying. It didn't seem to be helping. The prophet was tired of feeling like a punch line to an unintended joke. He was impatient, overwhelmed, and very tired. In the end, Jeremiah said, "I could not stay." There's an old saying: "God doesn't make you go against your will. He just makes you willing to go." Maybe this unknown author had Jeremiah in mind.

Prayer Starter

Father, may I play a willing part in Your plan. May I share what I know to be true about You. May I follow because You. . .

DAY 231
JEREMIAH 23–25

Prayer Scripture

Jeremiah the prophet spoke to all the people of Judah and to all the inhabitants of Jerusalem, saying: "From the thirteenth year of Josiah the son of Amon, king of Judah, even to this day, that is, the twenty-third year, the word of the LORD has come to me and I have spoken to you, rising early and speaking, but you have not listened. And the LORD has sent to you all His servants the prophets, rising early and sending them, but you have not listened."

JEREMIAH 25:2–4

Prayer Thought for the Day

It was a time for true confessions, and Jeremiah had already poured out his heart to God. Now, he shared his frustration with the people, who'd resisted listening to him in the past. This may be further indication that Jeremiah was overwhelmed. He talked about the total time he'd been preaching and the fact that the people wouldn't listen. This may have been less about shaming people into finally listening than it was an atypical prayer asking God for help. Jeremiah spoke the truth about people who refused to listen, but he was making his complaint to people who wouldn't listen. This was weariness personified.

Prayer Starter

Lord God, when I'm overwhelmed, let me ask for Your help, and may I be willing to accept the help You offer. May my strength come from You for the work You. . .

DAY 232
JEREMIAH 26–28

Prayer Scripture

It came to pass. . .that Hananiah the son of Azzur the prophet, who was from Gibeon, spoke to me in the house of the Lord in the presence of the priests and of all the people, saying: "This is what the Lord of hosts, the God of Israel speaks, saying, 'I have broken the yoke of the king of Babylon. Within two full years I will bring back into this place all the vessels of the Lord's house.'"

Jeremiah 28:1–3

Prayer Thought for the Day

There was cause for rejoicing, but it was based on a lie. Jeremiah had poured everything he had, all that God gave him, into sharing the news that the people would be exiled to Babylon for seventy years. It was a message he would have been happy to keep to himself. The people were tired of the message; but there was someone new in town, and his message contradicted what Jeremiah had been preaching for years. The people listened to Hananiah when he offered his made-up prophecy. This false prophet was boldly declaring everyone would return from Babylon within two years.

Not every bit of shared news is true. Pray for the wisdom to know what *is* true so you can avoid lies.

Prayer Starter

Father, I don't want to accept lies when You offer truth. Give me the wisdom to understand that not everything said is. . .

DAY 233

JEREMIAH 29–30

Prayer Scripture

"'I know the thoughts that I think toward you,' says the LORD, 'thoughts of peace and not of evil, to give you an expected end. Then you shall call on Me and you shall go and pray to Me, and I will listen to you. And you shall seek Me and find Me, when you shall search for Me with all your heart. And I will be found by you,' says the LORD."

JEREMIAH 29:11–14

Prayer Thought for the Day

God confirmed it wasn't two years of captivity for the people—it was seventy. The Israelites were urged to pray for the peace of Babylon, because, if there was peace for the nation that took them captive, then they would have peace during their seven-decade time-out. God provided reassurance and comfort that justice would be served. He made sure the people knew that His thoughts, or plans, included peace and a good outcome. He saw the day when the people would once more pray to Him. He would listen. . .they would seek Him. . .He would be found. The struggle Jeremiah faced had been transformed as hope was exposed. The people had a future to look forward to. Your future can have God included—always.

Prayer Starter

Lord God, seeking You means I find You. Praying to You means You hear me. Yesterday, today, and next year. Help me to refuse answers from anywhere else when I have questions about. . .

DAY 234
JEREMIAH 31–32

Prayer Scripture

"Ah, Lord GOD! Behold, You have made the heavens and the earth by Your great power and outstretched arm, and there is nothing too hard for You. You show loving-kindness to thousands and repay the iniquity of the fathers into the bosom of their children after them—the Great, the Mighty God, the LORD of hosts is His name; great in counsel and mighty in work, for Your eyes are open on all the ways of the sons of men, to give each one according to his ways and according to the fruit of his doings."

JEREMIAH 32:17–19

Prayer Thought for the Day

It's important to note that God didn't leave Jeremiah in a perpetual state of despair. This prophet was once considered the weeping prophet. He was willing to express his sense of being overwhelmed with God as well as with a crowd that didn't care for him or the God he served. Now? God had done great things, and nothing was too hard for Him. He was kind, loving, a counselor—and this God brought back mercy following a season of justice. This was good news, welcome news, and news worth a prayer of praise to a good God.

Prayer Starter

Father, Your Word says that joy comes in the morning. Help me to be patient for the morning light of mercy following a dark night of coexisting with justice. Give me a heart that praises You for. . .

DAY 235
JEREMIAH 33–35

Prayer Scripture

"This is what the Lord, the God of Israel, says concerning the houses of this city and concerning the houses of the kings of Judah, which are thrown down by the mounts and by the sword: 'They come to fight with the Chaldeans, but it is to fill them with the dead bodies of men whom I have slain in My anger and in My fury, and for all whose wickedness I have hidden My face from this city. Behold, I will bring it health and cure, and I will cure them and will reveal to them the abundance of peace and truth. And I will cause the captives of Judah and the captives of Israel to return."

Jeremiah 33:4–7

Prayer Thought for the Day

Here's more good news for the weeping prophet. Jeremiah was hearing from God, and things changed once the people had gone into captivity. What Jeremiah had endured was knowing that captivity was coming, but no one believed him, and those who listened to him were often hostile. With the people in exile, God was describing their future, and it was good. Coming to Israel's future? A healing and a cure—peace and truth—and ultimately a return home. Desperate prayers by a prophet were turning into an overwhelming tribute of praise.

Prayer Starter

Lord God, I want my hard times to bring me to a place of praise. May I start by remembering that. . .

DAY 236
JEREMIAH 36–38

Prayer Scripture

Zedekiah the king sent Jehucal the son of Shelemiah and Zephaniah the son of Maaseiah the priest to the prophet Jeremiah, saying, "Pray now to the LORD our God for us." Now Jeremiah came in and went out among the people, for they had not put him into prison.
JEREMIAH 37:3–4

Prayer Thought for the Day

The people of Israel were not all exiled to Babylon at the same time. Some were able to stay longer or permanently. But Babylon was in charge—they chose kings and enforced rules. So, the Babylonian-approved king, Zedekiah, sent an ally, Jehucal, to give Jeremiah a nine-word request, "Pray now to the LORD our God for us." The king's message actually shares one interesting word. That word is *our*. This message indicated the king agreed with Jeremiah and was placing himself on the side of the faithful, at least for the purpose of this request. There would be more trials for Jeremiah, but this time there seemed to be other men who were willing to walk with him to the best of their ability.

When you feel as if you have to walk with Jesus without friends, pray that God would bring human companionship with others who share the same journey.

Prayer Starter

Father, please send friends who also follow You. I could use their encouragement. Maybe they could use mine. I could benefit from faithful friends because. . .

DAY 237
JEREMIAH 39–41

Prayer Scripture

Nebuchadnezzar, king of Babylon, gave charge concerning Jeremiah to Nebuzaradan the captain of the guard, saying, "Take him and look after him, and do him no harm, but do to him even as he shall say to you." So Nebuzaradan. . .took Jeremiah out of the courtyard of the prison and committed him to Gedaliah the son of Ahikam, the son of Shaphan, that he should take him home. So he dwelled among the people.

Jeremiah 39:11–14

Prayer Thought for the Day

Jeremiah was one of the few who faithfully followed God when everyone else seemed content to wander. He must have seemed peculiar to most. When few do the right thing, they appear unusual. While most were on their way to exile, Jeremiah lived through unjust detention in horrid conditions. The king of Babylon told his soldiers to take care of Jeremiah and allow him to do what he needed to do. This foreign king was treating Jeremiah better than his own people had. This answer to prayer would allow Jeremiah to have a positive impact on those who were left in the promised land.

God's answer to your prayers may look very different from your expectations, but His answer is never a coincidence.

Prayer Starter

Lord God, kindness might come from a most unexpected place, yet it's always inspired by You. Help me to express kindness and accept kindness when. . .

DAY 238
JEREMIAH 42–44

Prayer Scripture

Then all the captains of the forces, and Johanan the son of Kareah, and Jezaniah the son of Hoshaiah, and all the people, from the least even to the greatest, came near and said to Jeremiah the prophet, "We beseech you, let our supplication be accepted before you, and pray for us to the LORD your God, even for all this remnant— for we are but a few left of many, as your eyes can see—that the LORD your God may show us the way in which we may walk and the thing that we may do." Then Jeremiah the prophet said to them, "I have heard you. Behold, I will pray to the LORD your God."

JEREMIAH 42:1–4

Prayer Thought for the Day

Jeremiah chose to stay with the remnant in Israel after the exile. This smaller group offered a glimpse at a better future. They came to Jeremiah to ask for prayer, but there was purpose behind their request. They wanted directions that they agreed to follow. Jeremiah hadn't previously heard this kind of willingness. Their seeking suggested a long-awaited return. God was working through bad circumstances to uncover a great outcome. He can do the same for you.

Prayer Starter

Lord God, help me to get—and stay—in a place where I recognize You and look to what You want for me. Give me purpose behind my prayer because I…

DAY 239
JEREMIAH 45–47

Prayer Scripture

The word that Jeremiah the prophet spoke to Baruch the son of Neriah, when he had written these words in a book at the mouth of Jeremiah, in the fourth year of Jehoiakim the son of Josiah, king of Judah, saying, "This is what the LORD, the God of Israel, says to you, O Baruch: 'You said, "Woe is me now! For the LORD has added grief to my sorrow. I fainted in my sighing, and I find no rest."'"

JEREMIAH 45:1–3

Prayer Thought for the Day

Baruch was Jeremiah's scribe. This passage suggests Baruch wasn't pleased with his career choice. It seems Baruch thought God should compensate him for his trouble. He thought he was being treated horribly and significantly inconvenienced. This was the frustrated prayer of a scribe. God essentially responded by saying that He was accomplishing something on a grand scale. God wanted to know if Baruch believed this was the right time to seek great things for himself. Baruch's prayer might have been the result of not understanding that God had a plan that was bigger than personal comfort. Is it possible to let comfort, wealth, and fame prevent you from being a part of God's plan? Can you be inconvenienced for God?

Prayer Starter

Father, I've learned that I can ask You questions. I'm also learning that Your plan may not always match my expectations. May I be willing to be inconvenienced when. . .

DAY 240
JEREMIAH 48–49

Prayer Scripture

"'I will set My throne in Elam and will destroy from there the king and the princes,' says the Lord. 'But it shall come to pass in the latter days, that I will bring back the captives of Elam,'" says the Lord.
Jeremiah 49:38–39

Prayer Thought for the Day

God was working to bring change. Jeremiah had messages for nearly a dozen cities and nations. All had inspired God to correct them. Each received what they viewed as a negative message.

Jeremiah wasn't a popular public speaker. The people of Elam were exiled as part of God's correction, but the captives would return. If God had wanted to free His people's lives from outside adversaries, He could have destroyed these enemy nations, yet in so many cases He promised to return the people to their lands. It seems this was another example of how God came for all people, in all places, for all time. This answer may have been for the unspoken prayer of nations who would have the opportunity to get acquainted with a God who wouldn't stop with this series of rescue operations.

What had begun then continues, and you've benefited from this mercy.

Prayer Starter

Lord God, thank You for showing me that even when correction is unpleasant, You restore what seemed lost, give what seemed to be taken, and help when hope was. . .

DAY 241
JEREMIAH 50

Prayer Scripture

[God said,] "My people have been lost sheep. Their shepherds have caused them to go astray; they have turned them away on the mountains. They have gone from mountain to hill; they have forgotten their resting place. All who found them have devoured them, and their adversaries said, 'We have not offended, because they have sinned against the LORD, the habitation of justice, even the LORD, the hope of their fathers.' . . . For behold, I will raise and cause to come up against Babylon an assembly of great nations from the north country, and they shall set themselves in formation against her; from there she shall be taken."

JEREMIAH 50:6–7, 9

Prayer Thought for the Day

People were exiled to Babylon because God chose to correct habitual law-breaking. Babylon saw this as a conquest. They mistook God's correction for punishment and then determined they could simply expand God's work and continue the punishment. Now the nation that was used by God to correct Israel would need correction.

You should allow God to make corrections in the lives of others without choosing to pile on punishment that God didn't intend. Remember: God corrects; enemies punish.

Prayer Starter

Father, I don't want to try to take Your place when it comes to other people. Help me to remain compassionate and let You correct. Give me the wisdom to. . .

DAY 242
JEREMIAH 51–52

Prayer Scripture

[God] has made the earth by His power; He has established the world by His wisdom and has stretched out the heavens by His understanding. When He utters His voice, there is a multitude of waters in the heavens, and He causes the vapors to ascend from the ends of the earth. He makes lightning with rain and brings forth the wind out of His treasuries.

Jeremiah 51:15–16

Prayer Thought for the Day

The book of Jeremiah was dedicated to God's correction. Jeremiah isn't the only book on the subject, but there may be more emotion detected here than in most accounts. Yet as the book comes to a close, there's a message in chapter 51 that might seem out of place. Perhaps it's actually a well-placed bit of encouragement. God had become known as the Great Corrector in this book. This passage suggests that humanity lives on a planet that God made by wisdom that is useful to people who need a personal friendship with Him.

The God who sustains also corrects. He corrects because He cares for you.

Prayer Starter

Lord God, may I choose to remember that You made what I enjoy and correct what I chose as a first response in favor of Your response. Help me to be patient when. . .

DAY 243

LAMENTATIONS 1–2

Prayer Scripture

They have heard that I sigh. There is no one to comfort me. All my enemies have heard of my trouble. They are glad that You have done it. You will bring the day that You have called, and they shall be like me. Let all their wickedness come before You, and do to them as You have done to me for all my transgressions. For my sighs are many, and my heart is faint.

LAMENTATIONS 1:21–22

Prayer Thought for the Day

Most scholars believe Lamentations was written by the Weeping Prophet, Jeremiah. This passage sounds like a prayer Job might have prayed. The writer feels his life experience has been less than ideal, so he shares his concerns with God through prayer. He doesn't feel comforted, enemies gloat, and personal sighing has become common. Of course what makes this a great prayer is that the prophet recognized his personal discomfort wasn't the only event happening in the world. The wickedness of others was noticed by God, and it would be dealt with.

When you're discouraged, don't think for a minute that God is unaware of anything that's going on. He will deal with it.

Prayer Starter

Father, remind me that You offer comfort even when I fail to recognize it. Help me to remember that You deal with everything and everyone, even when I don't understand. Give me the strength to follow, even when I wonder if. . .

DAY 244
LAMENTATIONS 3–5

Prayer Scripture

It is because of the LORD's mercies that we are not consumed, because His compassions do not fail. They are new every morning. Great is Your faithfulness. "The LORD is my portion," says my soul. "Therefore I will hope in Him." The LORD is good to those who wait for Him, to the soul who seeks Him. It is good that a man should both hope and quietly wait for the salvation of the LORD.
LAMENTATIONS 3:22–26

Prayer Thought for the Day

This is the third lamentation, and within this song of sadness there's a greater belief in a very big God. The scribe for these lamentations could have written this as a prayer, and if he had, it might have sounded something like "Your mercy keeps me in one piece. Your compassion holds me in hope. Your faithfulness astounds me. Keep me company while I wait. Help me to be patient as I wait for Your greater rescue."

This is a good example of how you can take a lesson in God's Word and make it a prayer that connects with your concern.

Prayer Starter

Lord God, keep me interested in Your Word, even those places in scripture that I'm not sure will teach me much. Thank You for showing me that others have experienced sadness but came to rely on You for. . .

DAY 245

EZEKIEL 1–3

Prayer Scripture

"You shall speak My words to them, whether they will hear or whether they will disregard, for they are most rebellious. But you, son of man, hear what I say to you. Do not be rebellious like that rebellious house."

Ezekiel 2:7–8

Prayer Thought for the Day

Ezekiel was a priest. He spoke God's words. He may seem like a prophet as you read the book that bears his name, but he was more at ease speaking to a congregation in the house of worship. Here's an important lesson on the subject of prayer that leads to the trust needed to do something that's very hard. The priest, Ezekiel, was asked by God to give a message in which there was no guarantee that those listening would respond favorably. The lesson isn't that this would be difficult but that the priest wouldn't be responsible for how people responded. He was responsible only for delivering the message.

If you've ever thought you're responsible for how people respond to God's good news, you should be reminded that you're responsible only for sharing—not convincing anyone to agree with you. This lesson can free you to share because the outcome has always been in God's hands.

Prayer Starter

Father, I need to share what You shared with me even when the outcome is uncertain. Give me a heart that agrees with You that. . .

DAY 246
EZEKIEL 4–7

Prayer Scripture

"This is what the Lord GOD says: 'This is Jerusalem; I have set her in the midst of the nations and countries that are all around her. And she has changed My judgments into wickedness more than the nations, and My statutes more than the countries that are all around her. For they have refused My judgments and my statutes; they have not walked in them.'"
EZEKIEL 5:5–6

Prayer Thought for the Day

Jerusalem had been honored to have a significant investment by the God of all things. This was an important location historically, because it was part of the promised land God gave to the people of Israel. This was where God's temple was built and would be renovated and rebuilt. It was the spiritual center of the region. In this place people prayed and God answered. But God noticed something. The people who should have blossomed because they had access to God traded good for bad, right thinking for wickedness, and commands for rebellion. In fact, the people who should have followed God because He was with them were actually more rebellious than the nations around them.

Why might it seem normal for people who know better to choose worse?

Prayer Starter

Lord God, knowing better and doing better should be companions, but that's not always true. Help me to know You more so I can do what. . .

DAY 247

EZEKIEL 8–11

Prayer Scripture

Moreover the Spirit lifted me up and brought me to the east gate of the LORD's house, which looks eastward. And, behold, at the door of the gate twenty-five men, among whom I saw Jaazaniah the son of Azzur and Pelatiah the son of Benaiah, princes of the people. Then He said to me, "Son of man, these are the men who devise evil and give wicked counsel in this city, who say, 'It is not near; let us build houses. This city is the caldron and we are the meat.' Therefore prophesy against them—prophesy, O son of man."

EZEKIEL 11:1–4

Prayer Thought for the Day

Have you ever heard of Jaazaniah and Pelatiah? No? Well, they were the resident troublemakers in Ezekiel 11. These two were architects of mischief and dispensed free advice described as "wicked." You might think of them as influencers, but their influence was never good. They believed that if the city was a large cooking pot, they provided the taste. But God knew their recipe was flawed. They didn't pray, and they didn't seem to care what He thought. God wanted this display of arrogance to stop.

You can pray for the opportunity to choose humility over a personal parade of honor.

Prayer Starter

Father, lead me to a place where I see You receive glory and I can say, "I follow Him." Help me to resist arrogance and learn how to. . .

DAY 248
EZEKIEL 12–15

Prayer Scripture

The word of the LORD came to me again, saying: "Son of man, when the land sins against Me by trespassing grievously, then I will stretch out My hand on it and will break the supply of its bread, and will send famine on it, and will cut off man and beast from it. Though these three men—Noah, Daniel, and Job—were in it, they should deliver only their own souls by their righteousness," says the Lord GOD.

EZEKIEL 14:12–14

Prayer Thought for the Day

The book of Daniel is yet to come, but he's mentioned here along with Noah and Job. These three men are written about in terms of their faithfulness to God. They started and finished well. They seem to be listed here to provide a comparison for people to understand the wickedness of the current generation. If these three men were present in this place, they would be the only ones to survive God's campaign against the ongoing sin of the nation. This is a great picture of why praying for God's mercy is an important and compassionate prayer. The lawbreaking tendencies of people should lead to never-ending correction. Pray for those who wrong you. You shouldn't desire this level of correction for anyone.

Prayer Starter

Lord God, society needs mercy because Your kindness leads people to turn from their current pursuits to something better. May I accept justice but pray for mercy because. . .

DAY 249
EZEKIEL 16–17

Prayer Scripture

"I will establish My covenant with you. And you shall know that I am the LORD, that you may remember and be confounded, and never open your mouth anymore because of your shame, when I am pacified toward you for all that you have done," says the Lord GOD.

EZEKIEL 16:62–63

Prayer Thought for the Day

The people needed to be reminded of the covenant God made with the people of Israel. He had kept the terms of this contract, while the people had chosen to violate them. There would come a new covenant, when Jesus arrived, but God expressed a willingness to reintroduce His already established covenant with a reminder that this contract was enforced and needed to be followed. If it weren't for this God-authored contract, the people would likely have been a footnote in history. This was an invitation for the people to change directions and then pray that God would give them the strength, wisdom, and interest in following Him once again. Obedience will always benefit from a position of prayer.

Prayer Starter

Father, You made an agreement to rescue, and I agreed that this is just what I needed. You offered to help me. I don't want to keep Your help at arm's length. Let me accept this connection, but when I fail to keep Your laws, help me to admit my rebellion and. . .

DAY 250
EZEKIEL 18–20

Prayer Scripture

"Yet you say, 'The way of the Lord is not equal.' Hear now, O house of Israel. Is My way not equal? Are not your ways unequal? When a righteous man turns away from his righteousness and commits iniquity and dies in them, he shall die for his iniquity that he has done. Again, when the wicked man turns away from his wickedness that he has committed and does what is lawful and right, he shall save his soul alive. Because he considers and turns away from all his transgressions that he has committed, he shall surely live—he shall not die."

Ezekiel 18:25–28

Prayer Thought for the Day

This time of national correction seemed overwhelming. The people thought God wasn't being fair. They thought what they were experiencing wasn't equality. God rightfully points out that humans are rarely interested in true equality. When they sin, they want mercy, but when other people sin, they want justice. God offered both when He could easily have determined justice was how He'd respond every time. The people really wanted situational mercy and justice—if they could decide who got each. God leveraged both. When you pray, thank God for offering mercy to whomever He chooses, and then champion His very real equality.

Prayer Starter

Lord God, thank You for Your equality, which has always been designed to keep me close. Be merciful even in Your justice. Without Your mercy no one could. . .

DAY 251
EZEKIEL 21–22

Prayer Scripture

[God said,] "And I sought for a man among them who should make up the hedge and stand in the gap before Me for the land, that I should not destroy it. But I found none."
EZEKIEL 22:30

Prayer Thought for the Day

How disheartening would it be to engage in a spiritual talent search and find no one qualified to compete? God wanted someone who stood between the way things were and the way things should be, and He found no one. Yes, there were prophets; yes, there were priests; and there were some in Babylon who refused to walk away from God. This seems to be a broad statement about any movement to God's side among the general population. The people had been exposed to the truth, and they simply didn't care enough to do anything to demonstrate a change of heart, attitude, or direction.

Would God find you willing to stand in the gap to bridge the distance between Himself and people who don't follow Him?

Prayer Starter

Father, following You shouldn't feel like standing alone, but even if that's true, strengthen my resolve to stand. I don't want to be shaken by the wind or blown off course by opinion. If this gap needs someone, let it be me so You can. . .

DAY 252
EZEKIEL 23–24

Prayer Scripture

"This is what the Lord God says: 'Because you have forgotten Me and cast Me behind your back, therefore you also bear your lewdness and your prostitution.'"
Ezekiel 23:35

Prayer Thought for the Day

God was using parables to help Ezekiel share His mind about the unfaithfulness of His people. In Ezekiel 23:36 the names Oholah and Oholibah most likely represented Judah and Israel. In this parable these two were unfaithful. It seems the thing the hearer should have taken away from this description is that their spirit was to be filled with God, but the people had systematically replaced Him with shards, fragments, and threads from surrounding nations and worldviews. In the end, they were left with a stew that was reprehensible to the God who'd done everything for the people. In return, the people chose to replace Him. Gone was the gratitude, faithfulness, and honor God was due.

Your choice to pray can reveal whether you've forgotten God and cast Him aside or if you're reaching in His direction and expressing a desire to follow your rescuer.

Prayer Starter

Lord God, it's easy to wander and even easier to replace what You've changed in me. May my everyday choice be to follow You and offer You my life, dedicated to. . .

DAY 253

EZEKIEL 25–27

Prayer Scripture

The word of the LORD came to me, saying, "Son of man, because Tyre has said against Jerusalem, 'Aha! She who was the gates of the people is broken; she is turned to me. I shall be replenished; now she is laid waste,' therefore this is what the Lord GOD says: 'Behold, I am against you, O Tyre, and will cause many nations to come up against you.'"

EZEKIEL 26:1–3

Prayer Thought for the Day

The known world viewed God's people as the region's greatest laughingstock. God's justice found many nations drawing the wrong conclusion, so they offered an incorrect response. These nations felt that if God was judging Israel and Judah, then they could too. But God was uniquely qualified to make any correction He knew would help. He didn't need anyone else to step in and add their own judgment to what He'd already established. He wasn't in the business of creating a feeding frenzy for those who were judgmental. One nation after another is condemned by God for their role in punishing when God was involved in correction. When you witness someone in the middle of correction, consider that they need something from you that is different from a penalty you were never asked to assess.

Prayer Starter

Father, I can make judgments about other people with very little information. Help me to let You correct, while I offer compassion and kindness when. . .

DAY 254
EZEKIEL 28–30

Prayer Scripture

"And they shall know that I am the LORD."
EZEKIEL 30:26

Prayer Thought for the Day

Part of one verse. Nine words. A single complete thought. These words work together to summarize what had been happening as God spoke to the priest Ezekiel. All the nations who acted as piranhas in the presence of a wounded fish, Israel, were under the judgment of God. He had a very compelling reason to correct. Beyond pointing out the worthlessness of being judgmental, God wanted other nations to believe He existed and know who He was. This seems to point out that God would one day introduce a covenant that would include all people from every land. These weren't perfect circumstances, but these nations would begin to realize the non-gods they'd relied on were worth nothing. These man-made objects of worship couldn't stand when God was in their land.

When you find that God's redirecting your life circumstances and others are amplifying your pain, it could be that God's also working to make Himself known to these wounded warriors at the same time. Pray for mercy. Pray that others would see God in your struggle.

Prayer Starter

Lord God, I cannot improve someone's life by keeping a scorecard of the infractions I observe. This is a practical reason for me to pray for them as I continue to seek You for my future and Your. . .

DAY 255
EZEKIEL 31–32

Prayer Scripture

"When I make the land of Egypt desolate, and the country is destitute of that of which it was full; when I strike all those who dwell in it—then they shall know that I am the LORD. This is the lamentation with which they shall lament her. The daughters of the nations shall lament her. They shall lament for her, even for Egypt, and for all her multitude," says the Lord GOD.

EZEKIEL 32:15–16

Prayer Thought for the Day

Justice delivers ill-timed news and a variety of emotions, including regret and grief. Justice may not seem like a short-term inconvenience. It descends like a dark cloud and leaves you wondering what the landscape will look like when light returns. Normal is no longer possible. Survival is a daily objective. When justice comes, everything changes. There's no easy path back to the past, and no human can tell you exactly what you need to do to move forward. This was the case for the majority of nations in the known world. Israel and Judah were in captivity, so many other nations drew God's corrective action against themselves, based on their willingness to antagonize God and ridicule Israel and Judah.

Regret is essential for the prayer of restoration, following wrong action.

Prayer Starter

Father, may I learn from regret and the emotions that arrive with it. Restore me from what caused me to venture away from. . .

DAY 256

EZEKIEL 33–34

Prayer Scripture

"Say to them, 'As I live,' says the Lord God, 'I have no pleasure in the death of the wicked but that the wicked turn from his way and live. Turn, turn from your evil ways.'"
EZEKIEL 33:11

Prayer Thought for the Day

It's interesting to see an unusual truth in Ezekiel 33. God would prefer wicked people live as long as it takes for them to change their wicked pursuits. He says in Psalm 116:15 that the death of His followers is precious. You might think the opposite would be true; but if you've accepted God's rescue, when you die, you meet Him face-to-face. Someone who resists God no longer has the chance to change their mind, heart, or opinion once they die. The longer you spend time praying to a good God, the more you look forward to being home with Him. Those who reject God have only their current life to enjoy. Maybe it makes sense why this option finds God saying, "I have no pleasure in the death of the wicked." It means there's no further opportunity to "turn from your evil ways."

Prayer Starter

Lord God, I'm glad I can talk to You, and I look forward to our time together now and in the future. I want to pray for people who are running out of opportunities to meet You. I think of friends and family members like. . .

DAY 257
EZEKIEL 35–36

Prayer Scripture

"But you, O mountains of Israel, you shall shoot forth your branches and yield your fruit to My people of Israel, for they are at hand to come. For, behold, I am for you, and I will turn to you, and you shall be tilled and sown. And I will multiply men on you, all the house of Israel, even all of it. And the cities shall be inhabited, and the ruins shall be rebuilt."

EZEKIEL 36:8–10

Prayer Thought for the Day

For the non-farmer types, *tilling* means God turns the soil over—breaking packed dirt and allowing new seeds to thrive in this conditioned soil. This is a picture God uses to describe His judgment. The people had become very set in their walkaway. God had to disrupt their "normal" life for new-decision seeds to grow and flourish. New fruit would grow, and God would be cheering new growth. He made it clear new life would grow from this hard soil, ruins would be rebuilt, and the people would once again know God. One of the great lines in this Ezekiel 36 passage is when God says, "I am for you." This should have instilled hope in those being corrected, and the echoes of this good news should be heard today.

Prayer Starter

Father, thank You for being for me. Thank You for turning the hard soil within me so new lessons can be learned and new choices can. . .

DAY 258

EZEKIEL 37–39

Prayer Scripture

"'I am the LORD their God, who caused them to be led into captivity among the nations. But I have gathered them to their own land and have left none of them there any longer. Nor will I hide My face any longer from them, for I have poured out My Spirit on the house of Israel,' says the Lord GOD."

EZEKIEL 39:28–29

Prayer Thought for the Day

God absolutely took responsibility for sending His people into exile and captivity. He had a reason: Mercy hadn't moved the nation's heart to return to Him. The people continued to find new ways to offend a holy God. Ezekiel 39:28–29 feels a bit like the promise Noah received after the Flood—an event also caused by God's judgment of lawbreaking humanity. God made a new promise. The first promise would be the gathering of His people. The second was that God would be approachable once more. Justice had been served, and mercy would return as a preferred response to people who sin. Pray with gratitude to the God who never gives up the right to pass sentence on lawbreakers but prefers to show mercy first.

Prayer Starter

Lord God, I can understand the reason for justice. Without it, lawlessness only accelerates. Change hearts and bring mercy to the way You respond to. . .

DAY 259

EZEKIEL 40–42

Prayer Scripture

In the twenty-fifth year of our captivity, in the beginning of the year, on the tenth day of the month, in the fourteenth year after the city was stricken, on this very same day the hand of the LORD was on me and brought me there. . . . And the man said to me, "Son of man, behold with your eyes and hear with your ears and set your heart on all that I shall show you. You have been brought here so that I might show them to you. Declare all that you see to the house of Israel."

EZEKIEL 40:1, 4

Prayer Thought for the Day

It had been twenty-five years since invading forces came and took some of the people away from the promised land. Nearly fourteen years since the destruction of the city, God was giving Ezekiel an amazing scoop. The news was big, and it would be very encouraging. Ezekiel would share the news with people who needed to hear it. This priest had shared God's words over and over again, and not everything he had to say was appreciated by the audience. This news meant a place of prayer would be reestablished and a new focus would correct the vision of the people.

Prayer Starter

Father, I welcome any good news that brings me closer to You. Help me to thank You for every good thing You do for me. This includes. . .

DAY 260
EZEKIEL 43–44

Prayer Scripture

"[The priests] shall teach My people the difference between the holy and profane, and cause them to discern between the unclean and the clean. And in controversy they shall stand in judgment, and they shall judge it according to My judgments. And they shall keep My laws and My statutes in all My assemblies."
EZEKIEL 44:23–24

Prayer Thought for the Day

The priests were called upon to represent God in how they spoke, in what they did, and in their willingness to keep God's commands. The priests were relied upon to judge disputes, to identify what was pure, and to be set apart for God's use. There was much to learn, share, and follow. There was much to avoid, resist, and condemn. Even priests needed a reminder that they were expected to do more than act like so many others in the society in which they lived and served. These priests would pray for and with those who came to them. They would be examples of what *following* looked like. God wanted them to know they had a big job.

God wants you to follow Him with the same goal of learning and sharing.

Prayer Starter

Lord God, allow me to think of myself as someone set apart to do what You want and what brings good to my life. I have much to learn so I can. . .

DAY 261

EZEKIEL 45–46

Prayer Scripture

[God said,] "When you divide the land for inheritance by lot, you shall offer an offering to the LORD, a holy portion of the land. The length shall be the length of twenty-five thousand rods, and the breadth shall be ten thousand. This shall be holy in all its borders all around."

EZEKIEL 45:1

Prayer Thought for the Day

This is a passage that would be easy to overlook. It seems that it might have been a legal description from Israel's planning and zoning commission. But this was more than just new information for the next published map; this was a visual object lesson. God is holy, set apart, unique, and has boundaries. This land set aside for His priests was holy, set apart, unique, and had boundaries. These priests would serve people designed to be holy, set apart, unique, with boundaries. And God's people need to pray prayers that are holy, set apart, unique, with boundaries. If it seems there's a recurring theme today, it's intentional, because God didn't make you to be a lawbreaker, a duplicate, just like everyone else, or someone who makes his own rules.

Prayer Starter

Father, may my life look like Your map of Israel, holy, set apart, unique, with boundaries. Give me a heart that pursues this with. . .

DAY 262
EZEKIEL 47–48

Prayer Scripture

"The sanctuary of the LORD shall be in the center. It shall be for the priests who are sanctified of the sons of Zadok, who have kept My charge, who did not go astray when the children of Israel went astray, as the Levites went astray."
EZEKIEL 48:10–11

Prayer Thought for the Day

Because humans can reason and make choices—and because those choices can be horribly wrong—it shouldn't be surprising that every human has broken God's laws. Some sinned and kept sinning. But there was a group of priests from the family of Zadok who paid attention to what God said, obeyed what He asked, and returned to His side when failed choices were identified. This wasn't universally true, so in the final chapter of Ezekiel the faithfulness of these priests was recognized. In this recognition you're reminded that the quick turnaround is important in your faith walk with God. Your prayer life should always seek to invite restoration. A refusal to talk to God about this struggle is like skipping wisdom class.

Prayer Starter

Lord God, not every day is a mountaintop experience. I don't always see where I should go, so I either stop or turn away. Keep my feet moving toward You so I can. . .

DAY 263

DANIEL 1–2

Prayer Scripture

Daniel went to his house and made the thing known to Hananiah, Mishael, and Azariah, his companions, that they would ask mercies of the God of heaven concerning this secret, that Daniel and his companions should not perish with the rest of the wise men of Babylon. Then the secret was revealed to Daniel.

Daniel 2:17–19

Prayer Thought for the Day

Four exiles in Babylon did something that was apparently unique. While God was judging Israel, the men Daniel, Hananiah, Mishael, and Azariah (the final three more commonly known as Shadrach, Meshach, and Abed-nego) had committed themselves to following God in this foreign land. Others hadn't followed God when they were in Israel, and this remained true in captivity. When the king had a perplexing dream, these four men prayed. God revealed the meaning of the dream to Daniel, and he gave the king his answer when no one else could. Prayer quite literally saved Daniel's life because the king had threatened to kill all the wise men of his kingdom if they couldn't interpret his dream. These four men were wise because they made the daily choice to listen to a very wise God.

Prayer Starter

Father, help me to rely on You for answers. Help me to ask those questions in prayer. May I walk with You so the questions I ask. . .

DAY 264

DANIEL 3–4

Prayer Scripture

A herald cried aloud, "It is commanded to you, O people, nations, and languages, that at the time you hear the sound of the cornet, flute, harp, lyre, stringed instruments, dulcimer, and all kinds of music, you fall down and worship the golden image that Nebuchadnezzar the king has set up. And whoever does not fall down and worship shall be cast the same hour into the midst of a burning fiery furnace."
Daniel 3:4–6

Prayer Thought for the Day

A worship band played in Babylon, but they worshipped a non-god. Three men were in the crosshairs of a very bad law. The king said everyone should bow down and worship his new statue whenever his band of merry musicians played. The biggest issue was that this statue wasn't God. Shadrach, Meshach, and Abed-nego were respected by the king, but he wasn't happy with their disobedience. The king heated the municipal furnace hotter than usual, and the three praying men were tossed in. They literally walked among the flames without injury. The result of this story is that God was honored by a king who had previously found honor only in a worthless metal statue. There's only one God who hears your prayer, and that God answers.

Prayer Starter

Lord God, when I worship, I want You to be the only one I think of. Give me courage to honor You even when others refuse. Give me courage to. . .

DAY 265
DANIEL 5–6

Prayer Scripture

When Daniel knew that the writing was signed, he went to his house, and—his windows being open in his chamber toward Jerusalem—he knelt on his knees three times a day and prayed and gave thanks before his God, as he did formerly.
Daniel 6:10

Prayer Thought for the Day

King Nebuchadnezzar had died. So had his son Belshazzar. The kingdom was now under the control of King Darius. Daniel had been relied on by each king to answer hard questions that only God could answer—and God answered because Daniel prayed three very specific times of day, morning, noon, and night. This is important because there was a bad case of wise-man jealousy. Other men who wanted King Darius to notice them plotted to eliminate their rival, Daniel. They convinced Darius to sign a law that the only prayers that could be prayed would be to the king. Daniel couldn't do that. He prayed at his usual time, in his godly way. The jealous men caught him and took him to the king, and Darius reluctantly sentenced him to the lions' den.

God was bigger than a bad law. And Daniel proved once again that he was wiser than the scheming of men.

Prayer Starter

Father, help me to learn to deal with people who want to harm me. May I trust You even when life is unfair. May I honor You by. . .

DAY 266
DANIEL 7–9

Prayer Scripture

It came to pass, when I—even I, Daniel—had seen the vision and sought for the meaning, then, behold, one having the appearance of a man stood before me. And I heard a man's voice between the banks of Ulai, which called and said, "Gabriel, make this man to understand the vision."

DANIEL 8:15–16

Prayer Thought for the Day

Sometimes you can have a dream and it seems especially real, maybe frightening. You wonder if there's some meaning behind what you saw with closed eyes. Daniel was one of the wisest men of his generation. He interpreted dreams, but the one he had would be interpreted only because God gave him the interpretation. That's how Daniel always interpreted dreams. God's messenger angel, Gabriel, was called on to help Daniel understand once Daniel prayed for help. The dream was all about kingdoms that would progress in dominance and decline. This was something he struggled to understand, but God had given a very accurate picture of the years of exile and a return home.

Sometimes you just need confirmation that God's in control. Search for it—you'll find it.

Prayer Starter

Lord God, I may not have dreams that I need interpreted, but I do live a life that's sometimes confusing. Help me to understand what You want me to do and the value in. . .

DAY 267
DANIEL 10–12

Prayer Scripture

I heard, but I did not understand. Then I said, "O my Lord, what shall be the end of these things?" And he said, "Go your way, Daniel, for the words are closed up and sealed until the time of the end."
DANIEL 12:8–9

Prayer Thought for the Day

Daniel's dream, or vision, was intense and disturbing. He saw what he saw. He wrote what he understood, but when he asked for a more complete understanding, God declined Daniel's request. Daniel was looking at the very end of earth's existence, and everything about it made no sense when viewed from the world that he knew. It likely felt a bit like time traveling, but the prophet had no one to decode the technological advances, the differences in the people, the way of speaking, and transportation that didn't include animals. God wanted these things written for a future generation, but it left Daniel confused. There's no record that he ever fully understood what he saw after the answer to prayer was "the words are closed up and sealed."

Sometimes God will say no to a prayer to protect you from something.

Prayer Starter

Father, thank You for saying no when that's absolutely the best answer. Even when I have no ability to understand why, help me to accept Your answer, knowing You love me and want me to. . .

DAY 268
HOSEA 1–5

Prayer Scripture

"I will have mercy on her who had not obtained mercy.
And I will say to those who were not My people, 'You are
My people.' And they shall say, 'You are my God.'"
HOSEA 2:23

Prayer Thought for the Day

Hosea's obedience to God made him one of the more unique object lessons in scripture. God asked him to marry a prostitute who had no intention of being faithful. They had three children to signify the choices God's people made and His choice to take a step back from mercy in favor of judgment. Hosea was a prophet during the time of national rebellion you've read so much about. Nothing about what God asked Hosea to do was normal or expected, yet it supplied visual clues to what He had to do to move people back to Him. It also points to the fact that God was for all nations in that He would make Himself known to people who didn't know Him (Gentiles) who could pray, "You are my God." (This was likely you.) Hosea heard from God ahead of time that this miracle would take place.

Prayer Starter

Lord God, thank You so much for making it possible for me to say that You're my God. Help me be a family member who looks forward to following You today and. . .

DAY 269

HOSEA 6–10

Prayer Scripture

Now they shall say, "We have no king because we
did not fear the LORD. What then should a king do
for us?" They have spoken words, swearing falsely
in making a covenant. Thus, judgment springs
up like hemlock in the furrows of the field.
HOSEA 10:3–4

Prayer Thought for the Day

You may remember a time when the people of Israel demanded a king while rejecting God as their king. He gave them a king, but it wasn't enough. They kept chasing things that seemed more important than God. In Hosea 10:3–4 the people recognize they no longer had a national leader because they'd rejected God. They even believed that if they had a king it wouldn't improve things. They recognized that the mess they made for themselves by rejecting God was bigger than any human could fix. The best they could do was make promises they couldn't keep and sign agreements they would break. In this way, if they had a king, that king couldn't really lead because they were just like everyone else. God was always the answer. The people just needed to spend more time with their questions.

Prayer Starter

Father, when I think about someone who really leads, help me to always think of You first. I'll need help getting to a better place. Only You can do that. Turn my attention to You and. . .

DAY 270
HOSEA 11–14

Prayer Scripture

Take words with you and return to the Lord. Say to Him,
"Take away all iniquity and receive us graciously, so we will render
the sacrifices of our lips. Assyria shall not save us. We will not
ride on horses, nor will we say anymore to the work of our hands,
'You are our gods.' For in You the fatherless find mercy."
Hosea 14:2–3

Prayer Thought for the Day

In this sample prayer, the people were encouraged to question their choices, review whom they trusted, and consider why compassion was something God offered in His mercy. This prayer was admitting that God was right when every other human choice was wrong. Every experiment that required a side trip from God's mercy resulted in disaster, but these side trips were common.

Admitting personal lawbreaking is key to a return to the only thing that actually works. God waits to hear from people who are often too stubborn to admit they're lost without Him. But this has never been news to Him. He waits for you to admit what He already knows, because until you make that choice, you're not really ready to return to the journey. So—He waits for you.

Prayer Starter

Lord God, turning from a pattern of lawbreaking damages my pride but is the only way to access real help. I don't want to be stubborn. I simply want to know You. . .

DAY 271

JOEL 1–3

Prayer Scripture

O Lord, to You I will cry, for the fire has devoured the pastures of the wilderness and the flame has burned all the trees of the field. The beasts of the field cry also to You, for the rivers of waters are dried up and the fire has devoured the pastures of the wilderness.

Joel 1:19–20

Prayer Thought for the Day

Many of God's people had been forcibly removed from their homes and were slaves in rival nations. Joel is just three chapters in length, and God did most of the talking; but in a few verses in the first chapter, it seems that even the land was suffering from the lawbreaking of the people. Pastures were burned and flames spread to trees, which meant a reduction in food and the elimination of shade. The streams were dry, and animals were looking for water, with little success. It seems to be more than a suggestion that the sin of the people caused a land once referred to as "flowing with milk and honey" to resemble an arid wasteland. Maybe your world seems just as desolate and in need of a refreshing only God can bring. Pray—for His kind of rain.

Prayer Starter

Father, let me pay enough attention to know that there's something wrong in my friendship with You. May You never have to take drastic action when inviting me to return when I have. . .

DAY 272
AMOS 1–5

Prayer Scripture

Can two walk together unless they are agreed? . . . Surely the Lord God will do nothing unless He reveals His secret to His servants the prophets. The lion has roared. Who will not fear? The Lord God has spoken. Who can but prophesy?

Amos 3:3, 7–8

Prayer Thought for the Day

The people of Israel and Judah had proven that they couldn't agree to walk with God. He used the prophets to amplify His message of judgment. He shared His message with the prophets, who shared it with those participating in the great walkaway. The prophets agreed to walk with God, and He kept speaking to them because they were the few that would walk with Him. They were the few who would listen. Nothing that was happening to the people was done in secret. God told His messenger-prophets, and they told the people. The people refused to listen, or if they did they rejected the message. They were invited to walk with God, but they wouldn't even talk with Him. When you agree with God, your walk begins—or continues.

Prayer Starter

Lord God, talk with me as I walk with You. Let me agree that Yours is a good plan and I'm in the best position when I'm with You learning, following, and. . .

DAY 273

AMOS 6–9; OBADIAH

Prayer Scripture

"On Mount Zion shall be deliverance. And there shall be holiness. And the house of Jacob shall possess their possessions. And the house of Jacob shall be a fire, and the house of Joseph a flame, and the house of Esau for stubble". . .for the LORD has spoken it.

OBADIAH 17–18

Prayer Thought for the Day

These verses are found in the shortest book of the Old Testament, from the prophet Obadiah. They contain truths that are worth another look. In the midst of exile, God had promised that there was a coming day of deliverance, holiness, and ownership. God said that though Israel was once a place for destruction, this would change. God also reminded other nations that while they were useful in correcting Israel, they weren't asked to be cruel to the exiles, and He would set this right in the end. The bold declaration is that God had not given up, was not giving up, and would not give up on those He corrects. He'll work to remove what isn't precious so there's room for what He's always said was important.

Prayer Starter

Father, thank You for refusing to give up on me. It can seem intimidating that You hold me to such a high standard. It's reassuring to know I can be forgiven. Give me a willingness to agree to walk with You so I can. . .

DAY 274
JONAH 1–4

Prayer Scripture

[Jonah prayed,] When my soul fainted within me, I remembered
the Lord, and my prayer came in to You, into Your holy temple.
Those who observe lying vanities abandon their own mercy.
But I will sacrifice to You with the voice of thanksgiving.
I will pay what I have vowed. Salvation is of the Lord.
Jonah 2:7–9

Prayer Thought for the Day

It's a familiar story—one man, one message, one big fish, one three-day time-out, and one reluctant act of obedience. Somewhere in the middle of a big fish in a big ocean this prodigal prophet named Jonah finally chose to speak to God instead of running from Him. To be fair, there wasn't much else he could do. He was God's captive audience. And in the internal fish juices, Jonah had a temporary change of heart. He prayed from the belly of a fish that ushered him to the throne room of God. He told God that he was ready to obey. He acknowledged that the only way out of his predicament was God's willingness to rescue. Running never solves your need to be found.

Prayer Starter

Lord God, when I want to turn away, keep me focused on Your willingness to forgive and show mercy. May I offer thanks for Your help even when I struggle with. . .

DAY 275
MICAH 1–7

Prayer Scripture

He does not retain His anger forever, because He delights in mercy. He will turn again. He will have compassion on us. He will subdue our iniquities. And You will cast all their sins into the depths of the sea.
MICAH 7:18–19

Prayer Thought for the Day

It's a good day when a prophet shares good news. It was even a good day when a prophet shared bad news. The reason that's true is that once bad days run their course the good days will return. The result of both pieces of news is that God will orchestrate the good and remove the bad. God's anger, observed by the people, wouldn't last forever. Mercy would make a comeback. Compassion could be expected. Sin could be overcome and forgiven. When God removed each instance of lawbreaking, it was completely expunged from the record. This sounded very much like the covenant that would be delivered when Jesus came.

Prayer Starter

Father, I'm amazed at the evidence that proves how You take bad circumstances and reshape them into impressive outcomes. I don't want to despair when I'm being corrected, because the outcome will be. . .

DAY 276

NAHUM 1–3; HABAKKUK 1–3

Prayer Scripture

[Habakkuk prayed,] "Although the fig tree shall not blossom, nor shall fruit be on the vines, the labor of the olive shall fail, and the fields shall yield no food, the flock shall be cut off from the fold, and there shall be no herd in the stalls, yet I will rejoice in the LORD. I will rejoice in the God of my salvation."

HABAKKUK 3:17–18

Prayer Thought for the Day

Make a list of everything that didn't go according to your plans over the last year. Recall the big and small things that were more than just standard irritants. Some probably seemed unfair. Some left you uncertain. All were unwanted. Habakkuk 3 provides one of these lists. There was no food nor growth, no harvest, and no livestock. The people were hungry, and everything they worked for came to nothing. But Habakkuk's choice in response was to rejoice, sing praise, and worship the God who saves. Don't get caught up in all the things that didn't go your way. Remember the God who rescues and whose long-term plan makes today's struggle seem a waste of concern.

Prayer Starter

Lord God, help me not to get so focused on whether I'm as comfortable as I want to be that I miss seeing the amazing things You do for me and in those around me. Help me to look to Your future for. . .

DAY 277
ZEPHANIAH 1–3; HAGGAI 1–2

Prayer Scripture

The word of the LORD came by Haggai the prophet,
saying, "Is it time for you. . .to dwell in your paneled
houses and this house to remain desolate?" Now, therefore,
this is what the LORD of hosts says: "Consider your ways.
You have sown much and bring in little. You eat, but you do
not have enough. You drink, but you are not filled with drink.
You clothe yourselves, but there is no one warm. And he who
earns wages earns wages to put it into a bag with holes."
HAGGAI 1:3–6

Prayer Thought for the Day

God pointed out, through Haggai, that the traditional pursuit of prosperity missed the point. The people were planting crops with nothing to harvest. They ate but were never satisfied. They drank but remained thirsty. They wore clothes but remained cold. They worked hard to earn money that they couldn't keep. At the end of the day it seemed things were worse than when they started. And all of this introspective thought went back to God's great request, "Consider your ways." If the people wouldn't pursue God, then they were bound to be let down by anything they accepted as a substitute.

Pray to know God's better pursuit.

Prayer Starter

Father, help me to resist chasing what will never satisfy or spending time and money on things that have no eternal benefit. Give me a better perspective on how You. . .

DAY 278
ZECHARIAH 1–4

Prayer Scripture

"Do not be like your fathers, to whom the former prophets have cried, saying, 'This is what the LORD of hosts says: "Turn now from your evil ways, and from your evil doings,"' but they did not hear or listen to Me," says the LORD. "Your fathers, where are they? And the prophets, do they live forever?"
ZECHARIAH 1:4–5

Prayer Thought for the Day

The prophets in the Bible weren't confined to one period of time. Zechariah was a prophet during the time of King Darius. Prophets spoke to the people on behalf of God in good times and bad. Sometimes these prophets were not giving God's message in the midst of justice. Some were given messages warning of coming judgment. This prophecy was linked to a future that included Jesus. The message seemed simple—if God wasn't followed by their parents, then the children needed to make a choice that didn't result in the same failed outcome.

Use your ears to hear and eyes to see. Pay attention. No one lives forever. How are you preparing for what comes next?

Prayer Starter

Lord God, help me learn from You and from the mistakes I see others make so I understand that You don't want me to make the same mistakes. May my prayers line up with Your desire to find me following. . .

DAY 279
ZECHARIAH 5–9

Prayer Scripture

"Rejoice greatly, O daughter of Zion; shout, O daughter of Jerusalem. Behold, your King comes to you. He is just and possessing salvation, lowly, and riding on a donkey, and on a colt, the foal of a donkey. . . . And He shall speak peace to the nations. And His dominion shall be from sea even to sea, and from the river even to the ends of the earth."

Zechariah 9:9–10

Prayer Thought for the Day

This is another prophecy—but, instead of judgment, this foretells a rescue with plot twists. The prophecy was about a coming King with worldwide dominion. No boundaries will prevent His rule and reign. This foretells the reign of Jesus. No one knew or had heard of Him, but this was a prophecy that looked forward to something God was—and is—still doing. What probably confused the hearers was that this incredible King, who was just and could rescue, was also lowly. Kings weren't lowly. People served kings. The God whom you pray to in Jesus' name was talking about His Son who would be king, but He was nothing like what people expected.

You know Jesus. You know the plot twists. This should make it easier to pray to the Great Rescuer.

Prayer Starter

Father, thank You for the plot twists that rescued my soul from a horrible ending. Thank You for showing me that serving is important to You. May I learn to follow Your example by. . .

DAY 280
ZECHARIAH 10–14

Prayer Scripture

It shall come to pass that everyone who is left of all the nations that came against Jerusalem shall even go up from year to year to worship the King, the LORD of hosts, and to keep the Feast of Tabernacles.
ZECHARIAH 14:16

Prayer Thought for the Day

Zechariah may have been offering a prophecy about the moments of earth's final years. It speaks of the people of Jerusalem who had been corrected by God before being brought home. Many enemies thought it was their job to continue punishing the nation that had disappointed God. Most of those nations also received God's judgment. But what Zechariah seems to be saying is that those nations that were being judged would one day worship the God who corrected them. This would be made possible by the soon coming Messiah who made the worship of God a freedom—worldwide.

The prayer you pray and the worship you offer is absolutely your right, and it's appropriate. *Pray.* Take the moment, make the time for the sake of worship.

Prayer Starter

Lord God, I'm honored that You accept my worship. Thanks for including me in Your rescue plan and for inviting me to make this worship a daily part of. . .

DAY 281
MALACHI 1–4

Prayer Scripture

You have wearied the LORD with your words. Yet you say, "How have we wearied Him?" When you say, "Everyone who does evil is good in the sight of the LORD, and He delights in them," or "Where is the God of judgment?"
MALACHI 2:17

Prayer Thought for the Day

The final book in the Old Testament is a warning about God culture. This was the idea that it was reasonable to keep God part of the national dialogue, but there was no real need to ask Him for help or follow Him most of the time. The people kept God around like a dusty family Bible. They didn't mind paying homage to what they thought was an increasingly archaic concept. It was a part of their family heritage, but God needed it to be more. The people had become lukewarm, and that's never been God's favorite temperature. This was true for those who heard that their twisted perspective was wrong in Malachi's message. It's true today for those who accept reminders of God without encouraging the act of following Him. Pray and ask God for wisdom. You'll need it in order to really follow instead of only agreeing that it's probably a good idea.

Prayer Starter

Father, may You be more to me than the object of a good song or a name on a piece of wall art. I want to be more serious about following than just. . .

DAY 282
MATTHEW 1–4

Prayer Scripture

When Jesus was born in Bethlehem of Judea in the days of Herod the king, behold, there came wise men from the east to Jerusalem, saying, "Where is He who is born King of the Jews? For we have seen His star in the East and have come to worship Him."
MATTHEW 2:1–2

Prayer Thought for the Day

God said Gentiles would worship Him, and that happened when a small contingent of wise men from way outside Jerusalem arrived to worship the baby Jesus. Prophecies about God's new covenant with the world had come true—and that covenant was inclusively exclusive. What does that mean? Well, it means that anyone can be included, but it's exclusive to those who actually accept God's rescue. Men from the east came to see the infant King, and their words, actions, and gifts spoke praise to God's perfect plan to rescue every willing human. This was worth prayers of praise then and now. It has never changed.

Prayer Starter

Lord God, as I read through Your statement of grace in the New Testament, help me to remember that You actually want me to be willing to tell You why I believe You're trustworthy and worth following today. So. . .

DAY 283
MATTHEW 5–7

Prayer Scripture

[Jesus said,] "Your Father knows what things you have need of before you ask Him. Therefore, pray according to this manner: Our Father who is in heaven, hallowed be Your name. Your kingdom come. Your will be done on earth as it is in heaven. Give us this day our daily bread. And forgive us our debts, as we forgive our debtors. And do not lead us into temptation, but deliver us from evil. For Yours is the kingdom and the power and the glory forever. Amen."
Matthew 6:8–13

Prayer Thought for the Day

Hearing Jesus teach must have been very strange for people who'd read the words of prophets about God's judgment and correction. Through His teachings they'd experienced life apart from the laws God offered their ancestors. They were waiting for the Messiah, but they didn't recognize Him when He arrived to teach them. Now, they were hearing a man teach on prayer, and it seemed something more than just obedience. It included others and invited the heart to join the acts of obedience. This must have seemed more personal—certainly different. This was a prayer that finally recognized God as King. This hadn't been the norm since Saul was chosen by Samuel and God was no longer considered their leader.

Prayer Starter

Father, this prayer that seems ordinary today was revolutionary when Jesus spoke it. This helps me to realize the blessing of knowing You personally and…

DAY 284
MATTHEW 8–9

Prayer Scripture

When [Jesus] saw the multitudes, He was moved with compassion for them, because they fainted and were scattered about, like sheep having no shepherd. Then He said to His disciples, "The harvest truly is plentiful, but the laborers are few. Therefore pray to the Lord of the harvest, that He will send forth laborers into His harvest."

MATTHEW 9:36–38

Prayer Thought for the Day

With no shepherds to teach them, God's people lived and died without understanding of the hope God offered them and how they could live for Him. Jesus not only noticed their need, but His compassion led Him to request prayer that all humanity would become wise. He asked His disciples to pray that God would send a solution—people who would work to bring knowledge of God to His scattered sheep. Jesus' prayer was well beyond simple instruction—it was for harvest laborers who would take what they were learning and share it with those who lived outside everything that led to understanding. The people simply existed. They experienced no hope because they were uncertain it existed. They needed someone to tell them.

It is the same need you once had. Perhaps you could be an answer to this prayer.

Prayer Starter

Lord God, help me to share what I learn while I seek to understand the needs around me. Give me a heart that cares for those who need You. May I become willing to. . .

DAY 285

MATTHEW 10–11

Prayer Scripture

[Jesus said,] "Come to Me, all you who labor and are heavy-laden, and I will give you rest. Take My yoke on you and learn from Me, for I am meek and lowly in heart, and you shall find rest for your souls. For My yoke is easy and My burden is light."

MATTHEW 11:28–30

Prayer Thought for the Day

Here Jesus compared God's people to an overburdened ox that struggled to pull a load. It may seem an unflattering comparison, yet people often feel overwhelmed by everyday burdens. The daily work of following God, providing for a family, and perhaps caring for aging parents was enough to burden any first-century Jew.

Jesus was not seeking to add more weight to their load. He invited these people to learn from Him how to carry a lighter load than the one their religious leaders had given them, which included many unnecessary additional rules and regulations. They also would find rest because Jesus takes all worry deposits. They'd be comforted because He's approachable.

Maybe you've prayed for just such an offer. It's always been available to you. Stay close, resist wandering, and let Jesus remove worry.

Prayer Starter

Father, if I'm to be compared to an ox, help me to admit that sometimes I'm insecure even when I act as strong as that animal. As I come close to You, please teach me, give me rest, and give me every opportunity to. . .

DAY 286
MATTHEW 12–13

Prayer Scripture

[The people of Nazareth] took offense at Him. But Jesus said to them, "A prophet is not without honor except in his own country and in his own house." And He did not do many mighty works there because of their unbelief.
MATTHEW 13:57–58

Prayer Thought for the Day

Jesus was well aware of the many prophets who were abused, neglected, overlooked, and ridiculed. He may have been thinking of men like Moses, Elisha, Jeremiah, and Isaiah who each faced their own struggle as they spoke the truth. Many prophets found willing listeners outside their own hometown, while friends, family, and neighbors rejected what they had to say. Jesus was saying that their experience was His experience. He had things to say, but many who knew Him His entire earthbound life seemed to consider His words foolish. They had no honor for the man who was once a boy who lived down the road.

God doesn't leave you where you once were. He has a plan for you that others may struggle to believe is possible. Pray to accept His plan and to withstand any rejection you may encounter.

Prayer Starter

Lord God, thank You for doing the hard work of changing me. Even when others can't believe it's true, help me to find the place where You can work in me to. . .

DAY 287
MATTHEW 14–16

Prayer Scripture

[Jesus] commanded the multitude to sit down on the grass, and took the five loaves and the two fish, and looking up to heaven, He blessed and broke and gave the loaves to His disciples, and the disciples to the multitude. And they all ate and were filled, and they took up twelve baskets full of the fragments that remained. And those who had eaten were about five thousand men, besides women and children.

MATTHEW 14:19–21

Prayer Thought for the Day

No other human knew what Jesus would do on the day described in Matthew 14. Thousands of people came to hear Him teach, and He taught. They were nowhere near a city where food could be found to feed the crowd. When this situation was discovered, the consensus seemed to be to send the people away so they could find food wherever possible. Jesus had other plans that involved a willing boy, a lunch, and faith. Jesus supplied the blessing. A miracle took place, bellies were filled, and the leftover fish and bread were more than what Jesus started with. Faith and blessing provided a miracle that was greater than anything the crowd could have expected.

Prayer Starter

Father, may I always understand that the benefit of prayer is an answer that defies explanation. Impossible only becomes possible with prayer. Help me to speak words that invite You to. . .

DAY 288
MATTHEW 17–19

Prayer Scripture

The disciples came to Jesus by themselves and said, "Why could we not cast him out?" And Jesus said to them, "Because of your unbelief. For truly, I say to you, if you have faith like a grain of mustard seed, you shall say to this mountain, 'Move from here to a distant place,' and it shall move, and nothing shall be impossible for you. However, this kind does not go out but by prayer and fasting."
MATTHEW 17:19–21

Prayer Thought for the Day

The disciples tested their faith by attempting big things on behalf of their teacher, but they couldn't heal an insane boy. Perhaps they thought that if they said words that sounded like what Jesus would have said, they could create a miracle where none had previously existed—but they couldn't. Maybe they thought that because they were close friends of Jesus this would be enough—it wasn't. Their faith appeared to be less than the power they assumed was found in words. Their prayers hadn't allowed God to intervene in the work they were attempting to do. The disciples would learn, but they hadn't on this day.

Prayer Starter

Lord God, may I never reduce my faith in You to a few magic words, believing You honor this kind of performance. Give me a heart that wants You to join me, because my strength will never be enough to. . .

DAY 289
MATTHEW 20–21

Prayer Scripture

The multitudes who went before and those who followed cried, saying, "Hosanna to the Son of David. Blessed is He who comes in the name of the Lord. Hosanna in the highest!" And when He had come into Jerusalem, all the city was moved, saying, "Who is this?" And the multitude said, "This is Jesus the prophet from Nazareth of Galilee."

Matthew 21:9–11

Prayer Thought for the Day

This was an example of the large-scale praise of Jesus. While it would become more common as time passed, this worship service was bold, loud, and short lived. Some weren't exactly sure what the noise of the people meant. For those who witnessed Jesus that day, this was a man worth worshipping. But the worship they offered may have been based on what they thought they could get by worshipping Him, not because anything meaningful happened in their hearts. Within a week many of these same people were making a new noise that was gaining equal attention. Instead of worshipping Jesus, they turned 180 degrees and were demanding His death. They moved from a vocal prayer of praise to the angry demonstration of the disillusioned.

Why might your opinion of Jesus change because of who you're around or how you feel?

Prayer Starter

Father, may I believe in You even when I'm unsure why You make certain decisions. Give me the endurance I need to worship You when. . .

DAY 290
MATTHEW 22–23

Prayer Scripture

Jesus said to him, "'You shall love the Lord your God with all your heart, and with all your soul, and with all your mind.' This is the first and great commandment. And the second is like it: 'You shall love your neighbor as yourself.' On these two commandments hang all the Law and the Prophets."

MATTHEW 22:37–39

Prayer Thought for the Day

The advice Jesus gave to a religious leader was sound and seemed simple. All the laws God had given in the Old Testament and the warnings given by the prophets were linked to a lack of two things: People didn't love God, and they didn't care about the people around them. The remedy was worth praying about.

When you struggle, evaluate whether you love God enough to follow. Ask Him if you're self-centered or if you show compassion to those who need it. To stay away from love will always diminish your willingness and ability to interact with God and the people He made. Isolation is not a suitable friend.

Prayer Starter

Lord God, You love me; You teach me to love You and others. This has always been my choice to make. I need to choose a closeness that demands no judgment and offers the closeness of friendship. May I make these good choices today when I. . .

DAY 291
MATTHEW 24–25

Prayer Scripture

"The King shall say to those on His right hand, 'Come, you blessed of My Father, inherit the kingdom prepared for you from the foundation of the world. For I was hungry and you gave Me food; I was thirsty and you gave Me drink; I was a stranger and you took Me in; naked and you clothed Me; I was sick and you visited Me; I was in prison and you came to Me.'"
MATTHEW 25:34–36

Prayer Thought for the Day

Jesus took the idea of loving God and others to another place when He described caring for people who were hungry, thirsty, sick, strangers, or prisoners and then stepping in to help them whenever possible. Jesus went so far as to say that when people do this for others, they're doing it for Him. Why? Because it's what He'd been doing while He was walking the earth. He didn't just look at helping others as an option—it was an extension of who He was.

When you choose to pray for those in need, it will be something that enhances your willingness to help. Your help is exactly what God wants from you. Start with prayer and then take another step.

Prayer Starter

Father, loving You and others is the reason I can step in to help when help's needed. This is Your example to me, and I want to. . .

DAY 292
MATTHEW 26

Prayer Scripture

[Jesus said to His disciples,] "My soul is exceedingly sorrowful, even to death. Remain here and watch with Me." And He went a little farther and fell on His face, and prayed, saying, "O My Father, if it is possible, let this cup pass from Me. Nevertheless, not as I will, but as You will."

Matthew 26:38–39

Prayer Thought for the Day

When Jesus prayed, "If it is possible, let this cup pass from Me," He was talking about His coming crucifixion. Jesus prayed prayers God wanted to answer, but if God answered this very specific prayer, then rescue would have looked very different. You never needed to worry about the alternative, because after Jesus spoke these words from a place of human struggle, He went on to say, "Nevertheless, not as I will, but as You will." Jesus was telling His Father that no matter what—He was all in. A key takeaway here is that when you pray you're free to express the way you think things should be, but be equally willing to accept that God may have better plans.

Prayer Starter

Lord God, there are things I never want to face, but if I need to, please go with me and give me everything I need to endure the challenge. Take my fear and make me willing to. . .

DAY 293

MATTHEW 27-28

Prayer Scripture

About the ninth hour Jesus cried with a loud voice,
saying, "Eli, Eli, lama sabachthani?"—that is to say,
"My God, My God, why have You forsaken Me?"
MATTHEW 27:46

Prayer Thought for the Day

This prayer from a dying Jesus was a fulfillment of prophecy. God had temporarily rejected His Son. It wasn't because He didn't love Jesus. But in order to be the sacrifice for the sins of mankind, all of the lawbreaking that would ever occur was placed on Him. God—who's holy, just, and set apart—couldn't remain in the presence of sin. Jesus died alone, rejected by mankind, with God's back intentionally facing Him for the first time.

He did this for you by saying a prayer you'll never have to pray. When you pray, remember these profound gifts that changed everything about how you can relate to God.

Prayer Starter

Father, it's sobering to remember that Your Son paid the penalty for my sin. It's humbling to know that this happened because Your Son's life was given for mine. It's gratifying to know that I can come to You because You. . .

DAY 294
MARK 1–3

Prayer Scripture

In the morning, rising up a great while before day, He went out and departed to a solitary place and prayed there. And Simon and those who were with Him followed after Him. And when they had found Him, they said to Him, "All men are looking for You."
MARK 1:35–37

Prayer Thought for the Day

Jesus counted time alone with God among His most welcome moments. He rose early, spent time without distraction, and talked to His Father. These times were likely filled with prayers for the people He taught and for guidance about how to best finish what He'd started by coming to live among humanity. Jesus' disciples sought Him because the people in the region were relentless in their pursuit of this teacher. They probably had no idea He was God's Son, but Jesus could do miracles, and the hope these miracles inspired was equal to the demands that He do more.

When you seek Jesus, come with more than a list of the things you'd like God to do. Include gratitude for what He's already done and share the needs of others around you.

Prayer Starter

Lord God, let me find many reasons to pray. I don't want to just pray because I believe You're the best one to ask for the things I want. Help me to seek You because You're a friend who. . .

DAY 295
MARK 4–6

Prayer Scripture

[Jesus] was in the stern of the ship, asleep on a pillow. And they awoke Him and said to Him, "Master, do You not care that we are perishing?" And He arose and rebuked the wind and said to the sea, "Peace, be still." And the wind ceased and there was a great calm. And He said to them, "Why are you so fearful? How is it that you have no faith?"

Mark 4:38–40

Prayer Thought for the Day

This is an example of a desperate prayer. The disciples were on a boat. Jesus was sleeping in the stern, and a storm greater than anything they'd ever seen threatened death with every aggressive wave. These men feared for their lives. They tried not to disturb the sleep of their teacher, but at some point their desperation became so deeply etched in their thinking that they said something very foolish: "Do You not care that we are perishing?" This was a man who performed amazing miracles, healed the sick, and invited them on the journey of their lives. Did they really think He didn't care? Did they really think He wasn't powerful enough?

Desperation can lead to very peculiar prayers. Start praying before desperation rewrites your words.

Prayer Starter

Father, may I refuse to wait to pray. I want to be so connected to You that praying is a first step and not the last. . .

DAY 296
MARK 7–9

Prayer Scripture

The Pharisees and scribes asked [Jesus], "Why do Your disciples not walk according to the tradition of the elders but eat bread with unwashed hands?" He answered and said to them, "Isaiah prophesied well of you hypocrites, as it is written: 'This people honors Me with their lips, but their heart is far from Me.'"

MARK 7:5–6

Prayer Thought for the Day

Maybe you've heard the old saying "Cleanliness is next to godliness." That was a favorite of moms and grandmas talking to their dirty offspring, but Mark 7 suggests that godliness is far superior to cleanliness. That's not to say cleanliness can't be considered a fine objective, but when the Pharisees got so caught up in whether the disciples had washed their hands, Jesus was quick to point out that this may have sounded like something that honored God but was not said from the heart of someone who loved or cared for Him. Your prayers can sound inspired, but when they don't make the foot-and-a-half connection between your head and heart, they will always miss the mark—and communication might not have really taken place.

Prayer Starter

Lord God, more than how I look, what I wear, or even the way I speak, You want to hear from me and know what's really bothering me. Help me to be honest every time I. . .

DAY 297
MARK 10–11

Prayer Scripture

[The rich young ruler] answered and said to Him, "Master, all these I have kept from my youth." Then, looking at him, Jesus loved him and said to him, "One thing you lack: go your way, sell whatever you have, and give to the poor, and you shall have treasure in heaven. And come, take up the cross and follow Me." And he was sad at that saying and went away grieved, for he had great possessions.

MARK 10:20–22

Prayer Thought for the Day

It almost seemed as if this rich young ruler was interested in getting a gold star for outstanding performance from Jesus. He knelt before Jesus as if in prayer and asked, "Good Master, what shall I do that I may inherit eternal life?" (verse 17). It sounded like a sincere question, so Jesus gave him good advice. He essentially said, "Follow the commandments." The man must have perked up. "Yeah, I do that." Then Jesus said something astonishing. He wanted the man to demonstrate his love for others by sharing all he had with the poor and following Him. That apparently was a deal breaker. He was willing to keep the law but failed to recognize the law was designed to inspire people to love each other.

Prayer Starter

Father, may I obey You and love all. May I accept Your good gifts and share my own. May I find my treasure when I follow. . .

DAY 298
MARK 12–13

Prayer Scripture

[Jesus] called His disciples to Himself and said to them, "Truly I say to you that this poor widow has cast in more than all those who have cast into the treasury, for all those cast in out of their abundance, but she, out of her need, cast in all that she had, even all her living."
MARK 12:43–44

Prayer Thought for the Day

In this giving parade, the more impressive floats seemed to already have passed by. Jesus saw it differently. At the end of the parade was one barely noticed woman with little to offer those who wanted to be impressed. Those who went before her made a grand show of their wealth. It was a veritable who's who of the rich-and-willing-to-flaunt-it. But this woman walked her living prayer to the collection box and deposited two small coins. The clink of her coins was barely discernible. Jesus watched, and for Him, this parade ended with a showstopper. The disciples were probably focused on the size of the gift, but Jesus was focused on the worship behind the gift. He determined that her generosity far exceeded that of the men who wanted recognition. Jesus didn't look at the value of the metal that formed her gift. He looked at the heart of the one who gave it.

Prayer Starter

Lord God, let me share without a parade. Give me a heart that isn't looking to be a headline act. Help me to remember. . .

DAY 299
MARK 14–16

Prayer Scripture

Being in Bethany in the house of Simon the leper, as [Jesus] sat at the table, a woman came with an alabaster box of very precious ointment of spikenard. And she broke the box and poured it on His head. And there were some who had indignation within themselves and said, "Why was this waste of the ointment made? For it might have been sold for more than three hundred pence and have been given to the poor." And they murmured against her.

Mark 14:3–5

Prayer Thought for the Day

The disciples were slow to learn. They assumed practicality was more spiritual than extravagance. They had witnessed the woman giving two coins, and instead of hearing what Jesus spoke about the heart of worship, they perhaps assumed He preferred small gifts. When a woman arrived at a home where Jesus was a guest, the disciples grew concerned. She poured expensive perfume over Jesus' head. Jesus accepted both acts of worship. One woman had little. One had much. But both worshipped. The disciples, unfortunately, seemed more concerned with what they could purchase with what the perfume was worth. There was still much to learn.

Prayer Starter

Father, let me refuse to judge how much someone loves You by what they're able to share. Let me only be concerned with the heart inside my chest that's either tuned to the rhythm of worship or not. I don't want to compare when. . .

DAY 300
LUKE 1

Prayer Scripture

The angel said to him, "Do not fear, Zechariah, for your prayer is heard. And your wife, Elizabeth, shall bear you a son, and you shall call his name John. And you shall have joy and gladness, and many shall rejoice at his birth. For he shall be great in the sight of the Lord."
LUKE 1:13–15

Prayer Thought for the Day

John the Baptist's birth had been predicted by the prophets Isaiah and Malachi. Yet it was also an answer to prayer by the priest Zechariah and his wife, Elizabeth. The angel Gabriel brought the very personal answer to prayer to the priest. John would be great, he would make a difference, and he would bring joy to his family. What may have sounded like an interest in verifying this report shows Zechariah questioning the validity of a claim from an angel. To prove the truth of the claim, Zechariah would be unable to speak until after John the Baptist was born. That presented a challenge to a priest.

A point to this answered prayer is you should truly believe God answers prayer so it's not a surprise when the answer arrives.

Prayer Starter

Lord God, I shouldn't wonder if You're big enough to answer prayer. I should be grateful when You do, instead of acting as if it must have been a mistake. Create in my heart a willingness to welcome Your answers with worship so I can. . .

DAY 301

LUKE 2–3

Prayer Scripture

Then [Simeon] took [Jesus] up in his arms and blessed God and said, Lord, now You are letting Your servant depart in peace, according to Your word. For my eyes have seen Your salvation that You have prepared before the face of all peoples, a light to enlighten the Gentiles, and the glory of Your people Israel.

LUKE 2:28–32

Prayer Thought for the Day

Simeon was an old man who met the eight-day-old Jesus. The elderly man had waited for this moment his entire life. He knew more about Jesus than most. He knew, for example, that Jesus came to rescue, that the prophets had written about Him, and that the Gentiles could receive the gift of this young boy. Eyes likely weakened by age looked in the face of God, and Simeon was content if not another day passed before his life journey ended. This was hope, joy, and answered prayer. It is also an example of how prayers may not be answered on the same day or in the same decade in which you pray. Be patient, knowing that with God's schedule it will show up just when it's needed most.

Prayer Starter

Father, it's hard to wait. When I pray for something, it's because it's important to me. Delay can make it seem as if You don't care. Help me to understand that Your answer may wait until I'm ready for it. Give me the patience to. . .

DAY 302
LUKE 4–5

Prayer Scripture

[The scribes and Pharisees] said to [Jesus], "Why do the disciples of John fast often and make prayers, and likewise the disciples of the Pharisees, but Yours eat and drink?" And He said to them, "Can you make the children of the bridechamber fast while the bridegroom is with them? But the days will come when the bridegroom shall be taken away from them."
Luke 5:33–35

Prayer Thought for the Day

The religious leaders noticed something you might not have. The disciples didn't seem to do much praying. This was important to the religious leaders. Maybe Jesus could do something about it and then thank them for showing Him the error of His ways—*or* Jesus could simply say that they had no real need to pray when they could talk to Him face-to-face whenever they wanted. This implied that Jesus believed He was God. He *is* God. Jesus said that His men would pray when He was physically removed from their everyday experience. Had anyone ever had the audacity to suggest that he was God and that those closest to him had no need to pray because they were hearing God's words? There really was something about Jesus. To some He brought comfort and to others suspicion. But God had come in the flesh, and changes were increasing.

Prayer Starter

Lord God, thank You for making needed changes in me. Help me to long to know Your answers when I have questions about. . .

DAY 303
LUKE 6–7

Prayer Scripture

[Jesus] spoke a parable to them: "Can the blind lead the blind? Shall they not both fall into the ditch? . . . And why do you look at the speck that is in your brother's eye but do not perceive the beam that is in your own eye?"
LUKE 6:39, 41

Prayer Thought for the Day

It may seem as if you're spiritually superior if you can point out every flaw. If this is a path you choose, be very careful. You could be giving good advice, but if you don't follow it, you may be called out for not practicing the very thing you're preaching. You're human and make mistakes. Anyone you talk to is human, and they also make mistakes. God *doesn't* make mistakes. Pray and ask God to intervene. Jesus is asking people to worry more about their own spiritual condition rather than condemning others for being in poor spiritual health. If God has helped you, He can help others. If God forgives you, He can forgive others. Because God loves you, it shouldn't be a surprise that He loves others. Pray before you point out others' flaws. Allow your interest in being a Pharisee to decrease.

Prayer Starter

Father, why is it always easier for me to see sin in the lives of other people, while I'm willing to excuse my own sin? Help me to cooperate with the change You want in me and love others by praying for. . .

DAY 304
LUKE 8–9

Prayer Scripture

It came to pass, as [Jesus] was alone praying, His disciples were with Him, and He asked them, saying, "Who do the people say that I am?" They answered and said, "John the Baptist, but some say Elijah, and others say that one of the old prophets has risen again." He said to them, "But who do you say that I am?" Peter answered and said, "The Christ of God."
LUKE 9:18–20

Prayer Thought for the Day

One of the most impulsive personalities in the Bible was with Jesus following a time of prayer. Jesus asked a question meant for the disciples, not for the crowds He encountered. After the disciples spent so much time with Jesus, they had a variety of answers. They suggested that some people thought He was one of several different prophets. Then Jesus looked at Peter and said, "Who do *you* say that I am?" It isn't clear if the answer was immediate, but Peter boldly suggested something not spoken openly: *You are the Messiah.* There was no question mark at the end of Peter's declaration. He believed it, no matter how unbelievable it sounded to others.

Prayer Starter

Lord God, may I be as firm in my belief about You as Peter was. But Peter would also deny You. I think most people struggle with that. Take my prayer time and give me a bold heart that. . .

DAY 305

LUKE 10–11

Prayer Scripture

In that hour Jesus rejoiced in spirit and said, "I thank You, O Father, Lord of heaven and earth, that You have hidden these things from the wise and prudent and have revealed them to infants. Even so, Father, for so it seemed good in Your sight."

LUKE 10:21

Prayer Thought for the Day

Have you ever wondered if Jesus needed to pray? That might be a bit like suggesting you should take a trip around the world and never check in with those you love most. Maybe you could do it, but why? Sometimes, when Jesus got alone with His Father, His prayer seemed like a progress report. Other times His prayer became an extended time of praise for God's wonderful plan that would result in the rescue of mankind. Notice this type of prayer in Luke 10. God took men who didn't seem wise by social standards and placed deep truths in their hearts, which would change the world. This ragged group of disciples would share God's good news that would impact nations. This knowledge allowed Jesus to praise God.

When you catch a glimpse of the good things God's doing, like Jesus, let Him know you realize you're witnessing something awesome.

Prayer Starter

Father, I've seen the good You do, and I've failed to let You know I'm grateful. Let me change my mind and tell You that today I'm in awe of. . .

DAY 306
LUKE 12–13

Prayer Scripture

[Jesus] said to His disciples, "Therefore I say to you, do not worry about your life, what you shall eat, nor for the body, what you shall put on. Life is more than food, and the body is more than clothing. Consider the ravens, for they neither sow nor reap; they have neither storehouse nor barn, and God feeds them. How much more are you worth than the fowls? And which of you by worrying can add one cubit to his stature?"
LUKE 12:22–25

Prayer Thought for the Day

In a worry? Luke 12 spotlights the fact that you're engaged in unproductive actions. You might respond to your concerns by prayerfully agonizing over all the things you worry about, and God will listen. He might remind you that He's told you often in His Word, "Fear not."

Or you could "cast all your burdens" in prayer, which means telling Him your struggles with fear and worry and asking Him to deal with what you can't. This is a better type of prayer. Surely God doesn't worry. He knows about all the things you need. Remember all the birds in the sky, which God feeds.

Worry can be deposited in prayer today. Pray now—God is standing by.

Prayer Starter

Lord God, worry only concerns You because it subtracts from my time to stay close to You. Help me to worry less and worship more. Take my worry so I can. . .

DAY 307
LUKE 14–15

Prayer Scripture

[Jesus said,] "There shall be more joy in heaven over one sinner who repents than over ninety-nine righteous people who need no repentance."
LUKE 15:7

Prayer Thought for the Day

Some might suggest this verse provides a free pass for a disobedient life. If at some point you come back to God, they would claim, He throws a bigger party than for those who have followed Him their entire life. Perhaps the greater point is that God doesn't want to see anyone separated from Him, based on their unwillingness to consider Him, even if they come to know Him late in life or just before death. The celebration is important because someone who was lost is found.

But when you know God earlier in life and pray, you get to spend years with God, time that a lawbreaker won't have. You get to experience life with God, while His deniers busily run away. You get daily rejoicing, while the sinner wastes time rejecting God.

Pray for that future rejoicing in heaven—because you want to see someone who should be very weary of running from God discover and take the better choice.

Prayer Starter

Father, may I join You in the choice to rejoice when someone willingly turns away from sin and follows You. May I reject criticism or even the expectation of instant perfection. May I just rejoice that You now have an influence, and they now have. . .

DAY 308
LUKE 16–17

Prayer Scripture

"Take heed to yourselves. If your brother trespasses against you, rebuke him. And if he repents, forgive him. And if he trespasses against you seven times in a day, and seven times in a day returns to you, saying, 'I repent,' you shall forgive him." And the apostles said to the Lord, "Increase our faith."

Luke 17:3–5

Prayer Thought for the Day

It almost seems amusing that when Jesus talked about forgiving difficult people, He said the offended ones should just continue to forgive. . .but from the disciples there was a very human response: "Increase our faith." It was almost as if they were admitting that they weren't sure they could do that—at least not without His help.

Make their three-word response your prayer: "Increase our faith." Gain some understanding that you'll always benefit from working through the hard instructions given in God's Word. The alternative is additional learning time and fewer opportunities to be as useful to God as you could be. The idea of asking God to increase your faith isn't selfish, because it's asking Him to help you be better prepared to be who He's always meant you to be.

Prayer Starter

Lord God, please boost my faith today. Do it again tomorrow and every day this week. When I lack, replenish my supply so I can forgive when. . .

DAY 309
LUKE 18–19

Prayer Scripture

"The tax collector, standing afar off, would not so much as lift up his eyes to heaven, but struck his breast, saying, 'God, be merciful to me, a sinner.' I tell you, this man went down to his house justified rather than the other. For everyone who exalts himself shall be humbled, and he who humbles himself shall be exalted."

LUKE 18:13–14

Prayer Thought for the Day

Jesus provided another object lesson for those willing to listen. This parable described a religious leader who used prayer to point out to God why he was better than most. In this man's view, his personal "righteousness" far exceeded those he considered bad—like tax collectors. So Jesus compared a tax collector's humble prayer to the "righteous" man's self-inflating one. The tax collector prayerfully admitted his sinful state and wasn't seeking any audience besides God. The result of this prayer comparison was that the one who wanted to get noticed was humbled and the already humble one would be remembered.

You don't need to compare yourself to others while you pray. You don't need to preach. Just use the time to connect with God. He already knows you and loves you very much.

Prayer Starter

Father, may I refuse to brag in my prayers. I'm more fortunate to have access to You than anything else I know. I'm unworthy, but You invite me to. . .

DAY 310
LUKE 20:1–22:38

Prayer Scripture

[Jesus] took bread, and gave thanks and broke it, and gave to them, saying, "This is My body that is given for you. Do this in remembrance of Me." Likewise He also took the cup after supper, saying, "This cup is the new covenant in My blood, which is shed for you."
LUKE 22:19–20

Prayer Thought for the Day

There were so many things going on when this prayer was prayed prior to the first communion. Jesus knew that among this group of men was Judas, who would betray Him; Peter, who would deny Him; Thomas, who would doubt Him; and the rest, who would temporarily run away when they witnessed trouble. Death was coming, and this is what Jesus acknowledged with the bread and the cup. Knowing all of this and more, Jesus chose to offer a prayer of thanks to God. The message of what these emblems represented didn't register with the disciples. Perhaps they thought it was just another lesson, and as with the parables, Jesus would tell them later what it meant.

Today you follow Jesus' example when you remember that the greatest response to His incredible sacrifice is "thanks."

Prayer Starter

Lord God, thank You for caring so much for my future that You provided assurance through something as simple as bread and a cup. Help me to remember Your sacrifice and gratefully say. . .

DAY 311
LUKE 22:39–24:53

Prayer Scripture

[Jesus] led them out as far as to Bethany, and He lifted up His hands and blessed them. And it came to pass, while He blessed them, He was parted from them and was carried up into heaven. And they worshipped Him, and returned to Jerusalem with great joy, and were continually in the temple praising and blessing God. Amen.

Luke 24:50–53

Prayer Thought for the Day

Jesus had been crucified. Then He rose from the dead. He spent time with His disciples. And then it was time for Him to leave and return to His place in heaven. He had helped the disciples move past their failings when soldiers came to take Him away. He had worked with Peter through his denial, and the disciples were finally coming to understand that while Jesus was no longer with them physically, He would always be with their spirits. This truth resulted in praise and joy. Why? While this seemed to many like an ending, for the disciples a new era had begun. The future had purpose—and it was very good.

Prayer Starter

Father, I can rejoice knowing that Jesus did what He came to do and left me with all the help I need to continue to be a part of the work He started. May I be willing to do what. . .

DAY 312
JOHN 1–3

Prayer Scripture

[John said,] "He who comes from heaven is above all. And what He has seen and heard, that He testifies. And no man receives His testimony. He who has received His testimony has certified that God is true. For He whom God has sent speaks the words of God, for God does not give the Spirit by measure to Him. The Father loves the Son and has given all things into His hand."

John 3:31–35

Prayer Thought for the Day

If you're going to pray, please understand that there's a connection between the message of the four Gospels in the New Testament and the God you've read so much about. John was declaring in this John 3 passage that Jesus came from heaven and is above everything. He speaks about heavenly things because that's His home. He can speak for God because God sent Him to speak. Jesus brought the new covenant with Him, and He fulfilled His roles and responsibilities to allow this covenant to become fully enforced. Jesus wasn't an underling. He wasn't an angel. He wasn't just a teacher, rabbi, or prophet. Jesus was God's Son and the key to the rescue from an eternity separated from God. This was His story, His mission, His plan. It was unexpected and absolutely perfect.

Prayer Starter

Lord God, Your Son is the reason I can choose to follow You. Thank You for Jesus. May I learn to be faithful by. . .

DAY 313
JOHN 4–5

Prayer Scripture

[Jesus said,] "The hour is coming, and now has come, when the true worshippers shall worship the Father in spirit and in truth. For the Father seeks such to worship Him. God is a Spirit, and those who worship Him must worship Him in spirit and in truth."

JOHN 4:23–24

Prayer Thought for the Day

Jesus spoke in a way that was both confusing to those who heard it for the first time and clarifying for those who were beginning to understand.

Worship had often been thought of as a time of prayer and singing within the temple. The location for worship was different for Israel and Samaria. Jesus had been talking to a woman from Samaria when the subject came up. Was Jesus suggesting that worship was something individual and apart from a specific location? Because Jesus came, worship was to be thought of in terms of a spiritual exercise that could be engaged in individually and anywhere. No one needed to wait for a special occasion in a special location to worship God. Neither do you.

Prayer Starter

Father, You've given me the gift of worship, and there are no restrictions on where I honor You. I can take You anywhere I go, and You can alter the steps we take together. May I always see You as worthy of worship, and when I do, may I. . .

DAY 314
JOHN 6–7

Prayer Scripture

Jesus said to the twelve, "Will you also go away?" Then Simon Peter answered Him, "Lord, to whom shall we go? You have the words of eternal life. And we believe and are sure that You are the Christ, the Son of the living God."
John 6:67–69

Prayer Thought for the Day

The religious leaders had no use for Jesus. He wasn't just a nuisance to them—He was viewed as a threat. The longer Jesus unpacked all the details of His purpose, the further He took some out of their comfort zone. In John 6 you read about some who'd followed and were out of patience. They turned their sandals in the direction of home. They performed their own exodus away from the very thing that could rescue them. As these unnamed followers abandoned Jesus, He asked the twelve disciples closest to Him if they too wanted to abandon Him. Peter summed it up nicely by saying that Jesus spoke words of eternal life that the disciples believed.

Going anywhere else made no sense. It still doesn't. You get to speak to the God who offered words that lead to eternal life. Don't go anywhere without Him.

Prayer Starter

Lord God, You don't abandon me, and I don't want to abandon You. The words You give are life, and I need them every day. May this friendship continue to grow, and may I. . .

DAY 315
JOHN 8–9

Prayer Scripture

[The religious leaders] called the man who was blind and said to him, "Give God the praise. We know that this man is a sinner." He answered and said, "Whether He is a sinner or not I do not know. One thing I know: that although I was blind, now I see." Then they said to him again, "What did He do to you? How did He open your eyes?" He answered them, "I have told you already, and you did not hear. Why do you want to hear it again? Will you also be His disciples?"

John 9:24–27

Prayer Thought for the Day

It wasn't the type of eye appointment you'd expect, but a blind man received vision restoration. Jesus did that, and the man was very happy. The religious leaders? Not so much. They were so concerned about who did the miracle that they paid almost no attention to the miracle itself. Interestingly, the religious leaders interrogated this man instead of Jesus. This man didn't give opinions—he offered facts. He was born blind but had a status change. Did the religious leaders want to become Jesus' disciples? No, that suggestion didn't make them happy. This story reminds us to offer praise instead of an interrogation when God performs a miracle.

Prayer Starter

Father, allow my praise to find a voice before anyone attempts to discredit Your gift that shows what's possible. May I rejoice for others when they. . .

DAY 316
JOHN 10–11

Prayer Scripture

They took away the stone from the place where the dead was laid. And Jesus lifted up His eyes and said, "Father, I thank You that You have heard Me. And I knew that You always hear Me, but because of the people who stand by I said it, that they may believe that You have sent Me." And when He had spoken this, He cried with a loud voice, "Lazarus, come out!" And he who was dead came out, bound hand and foot with grave clothes, and his face was bound about with a cloth. Jesus said to them, "Unbind him, and let him go."

John 11:41–44

Prayer Thought for the Day

Religious leaders claimed that Jesus' miracles were accomplished by demonic spirits. Jesus invited them to trust the results while they struggled with believing He was God's Son. A man named Lazarus had died of an illness just days before. Jesus prayed, addressing God as Father. He thanked God for listening to Him, and then? Lazarus was raised from the dead. Jesus hadn't prayed to some non-god. His prayer was a very intimate connection to His Father. Even if these leaders weren't convinced, they had a memory of an event with no logical explanation—orchestrated by a man they kept saying was a fraud.

Prayer Starter

Lord God, make me as comfortable talking to You as Jesus was. Even if others struggle, I believe. Help others to see You in the way I. . .

DAY 317
JOHN 12–13

Prayer Scripture

[Jesus said,] "My soul is troubled, and what shall I say? 'Father, save Me from this hour'? But for this reason I came to this hour. Father, glorify Your name." Then there came a voice from heaven, saying, "I have both glorified it and will glorify it again." Therefore the people who stood by and heard it said that it thundered. Others said, "An angel spoke to Him."

JOHN 12:27–29

Prayer Thought for the Day

God speaks, but not every person will be tuned in to what He's saying. The people heard thunder when God spoke to Moses on the mountain. Elijah heard God in a whisper. Most hear God best by reading the words written in the Bible. In John 12 God spoke to Jesus and Jesus heard Him. To others around Him it seemed as if there was a storm or perhaps angels were speaking. The people were getting sidetracked from what was happening. Jesus was announcing that everything was a go for His divine rescue plan, and His prayer expressed honor to God. Perhaps they would understand later, but in the midst of God answering a prayer, the people were distracted.

Prayer Starter

Father, listening for Your voice is something I would like. Knowing what You want is important to me and I want to honor You by listening. If that's through reading Your Word, then let me listen through. . .

DAY 318
JOHN 14–16

Prayer Scripture

[Jesus said,] "I will pray to the Father, and He shall give you another Comforter, that He may abide with you forever—even the Spirit of truth, whom the world cannot receive, because it does not see Him, nor does it know Him. But you know Him, for He dwells with you and shall be in you. I will not leave you comfortless; I will come to you."
JOHN 14:16–18

Prayer Thought for the Day

The prayers Jesus prayed are important to read, but there's always more to learn. In John 14, Jesus was praying for His replacement. He knew He would finish His time on earth, but the people would need continued comfort, advice, and teaching. They would miss these things when He left. The crucifixion and resurrection were on His calendar, and He wouldn't miss those dates. When He was gone, God would answer Jesus' request for His Spirit, who would lead all followers until Jesus returned. God's Spirit may be the hardest to understand, but this Holy Spirit has been at work in your life and the lives of all who follow God. He's here because God answered Jesus' prayer.

Prayer Starter

Lord God, Your Spirit helps me when I struggle, when I need courage, and when I have questions and concerns. The prayer Jesus prayed is the same prayer I'm praying: May Your Spirit bring comfort, truth, and companionship to me when. . .

DAY 319

JOHN 17–18

Prayer Scripture

[Jesus prayed,] "I do not ask that You take them out of the world, but that You would keep them from evil. They are not of the world, even as I am not of the world. Sanctify them through Your truth. Your word is truth. As You have sent Me into the world, even so I have also sent them into the world. . . . I do not ask for these alone, but also for those who shall believe in Me through their word."

John 17:15–18, 20

Prayer Thought for the Day

Jesus' prayer in John 17 promised His followers that trouble was coming. Sometimes, the only way to manage it was to go *through* it.

Jesus refused to ask that you be removed from trouble but did request that God safeguard you from evil. Learning, following, and sharing truth with others is how you'll be sent into the world so you can be useful as an agent of change in the life of someone who's also living through the promised struggle. That struggler will need to know hard times are part of God's design. We choose to go through them alone or with God's help. Spread that message, and you're an answer to Jesus' prayer.

Prayer Starter

Father, trouble isn't something I face with eagerness. Help me to walk through it with Your grace and share with others the help You can provide when they. . .

DAY 320
JOHN 19–21

Prayer Scripture

Jesus said to Simon Peter, "Simon, son of Jonah, do you love Me more than these?" He said to Him, "Yes, Lord; You know that I love You." He said to him, "Feed My lambs." He said to him again the second time, "Simon, son of Jonah, do you love Me?" He said to Him, "Yes, Lord; You know that I love You." He said to him, "Feed My sheep." He said to him the third time, "Simon, son of Jonah, do you love Me?" Peter was grieved.

John 21:15–17

Prayer Thought for the Day

Why you pray to and worship God, not humans, may be summed up in John 21. Jesus declared God's church would be built on Peter, who correctly identified Jesus as the Messiah. But he also denied knowing Jesus, resorted to violence when Jesus was arrested, and ran away. Later, when Jesus asked Peter if he loved Him, Peter's response was essentially "You're a really good friend." The word Jesus used for "love" was *agape* (God's unconditional love), but when Peter responded he used the word *phileo* (the affection of a friend). It was all Peter could offer, and it left him grieved. It's also why following Jesus is better than following any human. None can offer the love Jesus offers.

Prayer Starter

Lord God, because You love me without condition, help me to follow You—without condition. Let me love You with all my heart and. . .

DAY 321
ACTS 1–2

Prayer Scripture

Those who gladly received his word were baptized, and the same day about three thousand souls were added to them. And they continued steadfastly in the apostles' doctrine and fellowship and in the breaking of bread and in prayers.
Acts 2:41–42

Prayer Thought for the Day

When men who followed Jesus shared what they knew to be true about Him, it changed futures. Men without the credentials religious leaders required shared what they heard from Jesus. They had no need to make anything up. They simply shared His words and their experience. With an ever-increasing crowd, the men spoke boldly, and God's Spirit connected truth for three thousand who listened, believed what they heard, accepted rescue, and joined the movement. The prayers of righteous men were offered on behalf of mankind, and God answered in a big way. In this case three thousand more prayers were added—and the impact of their message continued to grow.

Prayer Starter

Father, if I would just be intentional about sharing Your message and my experience, I wonder what impact it would have on those around me. I don't want to be so concerned about what others might think that I let it affect my willingness to share good things like. . .

DAY 322
ACTS 3–5

Prayer Scripture

Peter and John answered and said to them, "Whether it is right in the sight of God to listen to you more than to God, you judge. For we cannot but speak the things that we have seen and heard." So when they had threatened them further, they let them go, finding no way in which they might punish them, because of the people, for all men glorified God for what had been done.

Acts 4:19–21

Prayer Thought for the Day

This was the opposite response to what happened in Acts 2. These religious observers stiff-armed anything having to do with Jesus. They heard the disciples speak; they saw the crowds, and their reaction resembled thuggery. Their confrontation attempted to hammer this movement into shards of ruin and decay.

Two apostles told the religious leaders they would need to decide if God was more important to listen to or if they, as religious leaders, were more important than God. That must have been awkward. The leaders chose to lash out with a few more threats and then admit the apostles had done nothing wrong. The end result? Those who gathered to listen glorified God in their actions and prayers.

Prayer Starter

Lord God, if there's opposition to sharing what You've done, give me the words to speak to open doors that continue the discussion. I need Your wisdom, and You have. . .

DAY 323
ACTS 6–7

Prayer Scripture

[The apostles] chose Stephen, a man full of faith and of the Holy Spirit, and Philip, and Prochorus, and Nicanor, and Timon, and Parmenas, and Nicolas, a proselyte of Antioch, whom they set before the apostles. And when they had prayed, they laid their hands on them. And the word of God increased, and the number of the disciples multiplied greatly in Jerusalem, and a great company of the priests were obedient to the faith.

Acts 6:5–7

Prayer Thought for the Day

As the early church continued to grow, the apostles determined they needed more help in managing the day-to-day things that took time away from sharing what they knew about Jesus. This new venture was also accomplished with prayer. The apostles wanted God to help them manage the growth as the good news brought by Jesus was finding a new audience throughout the known world. The number of followers was growing, and this included priests who saw the wisdom of following the Messiah. Their acknowledgment was also an answer to prayer. This was a revolutionary movement, and it was driven by the teachings of Jesus, the experience of those who were with Him, and the prayers of those who accepted the truth.

Prayer Starter

Father, You gave us a movement of Christ followers, and I chose to join. It's prayer that connects me to this change. Prayer has kept it growing and. . .

DAY 324
ACTS 8–9

Prayer Scripture

Peter put them all out and knelt down and prayed. And turning to the body he said, "Tabitha, arise." And she opened her eyes. And when she saw Peter, she sat up. And he gave her his hand and lifted her up. And when he had called the saints and widows, he presented her alive.
Acts 9:40–41

Prayer Thought for the Day

God was moving. The church was growing. Despite plenty of opposition, there were many amazing events that made the opposition seem less impressive. Saul was the poster boy for persecution. When Stephen was being stoned to death, Saul held the coats for the attacking mob. But God redirected this bad situation when Saul the persecutor became Paul the apostle. A man named Simon tried to buy the power of the Holy Spirit and instead learned of the power of God. Then there's the story of Tabitha, who had always shown kindness within the church. The apostles were told she had died. Peter rushed to her home and prayed. Tabitha rose from the dead that day. All these incidents found answers after a prayer consultation with God.

Prayer Starter

Lord God, it's clear that prayer was very important to the growth of Your church. This seems so different from the time in Israel's history when no one wanted to follow You. Help me to learn from the early church so I can. . .

DAY 325
ACTS 10–12

Prayer Scripture

There was a certain man in Caesarea called Cornelius, a centurion of the cohort called the Italian cohort, a devout man and one who feared God with all his house, who gave many charitable gifts to the people and always prayed to God. About the ninth hour of the day he clearly saw in a vision an angel of God coming to him and saying to him, "Cornelius." And when he looked at him, he was afraid and said, "What is it, Lord?" And he said to him, "Your prayers and your charitable gifts have come up for a memorial before God. And now send men to Joppa and call for Simon, whose surname is Peter."

Acts 10:1–5

Prayer Thought for the Day

God used a Gentile's prayer to change Peter's heart. Cornelius, a Roman soldier, wasn't Jewish, and most early Christians struggled to share God with "outsiders." But this soldier prayed, honored God, and financially assisted the Jewish people. God answered Cornelius' prayer by asking him to find Peter. This one Gentile enlarged Peter's vision. This apostle, who believed God was only for the Jewish people and was against all others, had to learn that God was for everyone. Hadn't He commanded the disciples to make disciples of all nations? Of course He had (see Matthew 28:19–20).

Prayer Starter

Father, may I remember that You're big enough to be the God of all and not just some. This is important because. . .

DAY 326
ACTS 13–14

Prayer Scripture

When they had ordained elders for them in every church, and had prayed with fasting, they commended them to the Lord in whom they believed.
ACTS 14:23

Prayer Thought for the Day

The first-century church was on the move. It was growing, and people were coming to know, love, and serve the cause of Jesus. It was a case of spiritual rescue when people recognized they were in desperate need of what only Jesus could offer. Paul and Barnabas traveled from town to town, established churches, and identified leaders for each congregation. This involved prayer and fasting because it wasn't a decision they took lightly. They wanted each body of believers to be led by those who took their jobs as seriously as the selection process. Because Paul and Barnabas wanted their choices to connect with God's plan, they prayed.

Your choices can connect with God's plan too. The not-so-secret secret is prayer.

Prayer Starter

Lord God, it's informative to read the method Paul and Barnabas took in making an important decision. I have important choices to make every day. May I not be so confident in my own decision-making that I refuse Your guidance. When my choice is prayer, may I. . .

DAY 327
ACTS 15–17

Prayer Scripture

At midnight Paul and Silas prayed and sang praises to God, and the prisoners heard them. And suddenly there was a great earthquake, so that the foundations of the prison were shaken. And immediately all the doors were opened, and everyone's chains were loosened.

Acts 16:25–26

Prayer Thought for the Day

Something you might not hear about every day is prisoners praising God and praying at midnight while other prisoners listen. Many vibrant prison ministries might have gotten their inspiration from Acts 16. This is where incarceration meets the freedom of a life with Jesus. Even when a body is imprisoned, a spirit can be free. That freedom changes the prisoners' outlook on any present circumstance. In the case of Paul and his ministry partner Silas, God gave His own verdict and brought them out of their prison cell. In doing so, God opened an opportunity for these two missionaries to move beyond prayer and praise to sharing faith with the keeper of the prison—who accepted rescue and followed Jesus. Don't be surprised when prayer and praise open opportunities you never expected. Praise should never be an afterthought.

Prayer Starter

Father, I haven't always thought of praying to You and praising Your name as opportunities. Help me to accept prayer as my connection with You and an extension to. . .

DAY 328
ACTS 18–19

Prayer Scripture

[Paul] departed from there and entered into the house of a certain man named Justus, one who worshipped God, whose house was adjoined to the synagogue. And Crispus, the chief ruler of the synagogue, believed in the Lord with all his house. And many of the Corinthians, hearing, believed and were baptized.

Acts 18:7–8

Prayer Thought for the Day

Because Paul was a missionary apostle he didn't seem to stay in one place very long. He preached, he met people, and he developed and launched local leaders to grow the local church. Paul met people in Corinth, and it seemed he wasn't just among friends but had found a spiritual family. Two of those men were Justus and Crispus, who were recognized as leaders.

The local synagogue was a common gathering place, but this friendship was part of the growth of the church in Corinth. In a vision, God told Paul that, unlike some places, this was a location that would be friendly to him. Paul stayed there for a year and a half, taking a role in the long-term development in the Corinthian church. Paul would later write letters to help the church in which he'd invested time, prayer, and instruction.

Prayer Starter

Lord God, may prayer be a refining part of friendship. I should pray for others and encourage them to pray for me. Give me a heart that sees the needs of a friend and invites You to. . .

DAY 329
ACTS 20–22

Prayer Scripture

When [Paul] had said these things, he knelt down and prayed with them all. And they all wept greatly and fell on Paul's neck and kissed him, sorrowing most of all for the words that he spoke, that they should no longer see his face. And they accompanied him to the ship.

Acts 20:36–38

Prayer Thought for the Day

Paul had spent a lot of time in Miletus and the church in Ephesus. You can't spend so much time with a group of people and not get a lump in your throat when it's time to leave. He spent time in prayer, and the people spent time weeping "greatly." One of the big reasons for this very emotional prayer meeting was that it was a send-off for Paul by people he'd invested so much time into, with all knowing this was likely the last time they would see him. By this time Paul had survived a stoning, but he was heading toward a shipwreck, a snake bite, and a long-term prison stay. This event would likely be remembered for the joy of a growing ministry at a time when everyone was moving in a similar direction.

Prayer Starter

Father, help me to appreciate the moments I spend with believers when we all share the same passion for following You. In those moments these people are true family that I should share life with. Thank You for allowing me to find people who. . .

DAY 330
ACTS 23–25

Prayer Scripture

Some of the Jews banded together and bound themselves under a curse, saying that they would neither eat nor drink until they had killed Paul. And there were more than forty who had made this conspiracy. And they came to the chief priests and elders and said, "We have bound ourselves under a great curse that we will eat nothing until we have slain Paul. Now therefore you, with the council, signify to the chief captain that he bring him down to you tomorrow, as though you were going to more thoroughly inquire about something concerning him. And we are ready to kill him before he ever comes near."

Acts 23:12–15

Prayer Thought for the Day

Paul could have played it safe by staying in Corinth or Miletus, but he felt called by God to go to Jerusalem. This option was dangerous; there he was arrested. Then a murder plot was uncovered by Paul's nephew. More than three dozen men promised to refrain from eating until they killed Paul. But God was sending Paul to Rome. God kept this missionary safe. It's quite probable that the people he encouraged in other towns were joining him in prayer that God's will would happen just the way God wanted. And, as always, it did.

Prayer Starter

Lord God, sometimes it seems I can be in danger, yet You protect me in ways I never thought possible. Give me the confidence to trust You when…

DAY 331
ACTS 26–28

Prayer Scripture

In the same region were lands of the chief man of the island, whose name was Publius, who received us and lodged us courteously three days. And it came to pass that the father of Publius lay sick of a fever and of dysentery. Paul went in to see him and prayed and laid his hands on him and healed him. So when this was done, others on the island who had diseases also came and were healed.

Acts 28:7–9

Prayer Thought for the Day

A shipwreck left Paul on the island of Malta in wintertime. The people showed kindness to the soldiers and their prisoners headed for Rome. But this detour was God's idea. There were people who needed to hear about Jesus. Paul was perfectly willing to share what he knew. One islander named Publius had taken shipwrecked individuals into his home, but his father was very sick in another room of the house. Paul went to this older man and offered a prayer to the God who brought him to Malta. The God who answers prayer healed this man. That healing brought all kinds of people to Paul, and God healed them too. Rest assured that Paul was able to share Jesus with them once he prayed for them.

Prayer Starter

Father, help me to see unexpected circumstances as opportunities to make You known to others. Give me courage and a receptive audience when You…

DAY 332
ROMANS 1–3

Prayer Scripture

First, I thank my God through Jesus Christ for you all, that your faith is spoken of throughout the whole world. For God, whom I serve with my spirit in the gospel of His Son, is my witness that without ceasing I always make mention of you in my prayers, making request, if by any means, now, finally, I might have a prosperous journey by the will of God to come to you.

Romans 1:8–10

Prayer Thought for the Day

The message originated by Jesus had come to Rome, and the church was growing. Paul wrote to the believers and was quick to let them know he was praying for them. He was also making requests that God would see fit to send him to the Roman believers. But in the meantime he sent this letter to encourage them. It remains an encouragement to those who read God's Word today. Paul was grateful for these believers and their strong faith.

It may be helpful to remember that this letter was shared from the heart of Paul to people he knew and cared deeply about. This can help you connect with the instructions and the reason for personal prayer for all who would read these words.

Prayer Starter

Lord God, thank You for Your personal friendship and the friendships found in the writings of Paul. Help me to pray for friends with the same. . .

DAY 333
ROMANS 4–7

Prayer Scripture

O wretched man that I am! Who shall deliver me from the body of this death? I thank God through Jesus Christ our Lord. So then, with the mind I myself serve the law of God, but with the flesh, the law of sin.
ROMANS 7:24–25

Prayer Thought for the Day

This was a letter to friends about real life. No pretending. No acting as if there were no issues. Paul said what most have felt. Does it connect with you? He essentially said, "I want to do what God wants me to do, but I blow it." This is an everyman battle between what the spirit instructs and what the flesh demands.

On good days, when the spirit wins out and good choices are made, you might feel hope. Then the flesh steps in and demands a detour, and you wonder what it could hurt. But sin always does. Regret sets in, and you might agree with Paul when he applied the term "wretched" to himself. It's important to know that what you struggle with is a part of humanity's common struggle. That makes prayer an even greater source of sin resistance.

Prayer Starter

Father, I fight an inner war, but I don't want to fight alone. Keep me from evil, change my choices, and forgive me when the flesh is victorious. Lead me when. . .

DAY 334
ROMANS 8–10

Prayer Scripture

Likewise the Spirit also helps our infirmities. For we do not know what we should pray for as we ought, but the Spirit Himself makes intercession for us with groanings that cannot be uttered. And He who searches the hearts knows what the mind of the Spirit is, because He makes intercession for the saints according to the will of God.
ROMANS 8:26–27

Prayer Thought for the Day

Have you ever struggled to find the words to pray? You might be overcome with emotions as different as anger or sorrow. You might be confused and nothing you try to say makes sense. You wonder why you should try praying when you can't find the words. Is that even remotely helpful? Yes, it is. Paul was telling the church in Rome that when those times come—when maybe tears fall before words or a lump in the throat comes before a word on the tongue—there's another option. You may remember that Jesus prayed for the arrival of the Holy Spirit to help His followers. That same Holy Spirit prays for you when you just can't. That doesn't mean you don't try. It means He takes over when you hit a roadblock you just can't get around.

Prayer Starter

Lord God, when I can't pray. . .

DAY 335
ROMANS 11–13

Prayer Scripture

O the depth of the riches both of the wisdom and knowledge of God! How unsearchable are His judgments and His ways past finding out! "For who has known the mind of the Lord? Or who has been His counselor? Or who has first given to Him and it shall be repaid to him?" For from Him and through Him and to Him are all things, to whom be glory forever. Amen.

ROMANS 11:33–36

Prayer Thought for the Day

The more time you spend recalling the goodness of God in your prayer time, the bigger He becomes. Being overwhelmed should be expected. Things like wisdom, knowledge, judgment, and leading are things He offers as part of a day's work. It's not hard for Him but outside your ability without His help. He keeps everything going. All things owe Him honor. Not just today, but for every day and then for all eternity. You can take Romans 11:33–36 and make it a prayer of the overwhelmed but grateful.

Prayer Starter

Father, more than my effort, there's Your strength. More than I can think, there's Your wisdom. I stand humble and grateful for. . .

DAY 336
ROMANS 14–16

Prayer Scripture

I beseech you, brothers, for the Lord Jesus Christ's sake and for the love of the Spirit, that you strive together with me in your prayers to God for me, that I may be delivered from those in Judea who do not believe, and that my service that I have for Jerusalem may be accepted by the saints, that I may come to you with joy by the will of God and may be refreshed with you. Now the God of peace be with you all. Amen.

Romans 15:30–33

Prayer Thought for the Day

Paul expected trouble. He was often right. Among his Roman friends Paul very specifically made a request. If they loved God's Spirit at work in their lives, and for the sake of Jesus' work in the world, would they pray to God for him? He expected trouble in Judea and wasn't sure he'd be accepted in Jerusalem. Paul asked for prayer that he wouldn't be prevented from making a visit to Rome to spend time with these believers.

When you're asking others to pray for you, it's all right to be specific about your concerns. Unspoken requests may be more common, but consider Paul's frank request.

Prayer Starter

Lord God, sometimes I don't think much about asking others to pray for me. Maybe I think it makes me look weak, but I *am* weak without Your help. May the prayers of others bring a willingness to. . .

DAY 337

1 CORINTHIANS 1–6

Prayer Scripture

It pleased God by the foolishness of preaching to save those who believe. For the Jews require a sign, and the Greeks seek after wisdom, but we preach Christ crucified, a stumbling block to the Jews and foolishness to the Greeks, but to those who are called, both Jews and Greeks, Christ the power of God and the wisdom of God. Because the foolishness of God is wiser than men, and the weakness of God is stronger than men.

1 Corinthians 1:21–25

Prayer Thought for the Day

Those who followed Christ recognized Him as the Messiah. The Jewish people looked for the sign they'd missed when Jesus was alive. The Greeks were all about what a person could know, and while Jesus' life was fairly easy to explain, it seemed hard to understand. He came to rescue mankind from the penalty for breaking God's law. Jews didn't want to accept it, and Greeks thought it was foolish. God took the prayers of those considered foolish and simply set about the job of changing the world. Some choose not to believe.

Pray for others. You don't need their approval. What they think is foolish might just be the thing God uses to help them finally recognize His Son.

Prayer Starter

Father, help me to accept that some will hear what I have to say about You and think it's foolish. Use my words so someone might consider You for. . .

DAY 338
1 CORINTHIANS 7–10

Prayer Scripture

Let him who thinks he stands take heed lest he fall.
No temptation has taken you but such as is common to man.
But God is faithful, who will not allow you to be tempted
above what you are able, but with the temptation will also
make a way of escape, that you may be able to bear it.
1 CORINTHIANS 10:12–13

Prayer Thought for the Day

Paul had apparently witnessed Christ followers becoming arrogant. They compared how well they personally performed and not so discreetly pointed out that others had failed where they found success. This wasn't the act of the humble; it showed the heart of the proud. When you think you've become inoculated against the virus of sin, you need to remember that temptation has regularly scheduled deliveries. That's nothing new and is something everyone faces. God has always advised prayer, but He wants you to remember He'll always provide an off-ramp where you can exit the Temptation Toll Plaza. Without God's intervention, you wouldn't be able to stand against any temptations you face.

Prayer Starter

Lord God, please stand between me and temptation. Show me the exit and give me the courage to leave. Give me the heart of a man who knows that You. . .

DAY 339
1 CORINTHIANS 11–13

Prayer Scripture

Love endures patiently and is kind; love does not envy; love does not boast, is not puffed up, does not behave improperly, does not seek its own, is not easily provoked, does not think evil, does not rejoice in iniquity, but rejoices in the truth; it bears all things, believes all things, hopes all things, endures all things.
1 Corinthians 13:4–7

Prayer Thought for the Day

Prayer is an act of love. It is. When you make prayer an expression of love, you can endure by bringing the struggle to God. You can cheer someone who needs encouragement without passing out flyers that list your latest accomplishments. Prayer is a positive behavior. Prayer includes others. It helps reduce frustration. It places a spotlight on God's goodness. Prayer refuses to celebrate sin. It recognizes truth and encourages a belief in the God who defines truth. Prayer can help you carry struggles, because you'll be giving them to God. Prayer encourages believers, inspires hope, and leads to endurance. Take these ideas of love with you the next time you meet with God.

Prayer Starter

Father, thanks for encouraging me to take Your love and make it a motivation to pray. When I think of others, I pray to You to help me. . .

DAY 340
1 CORINTHIANS 14–16

Prayer Scripture

[Paul said,] "I am the least of the apostles, and am not suitable to be called an apostle, because I persecuted the church of God. But by the grace of God I am what I am, and His grace that was bestowed on me was not in vain."
1 CORINTHIANS 15:9–10

Prayer Thought for the Day

Someone needs to read that again. Maybe it's you. Paul admitted he once had no use for Jesus. He persecuted those who believed in Him. Paul considered himself the least suitable to be an apostle. But Jesus changed Paul. He was a forgiven, remade clay pot with self-inflicted flaws removed. He was suitable for the purpose God had for him. And all the grace poured into his life made a deep and lasting change in Paul. That difference was used to inspire change in others. It's easy to say that God got a bad deal when He rescued you, because you seem to need to be rescued often. You read a truth from God, and you want to do what He asks, but you do the opposite. You feel you're the least among Christians. . .yet God. He keeps pouring into you. It's a personal investment that may have an eternal impact in someone else's life.

Prayer Starter

Lord God, help me to stop considering that You're wasting Your time on me. May I learn to follow. When I fail, give me the courage to. . .

DAY 341

2 CORINTHIANS 1–5

Prayer Scripture

Blessed be God, even the Father of our Lord Jesus Christ, the Father of mercies and the God of all comfort, who comforts us in all our tribulation, that we may be able to comfort those who are in any trouble, by the comfort with which we ourselves are comforted by God.

2 Corinthians 1:3–4

Prayer Thought for the Day

The opening of Paul's second letter to the church at Corinth was a great opportunity to offer gratitude to God. The church would be reminded God provided comfort, because they would hear of the obedience struggles that Paul saw in the church. Paul was also very aware that there were those who said they spoke for God but were saying things He never said. People were believing lies. When struggles come, use your prayers to thank God that when you think things are so far out of control that they can't be fixed, there's a God who offers mercy and comfort when no one else will. When this is offered to you and you share it—this gift grows to include others.

Prayer Starter

Father, help me to understand that with You everything is just right. Let me trust that You don't give up control. May this good news change my mind about. . .

DAY 342
2 CORINTHIANS 6–9

Prayer Scripture

For though I made you sorrowful with a letter, I do not regret it, though I did regret it, for I perceive that the same letter has made you sorrowful, though it was but for a time. Now I rejoice, not that you were made sorrowful, but that you sorrowed to repentance. For you were made sorrowful according to a godly manner, that you might suffer loss from us in nothing. For godly sorrow produces repentance to salvation, not to be regretted.

2 CORINTHIANS 7:8–10

Prayer Thought for the Day

Paul was a master letter writer. God used many letters from the early church era, often called epistles, to make up our New Testament. Not all of the letters Paul sent included good news and attaboys. Paul referenced a letter that spoke truth that hurt primarily because it called out the sin of the people. Paul was clear that it made him sad that the people were sad. But the sorrow they expressed led to an impressive turnaround. They were confronted with an uncomfortable truth, and by believing truth, they were set free from the bondage of the lies they had been accepting.

Prayer Starter

Lord God, I need to feel sorrow for believing a lie. When I know Your truth, bring on the sorrow and let it lead me back to You so I can. . .

DAY 343

2 CORINTHIANS 10–13

Prayer Scripture

The weapons of our warfare are not of the world but mighty through God in the pulling down of strongholds, casting down imaginations and every haughty thing that exalts itself against the knowledge of God, and bringing into captivity every thought to the obedience of Christ.

2 Corinthians 10:4–6

Prayer Thought for the Day

What does it mean when Paul told the believers at Corinth to take thoughts captive? How do you make thoughts obedient? There are two perspectives on this, and both could be correct. The first is to take everything you hear and read then learn to discern truth and reject fiction. Make all input conform to what God actually said. If it can't connect, then dispose of those thoughts. The second potential meaning is a time when thoughts come to your mind when you haven't asked for their presence. They suggest things you haven't considered, and they seem friendly enough that you play host to their twisted logic. Bring thoughts that come from the outside—or the inside—to God in prayer. Seek to bring these imperfect, impure, inopportune thoughts under His control, allowing God to give them an eviction notice with your consent. You don't have to accept wrong thinking.

Prayer Starter

Father, I don't want, and I don't need, thoughts that convince me to believe lies. Help me to interrogate my thoughts and send wrong thinking. . .

DAY 344
GALATIANS 1–6

Prayer Scripture

Whatever a man sows, that he shall also reap. For he who sows to his flesh shall of the flesh reap corruption, but he who sows to the Spirit shall of the Spirit reap life everlasting. And let us not be weary in doing good, for in due season we shall reap, if we do not lose hope. Therefore, as we have opportunity, let us do good to all men, especially to those who are of the household of faith.
GALATIANS 6:7–10

Prayer Thought for the Day

Like Jesus, Paul understood that farming was a primary part of life in the first century. Using agricultural terms meant that most people would know what he was talking about. In Galatians 6 Paul wrote about planting and nurturing seeds. One of the descriptions for what Paul was suggesting was kindness. All elements of goodness are seeds that can be planted. These seeds may seem to disappear in the soil. You may wonder if it was worth the effort, but seeds may grow later than you think and may produce more abundantly. So the choice of giving up because you're weary is simply giving up too soon. Pray for strength when your spiritual tank is empty. Offer kindness, compassion, and a helping hand. Even if it's rejected, the seed is planted and has an opportunity to grow.

Prayer Starter

Lord God, help me to plant good seeds. Help me to be patient. Help me to see these seeds. . .

DAY 345

EPHESIANS 1–6

Prayer Scripture

I bow my knees to the Father of our Lord Jesus Christ,
from whom the whole family in heaven and earth is named,
that He would grant you, according to the riches of His glory, to
be strengthened with might by His Spirit in the inner man,
that Christ may dwell in your hearts by faith, that you, being
rooted and grounded in love, may be able to comprehend with
all saints what is the breadth and length and depth and height.
EPHESIANS 3:14–18

Prayer Thought for the Day

Paul draws from a variety of word pictures to let the church in Ephesus know they serve a big God, that their strength would come from Him. You can learn other things from this prayer. God's family was named for Jesus. Your inner man is strengthened by God's Spirit. Jesus dwells with you. God gives His love so you'll take the full measure of His gift and understand there's nothing beyond or outside of His compassion for you. His love reaches in all directions and is all-encompassing.

The promise of this prayer by Paul could likely inspire a greater depth to your own prayer time. Allow your mind to think of God as big as possible and know that it's still too small.

Prayer Starter

Father, wide, tall, deep, and long—Your love is what strengthens me. Give me just a small glimpse of Your amazing compassion and let it. . .

DAY 346
PHILIPPIANS 1–4

Prayer Scripture

I thank my God on every remembrance of you, always in every prayer of mine for you all, making request with joy for your fellowship in the gospel from the first day until now, being confident of this very thing, that He who has begun a good work in you will perform it until the day of Jesus Christ.

Philippians 1:3–6

Prayer Thought for the Day

Someone has impacted your life. Certainly God would be included, but think about people with flesh and bones who breathed life into your existence. It could be a relative or a lifelong friend. Someone who helped you (or you helped) might have started as an adversary. Paul wanted to make sure that the church in Philippi knew that he was grateful for the memory of time spent with them. He took it a step further by declaring that he talked to God about them. Paul was confident that the good work he observed in their lives was just the beginning. Paul had seen these planted seeds and knew this work would be ongoing. It would enlarge influence. How meaningful would it be to let others know you believe in them and that you're praying for them?

Prayer Starter

Lord God, help me to catch a glimpse of the good things You're doing among those who've impacted my life. Thanks for so many growing seeds, in my life and the lives of. . .

DAY 347

COLOSSIANS 1–4

Prayer Scripture

Beware lest any man seduce you through philosophy and vain deceit, according to the tradition of men, according to the rudiments of the world, and not according to Christ.

Colossians 2:8

Prayer Thought for the Day

Beyond the prayers that Paul might pray (Colossians 1:18), he was vocal concerning his fears for the fledgling church in Colossae. Sitting in the same congregation were people who really wanted to follow God and those who were content to simply occupy space. These space-taking individuals were creating mash-ups between what God said and what they'd always believed. They wanted God to fit in where they decided He should. So Paul issued a word of caution and mentioned four points of diversion that were causing issues in the Colossian church. People were leaving the straight path of God by accepting a mix of philosophy, clever arguments, human guesses, and a long list of traditions. As a result, many people were led to something that wasn't a clear picture of the good news Jesus brought.

Instead of redefining God's truths, this church would have done well to seek to know God better through prayer.

Prayer Starter

Father, may I refuse to add ingredients to Your perfect recipe of grace. The result will never be an improvement. Help me to seek a pure understanding of who You are so I can. . .

DAY 348

1 THESSALONIANS 1–5; 2 THESSALONIANS 1–3

Prayer Scripture

What thanks can we render again to God for you, for all the joy with which we rejoice for your sake before our God, night and day praying exceedingly that we might see your face and might perfect what is lacking in your faith?

1 Thessalonians 3:9–10

Prayer Thought for the Day

The Thessalonian church was primarily filled with Gentiles. They didn't have a background that included God, but they'd heard about Jesus and His good news. Following God was uncomfortable. The people may have followed to the best of their ability, but they were young believers with little experience. Paul sent two letters to these Christians to let them know he was concerned and wanted to encourage them. He let them know he was praying for the things that would shrink their gap in understanding. These people who meant something to Paul meant everything to God. They were like a lot of people who have chosen to start their journey but still struggle to learn so they can follow better. It's much more helpful to pray that God would take care of their knowledge gap than to criticize them for not knowing something that many think is commonplace.

Prayer Starter

Lord God, I pray for growth that leads to change—in me and in others. May we all learn more so we know how to follow You with. . .

DAY 349
1 TIMOTHY 1–6

Prayer Scripture

I exhort therefore, first of all, that supplications, prayers, intercessions, and giving of thanks be made for all men, for kings and for all who are in authority, that we may lead a quiet and peaceful life in all godliness and honesty. For this is good and acceptable in the sight of God our Savior, who wants all men to be saved and to come to the knowledge of the truth.

1 Timothy 2:1–4

Prayer Thought for the Day

Paul's instructions in 1 Timothy 2 likely had people asking if there was a loophole. Praying for leaders they didn't even like? No thanks. God wants every human to come to Him—this includes leaders. Some may already know God. Some may have run away from Him all their lives. But God has used leaders of countries who didn't follow Him to play a role in the return of the people to the heart of God. Leaders have been responsive to requests made by respectful believers who weren't demanding rights but prayed for the favor of those leaders first. Showing respect may be the easiest way for anyone in any position of leadership to discover a willingness to have concerns heard.

Prayer Starter

Father, it has always been easier to complain than show respect to those in positions of leadership. Give me a heart that's willing to pray for whoever is in a position to. . .

DAY 350
2 TIMOTHY 1–4; TITUS 1–3

Prayer Scripture

I thank God, whom I serve as my forefathers did, with pure conscience, that without ceasing I remember you in my prayers night and day, greatly desiring to see you, being mindful of your tears, that I may be filled with joy when I am reminded of the sincere faith that is in you.
2 Timothy 1:3–5

Prayer Thought for the Day

This letter from Paul seems among the most personal. Maybe there's a good reason for that. Timothy was considered one of Paul's sons in the faith. He was given a position of leadership and told not to let people look down on him for his age. He had something to teach, and age wasn't an issue. Paul took the time to say that there wasn't a day that passed that he wasn't praying for Timothy—and those prayers weren't just the once-a-day variety. Timothy's faith was strong, and the apostle Paul absolutely wanted to return to spend time with the young man he mentored.

Finding someone older to help you grow is a good plan. Finding someone younger to share your faith with is a brilliant plan. Finding others to live life with is a perfect plan when God is the thing that connects the heart of friends.

Prayer Starter

Lord God, thank You for people who care for me and for people that I can care about. Both can help me to grow, and both. . .

DAY 351

PHILEMON; HEBREWS 1–6

Prayer Scripture

"You, Lord, in the beginning have laid the foundation of the earth, and the heavens are the works of Your hands. They shall perish, but You remain. And they all shall become old as does a garment, and you shall fold them up like a garment, and they shall be changed. But You are the same, and Your years shall not fail."

Hebrews 1:10–12

Prayer Thought for the Day

This is a prayer that recognizes both the temporary things and eternal things. For instance, your physical body wasn't meant to last forever. The earth has an expiration date. Plants and animals grow and eventually pass from existence. As depressing as that may sound, this prayer talks about what lasts forever. What won't change is the God who created all the temporary things with a way to access an eternal existence. Fashions end, cars stop working, and refrigerators wear out. Face it, you're used to so many disposable things in life. To God, you're *not* disposable. He gave you life so you'd have the opportunity to make the decision to join Him in eternity. This opportunity is worth the prayer.

Prayer Starter

Father, thank You for offering eternity to someone who has no reason to expect anything beyond a last breath. Thank You for the offer of rescue and the beginning of life with. . .

DAY 352
HEBREWS 7–10

Prayer Scripture

As it is appointed for men to die once, but after this the judgment, so Christ was offered once to bear the sins of many. And to those who look for Him, He shall appear the second time without sin for salvation.
HEBREWS 9:27–28

Prayer Thought for the Day

This passage gets very pointed in explaining who's responsible for making forever life possible. Jesus did something that took the sins of all and made it possible for them to be forgiven. The temporary life means every human will die once, but there will come a time when Jesus returns to earth for a second time to rescue temporary humanity—those who've admitted their need for Him and have accepted rescue—to their permanent and forever home with God. This is part of the new covenant that became effective when Jesus died on the cross. With this sacrifice all the terms and conditions of grace, hope, and a future home were fulfilled, and all the shortcomings of a temporary life were removed. The prayer of a righteous man might well include gratitude for God's perfect contract with mankind. He fulfills His terms and conditions, which are yours upon personal acceptance.

Prayer Starter

Lord God, help me to consider and believe the value of the covenant You offer. May it change choices now, and may I be grateful that it will change forever when You. . .

DAY 353
HEBREWS 11–13

Prayer Scripture

Since we also are surrounded by so great a cloud of witnesses,
let us lay aside every weight, and the sin that so easily besets
us, and let us run with patience the race that is set before us,
looking to Jesus, the author and finisher of our faith, who for
the joy that was set before Him endured the cross, despising the
shame, and is seated at the right hand of the throne of God.

HEBREWS 12:1–2

Prayer Thought for the Day

Hebrews 11 is often referred to as faith's Hall of Fame. It mentions a long list of heroes who were faithful in their pursuit of God. They weren't perfect, but they kept coming back to God and sought to follow Him when they got off track. Many scholars see this list of the faithful as being the cloud of witnesses who cheer you on in your own act of following God. Because you have a journey and because lawlessness will tempt you to take an off-ramp, these heroes would like nothing more than for you to seek Jesus, who writes your story and will help you finish your race. This is the same Jesus who paid the price for all lawbreakers and now sits with God waiting to meet you face-to-face.

Prayer Starter

Father, thinking of those I've read about cheering Christ followers on is encouraging. I'm running this race with You. Help me to finish. . .

DAY 354
JAMES 1–5

Prayer Scripture

If any of you lacks wisdom, let him ask of God, who gives to all men generously and without reproach, and it shall be given him. But let him ask in faith, without wavering. For he who wavers is like a wave of the sea driven with the wind and tossed. For do not let that man think that he shall receive anything from the Lord. A double-minded man is unstable in all his ways.

James 1:5–8

Prayer Thought for the Day

Everyone has a knowledge gap. You can hear someone talk about something complex, and it seems as if they could be speaking a foreign language—the impact would be the same. Likewise, the difference between what you know and what God knows is huge. But you get to ask God to bridge the gap. This means prayer. This means courageous prayer. This means intentional prayer. Ask—and believe that God will give you what you need so you can understand. This understanding probably won't be everything God knows, but more likely it will include whatever you need to know for the circumstances you're facing. In every knowledge gap, pray. This is a prayer God wants to answer.

Prayer Starter

Lord God, I don't know all You know about my current struggle. Give me wisdom that only comes from You so I can. . .

DAY 355

1 PETER 1–5

Prayer Scripture

In this you greatly rejoice, though now for a season, if need be, you are in heaviness through many different temptations, that the trial of your faith, being much more precious than gold that perishes, though it is tried with fire, might be found to praise and honor and glory at the appearing of Jesus Christ. Having not seen Him, you love Him. . .though now you do not see Him, yet believing, you rejoice with joy unspeakable and full of glory.

1 Peter 1:6–8

Prayer Thought for the Day

The struggle was real and common. Peter was talking to people who didn't seem to be prospering. Some people coming into the church were introducing ideas that weren't inspired, endorsed, or accepted by God. The conflict in thought resulted in a trial by fire for the believers. Their faith, when tested, should have brought three things: praise, honor, and glory because of Jesus.

The people couldn't see Jesus, but they loved Him. They struggled yet found reasons to rejoice. This place of conflict was useful in refining their faith and increasing their prayer connection with God. This sort of friction could bring heat that removed impurity and light that identified the difference between God's wisdom and the uninspired ideas being introduced by those who discredited truth.

Prayer Starter

Father, when I struggle, help me to seek truth and reject theory. Give me a refined heart so I can. . .

DAY 356
2 PETER 1–3

Prayer Scripture

Giving all diligence, add to your faith, virtue; and to virtue, knowledge; and to knowledge, self-control; and to self-control, patience; and to patience, godliness; and to godliness, brotherly kindness; and to brotherly kindness, love. For if these things are in you and abound, they make you that you shall be neither barren nor unfruitful in the knowledge of our Lord Jesus Christ.

2 Peter 1:5–8

Prayer Thought for the Day

Peter asked fellow Christ followers to build a chain. Each link connected with another, and all connected to a purpose. The first link any follower needs is faith—and God makes sure you have it when you ask. Virtue is next because faith changes choices. Next is knowledge to help fill the knowledge gap everyone has in their journey. This is followed up by self-control, showing that you're applying what you're learning. You'll need the link of patience because others aren't in the same place you are. Be sure to grab the link of godliness, because you've been set apart. God is working, and you'll need kindness because kindness changes things. The final link is love, which connects to God, others, as well as the first link of faith. Pray for access to every link—keep them together.

Prayer Starter

Lord God, can I have all the links that hold my life together? Teach me how to use each link for my good, for Your glory, and as a way to help. . .

DAY 357
1 JOHN 1–5

Prayer Scripture

He who says he is in the light and hates his brother is in darkness even until now. He who loves his brother abides in the light, and there is no cause of stumbling in him. But he who hates his brother is in darkness and walks in darkness, and does not know where he goes, because that darkness has blinded his eyes.

1 JOHN 2:9–11

Prayer Thought for the Day

Did you know you can't say, "I love Jesus, but not that guy"? If you love Jesus, then you'll love others. If you pray to Jesus, then forgive those whom you might otherwise think of as enemies. God doesn't give you the option of being selective with compassion, kindness, and love. If you insist on believing that you can hate someone, John says this choice leaves you in the dark, making it very hard to notice the illumination of God's truth. If you think hating someone will change them, it won't. If you think that hating someone won't change you, it already has. There's a practical reason you're asked to love others and forgive them: It means you're seeking the light of wisdom that brings you close to Jesus and the people He created to be loved.

Prayer Starter

Father, I don't want to walk in darkness without You. Help me to resist hate, embrace love, and share Your light with. . .

DAY 358

2 JOHN; 3 JOHN; JUDE

Prayer Scripture

To Him who is able to keep you from falling and to present you faultless before the presence of His glory with exceeding joy, to the only wise God, our Savior, be glory and majesty, dominion and power, both now and forever.

JUDE 24–25

Prayer Thought for the Day

Jude is most likely the half brother of Jesus. James was another half brother. They would both follow Jesus and both share words that God inspired them to write in books that bear their names. The book of Jude is just one chapter long, but it includes a blessing that can be thought of as a prayer covering the people who would hear (or read) it. This blessing sought to ensure that God was recognized as one who upholds His people, cleanses their hearts, and is the only wise God—the rest were non-gods with no wisdom or power. Jude offered his rescuer a tribute of majesty, glory, and a recognition of His power and authority that have no end. You too can pray this kind of prayer blessing.

Prayer Starter

Lord God, I'm upheld by You. I'm forgiven by You. Everything that exists is because of You. I'm blessed because of You. Let me never forget to. . .

DAY 359
REVELATION 1–3

Prayer Scripture

[Jesus said,] "I know your works, that you are neither cold nor hot. I wish that you were cold or hot. So then, because you are lukewarm, and neither cold nor hot, I will spew you out of My mouth. Because you say, 'I am rich and increased with goods and have need of nothing'—and do not know that you are wretched and miserable and poor and blind and naked."

Revelation 3:15–17

Prayer Thought for the Day

Jesus was sharing messages for several churches in this book of Revelation. Most of these churches had room for improvement and growth, but at the church at Laodicea there was something seriously wrong. The people weren't close to God. They didn't deny His existence. They filled familiar seats on the weekend but left church unchanged. Jesus likened their faith walk to tepid food or liquid. It wasn't satisfying. Jesus found no refreshment in their choices. They felt their lives were pretty good and concluded that God must be blessing them. In spite of their prosperity, Jesus concluded that they all had five attributes worth avoiding. They were wretched, miserable, poor, blind, and naked. They needed God but weren't convinced that's what they wanted.

Prayer Starter

Father, when I get to the place where I think I don't need You, open my eyes so I can see that I have become lukewarm. Help me to become passionate about. . .

DAY 360
REVELATION 4–6

Prayer Scripture

"You are worthy, O Lord, to receive glory and honor and power, for You have created all things, and for Your pleasure they are and were created."
REVELATION 4:11

Prayer Thought for the Day

Hidden among the hope of a future reunion between Christ followers and the God they've yet to see are some prayers worth noting. Revelation 4:11 is one of these prayers. Who's worthy to receive glory? Who should receive honor? Who's all powerful? If you answered the Lord, God, or Jesus, then you'd be right. The earth was created by this honorable and powerful God. He made everything for Himself and for the enjoyment of those He created. This was a prayer during a time of trouble. It wasn't a prayer of complaint or suggesting God was misguided. John observed things he didn't understand, and he wrote what he saw and heard. In the midst of what he couldn't explain, he kept catching wonderful glimpses of God's goodness and why God was worth every moment anyone could spend showing honor and respect. So Revelation 4:11 is an invitation to you to notice God and describe to Him all the goodness you see.

Prayer Starter

Lord God, everywhere I look I see Your fingerprints. You're good. You're great. You created all, and You are worthy of my. . .

DAY 361
REVELATION 7–10

Prayer Scripture

"Blessing and glory and wisdom and thanksgiving and honor and power and might be to our God forever and ever. Amen."
REVELATION 7:12

Prayer Thought for the Day

Revelation 7:12 is a prayer created for those who lived through the world's final tribulation. They wouldn't have had a prosperous or easy existence. Yet before them the angels and elders gather to declare just seven common themes of God: blessing, glory, wisdom, thanksgiving, honor, power, and might. These were all useful in describing the one who planned for the future, loved His family, and would remove all pain and suffering in heaven. Perhaps those who had suffered finally understood that at the end of any physical pain there's a blessed relief in God's presence. This is true whether you're considering the end of the world or just communicating with God in the everyday physical and emotional pain you encounter.

Prayer Starter

Father, when I've no particular reason for joy, praise, or thanksgiving, I want to recognize You and then take the time to let You know that I've noticed. Stand with me in the struggle, and when I offer my prayers to You, may I. . .

DAY 362
REVELATION 11–13

Prayer Scripture

"We give You thanks, O Lord God Almighty,
who is and was and is to come, because You have
taken to You Your great power and have reigned."
REVELATION 11:17

Prayer Thought for the Day

Thank God. Seriously. He's in control and has intervened in lives that are all prone to deceitfulness, hatred, envy, and fighting. No one is godly on their own. No one is kind without encouragement. No one tells the truth without a change of heart. Join in this prayer of thanks to a mighty God who's always been and always will be. His power is unrivaled, and this allows Him to reign as King even when a majority believes He isn't real and therefore can't really effect any change in a world that's gone crazy. The craziness isn't because God doesn't have control but because the choices people make prove the world is rebelling against Him. None of this is a surprise to God, and it doesn't derail His overall plan for you. So why not pass some thanks along to the God who continues to reign.

Prayer Starter

Lord God, things don't always seem under control. They can feel downright chaotic. But You're not a God of chaos. You keep everything together, and the sun doesn't rise or set without You. Help me to remember this when. . .

DAY 363
REVELATION 14–16

Prayer Scripture

"Who shall not fear You, O Lord, and glorify
Your name? For You alone are holy. For all nations
shall come and worship before You."
REVELATION 15:4

Prayer Thought for the Day

Whether it's a stroll or a sprint, everyone's participated in the great walkaway from God. It may be temporary, or it may seem as if it's unending. The gift of choice can inspire the most unusual decisions. Many are devastating and leave lasting scars. This prayer suggests that there will come a time when everyone will finally demonstrate honor and respect for God. He's the one who's set apart. His plan is something that may not be explained or understood. Perhaps this is why so many participate in a spiritual exodus. They don't understand God and aren't especially interested in learning. But a time will come when every knee will bow in honor of the God who made all, sees all, and knows all. How much better would it be to offer that honor now?

Prayer Starter

Father, even when it seems I stand alone, help me to remember that a day is coming when people will recognize and honor You. I want to walk faithfully with You and learn from You. May I carefully choose my steps as You. . .

DAY 364
REVELATION 17–19

Prayer Scripture

"Alleluia. For the Lord God omnipotent reigns. Let us be glad and rejoice and give honor to Him, for the marriage of the Lamb has come."
REVELATION 19:6–7

Prayer Thought for the Day

One day, on God's return to find His people, there will be a time of rejoicing and gladness. God will accept the rescued as a groom accepts his bride. His is a forever acceptance, and God's unmatched power means that everyone rescued will be taken care of. On the day of His return all doubts will evaporate, lawbreaking will be relegated to history, hope will be realized, and honor will be given. Gone will be days of rebellion, worry, and regret. Gone will be tears, pain, and broken hearts. The past can no longer hurt you, because God will be giving you something entirely new, and what once *was* is no longer a concern, in heaven, with God forever.

Prayer Starter

Lord God, this coming day seems foreign and somewhat unbelievable, yet You promised, and Your promises are kept. I look forward to a day of no rebellion or regret. I want to know my past is not held against me when You. . .

DAY 365
REVELATION 20–22

Prayer Scripture

Even so, come, Lord Jesus. The grace of our Lord
Jesus Christ be with you all. Amen.
REVELATION 22:20–21

Prayer Thought for the Day

Mankind was given rules they couldn't keep. They received instructions they wouldn't follow. They were given warnings they routinely ignored. People started making rebellious decisions, and they couldn't seem to stop themselves. Some followed God, and their unusual but right way of living inspired others to seek Him too. Jesus came to rescue those who would accept it. He gave a new covenant that was paid for by His death. Then, by rising again, Jesus proved His power and allowed His followers to see the world in a new way. They observe common decision-making and increasingly look forward to an end to injustice, rebellion, and mockery. This second-to-last verse is the Bible's very last prayer, and it sums up what many Christ followers long for: "Come, Lord Jesus."

Prayer Starter

Father, there are days when I think what I'm experiencing right now is all there ever will be, so I try to make the best of it. Help me to remember that my physical life isn't the end and that You're preparing for all that comes next. You rescued my soul, now please rescue me from this body of death when You return for. . .

SCRIPTURE INDEX

OLD TESTAMENT

Genesis

Exodus

Leviticus

Numbers

2 Kings

1 Chronicles

2 Chronicles

Ezra

Nehemiah

Esther

Job

NEW TESTAMENT

MORE GREAT READING FOR MEN

Follower of Jesus, there's always a better day ahead—whether by the miraculous intervention of a loving, resourceful God or the ultimate perfection of His eternal presence. These encouraging devotional readings show that no matter how disappointing or frustrating this life is, you as a Christian ultimately can't lose.

Flexible DiCarta / ISBN 979-8-89151-083-8